Education of a Humanist

Education
of a Humanist

ALBERT GUERARD

HARVARD UNIVERSITY PRESS

1949

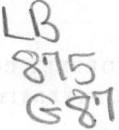

COPYRIGHT · 1949 · BY THE
PRESIDENT AND FELLOWS OF HARVARD COLLEGE
AND PRINTED IN THE UNITED STATES OF AMERICA
BY THE WILLIAM BYRD PRESS · INC ·
RICHMOND · VIRGINIA

LONDON · GEOFFREY CUMBERLEGE
OXFORD UNIVERSITY PRESS

TO
THOSE PROMISING YOUNG HUMANISTS
AND WORLD CITIZENS

John Stuart Pearson

Gregory Anders Pearson

Foreword

I have taught forty years in American universities; this is my final report. I have expressed myself repeatedly on all the subjects discussed therein. I could not always find new words to clothe familiar thoughts. So resemblances between some of these pages and others previously published by me are not purely coincidental.

I can, however, pledge my word to my readers that this is not a collection of miscellaneous essays. Every chapter has been thought anew, in the purer air of Emeritus Heights. Every page has been written afresh—three times over—for the present work.

I wish to thank my good friends, the editors of the following publications, *The American Scholar, The Antioch Review, Free World, The Nation, The New Republic, The Pacific Spectator, The Southwest Review, Stanford Studies in Language and Literature,* first for their generous hospitality, and particularly for permission to reprint passages from articles which have appeared in their columns.

This is a teacher's book; it is not written exclusively for teachers. Works on foreign policy are not all intended for professional diplomats; neither are religious works addressed solely to ordained ministers. These pages are not a pedagogical treatise, but reflections on education; and education is our common concern, the keystone of our democracy.

This book deals with the subjects I have taught and attempts to show their organic unity. It is not an epitome of my courses: *France: A Short History, Preface to World Literature,* and *Europe Free and United* serve that purpose. On these subjects, French

Foreword

Civilization, the principles of Literature, History, International Affairs, I may claim some professional knowledge: how limited, how relative, I am perhaps better aware than my readers.

What lies beyond this tight little island of technical knowledge —what I believe, or better, what I surmise and what I yearn for, my ideal Commonwealth, my conception of art and love, my philosophy, my religion—will be found, God willing, in a farewell book, *Bottle in the Sea.*

ALBERT GUÉRARD

Contents

I. Evening Thoughts of a Schoolmaster

EDUCATION · TEACHING · SCHOOLING	3
SCHOLAR AND SCIENTIST	14
HUMANE LEARNING	26

II. French Civilization

THE TEACHING OF FRENCH	41
GERMANY AND MEDIEVAL PHILOLOGY	48
TRIBULATIONS OF AN INTERPRETER	59
FOR ALL THE GODS OF THE NATIONS ARE IDOLS . . .	69
IS THERE A FRENCH "CULTURE"?	85

III. Literature

RESEARCH AND CRITICISM	101
LITERATURE AND LANGUAGE	113
THE WORLD OF BOOKS AND THE WORLD OF MEN	123
TEACHING LITERATURE OR TEACHING MEN?	141

IV. History

GROWTH OF THE HISTORICAL SPIRIT	155
THE FITFUL STREAM: "PERIODS" AND "GENERATIONS"	169
HEROES, LEGENDS, AND MYTHS	185
VAE VICTIS!	203
VAE VICTORIBUS!	214

Contents

V. World Citizenship

TRUST THE EXPERT AND KEEP YOUR OWN COUNSEL	225
THE LANGUAGE APPROACH	237
A FREE EUROPE, AND REGIONAL UNIONS	255
THE ATOMIC REVOLUTION	275
THE GREAT REPUBLIC—AND THE PRICE TO PAY	285

Education of a Humanist

I. Evening Thoughts of a Schoolmaster

EDUCATION · TEACHING · SCHOOLING

In September 1906, a young Frenchman, with piebald beard on his chin and wild surmise in his heart, met his first American classes at Williams College. In September 1946, a grizzled American veteran, shaven and shorn, but still eagerly scanning the horizon, took leave of his last classes at Stanford University. It is the story of this forty-year educational pilgrimage that I am proposing to relate.

My academic career has been uncheckered, but by no means monotonous. It has taken me from the Eastern seaboard to the Pacific Coast, with a long and pleasant sojourn in the deepest South. It has brought me into intimate touch with every section of this country. I have been on the regular staff of only four institutions, Williams, Stanford, Rice, and the University of California at Los Angeles; but summer teaching in Chicago, in Oregon, in Utah, in Hawaii, has greatly enriched my experience. I have had a foot solidly planted in four departments, Romance Languages, English, History, International Affairs—a quadrupedal arrangement which I found most comfortable. Wherever I was, and whatever my formal title, my essential conception has never varied: the first aim of education is to develop men. We are in the Machine Age, and we should return thanks for the marvelous opportunities which it is offering us. But if

Education of a Humanist

man is not to be enslaved by his own robots, he will have to assert, refine, and strengthen his humanity more sedulously than he ever did before. The efficiency which applied science confers upon us could easily turn into a thing of evil, unless power were controlled by understanding, and understanding illuminated by sympathy. Let the machine increase, provided it remain a manageable servant; but the human factor still is paramount, and we must preserve the balance between our responsibilities and our capacity. It is evident that in certain countries knowledge had far outstripped wisdom; and the peril is with us too. Training men so that they will not let the machine run out of hand is the first task of the Humanities.

The first: but only in the sense of the most obvious, the most pressing. Not the highest. I closed my book *Personal Equation* with these words: "I, who am not a scientist, hail this conquest of the world by the scientific spirit without humility and without jealousy. What I expect of science is that it will free mankind from ancestral fear. Then man will be able to address himself to problems which physical science cannot even define. Science is the deliverer: but what shall we do with our liberty?" This was the problem when Socrates taught in Athens, and it remains our problem today. To help individual man face that problem is the chief purpose of the Humanities.

For something like sixty years, I have been attending school—learning, teaching, unlearning. In celebration of our diamond jubilee, I am planning at last to raise my eyes from my desk and to appraise Dame Pedagogy, the stern companion of a studious life. I am not sure that our union was founded on romantic love; it has been an ideal marriage of convenience. I have scrupulously kept my vows. I have never wandered into the paths of profitable business, practical politics, or mere literature. I have well deserved the praise that François Coppée bestowed on the little groceryman at Montrouge:

> *Il avait ce qu'il faut pour un bon épicier:*
> *Il était ponctuel, sobre, chaste, économe.*

Evening Thoughts of a Schoolmaster

I too have been punctual, abstemious, chaste, and thrifty, according to the scholar's rule of life. Of course, I am not without regrets: regrets are the leaves which prove that the old tree is not dead timber. But I am persuaded that I chose wisely. On second thought: did I choose, or was I chosen? Perhaps I should say: I believe that fate was kind.

Let not the reader be misled by the apparent coolness of my tone. Education and I have lived so long together that we find it hard to rave about each other. To praise her would be unbecoming. If I were not a teacher, I too could sing a hymn of praise to all-conquering knowledge, holy research, and the guidance of the young. But, in America, the virtues of education need not be extolled. Let us bow to the obvious, and proceed. The educated mind is the critical mind. Education is criticism: it trains for criticism through criticism. So our very first task is to submit education itself to the critical process.

Let us first establish elementary distinctions. Education is not synonymous with teaching. Just as there are carriers immune to the disease they spread, so it is possible for educators to be uneducated. I shall waste little time in taking stock of teaching as a profession. There is nothing mysterious about either its drawbacks or its rewards. The material compensation is seldom adequate, perhaps because the trade has not yet found its John L. Lewis, perhaps because a teachers' strike would not paralyze the community. Servants of the spirit should be free from worldly care; perhaps they could be, even under the present dispensation, if they were willing to forego worldly pleasure. But I am not advocating the celibacy of the pedagogical clergy.

After forty years, I am not fully convinced that the prestige of the teaching profession is high enough to offset the poor pay. America worships education, but finds it difficult to conceal her distrust of educators. A paradox, but a familiar one. In the Middle Ages, faith was so ardent that the people could afford a healthy dose of anticlericalism: the higher your ideal, the more flagrant will

Education of a Humanist

be the inadequacy of its instruments. On a different plane, America has an almost fanatical belief in the excellency of her political system, coupled with a thorough contempt for politicians. The professor is tolerated so long as he allows you to forget that he is a professor. If he fails to conceal his knowledge, he is called a pedant. If he reveals any originality of thought, he is voted a crank.

The teacher's life is pleasantly monotonous, but not dull. I had my share of drudgery, but I realize that it would have been worse in the two other professions which I considered in my boyhood: engineering and the clergy. The classroom offers few dramatic possibilities, although there are Abélards and Héloïses in the twentieth century. For a few privileged businessmen, statesmen, soldiers (once or twice in a lifetime), opportunities may expand suddenly. For the discoverer, the inventor, the creative artist, the poet, the mystic, the miraculous door may yield at any moment. This is infinitely rarer in the teacher's experience, especially if his field be the Humanities. Even if he is engaged in original research, it is seldom given to him visibly to alter the past or shape the future. Shakespeare grows richer with every monograph, but the change is barely perceptible. For the mature teacher there are few peaks in Darien.

If, in the Humanities, the subject alters as slowly as humanity itself, the audience is ever new. Every student is in sooth a fresh man, a novel experiment in world history. It is the rare reward of the true teacher to meet individual minds at the delightful and elusive moment when they are full grown, yet not hardened. But alas! that rare reward is all too rare. I envy Emile's tutor or Mark Hopkins on his log: but both cases are fabulous. In spite of all efforts, American education is still big business and mass production. In the main, the teacher has to think in terms of classes, not of personalities: the tutorial system is at best a compromise, and it has remained a luxury.

The composite picture of classes I have met through four decades has barely changed. I have known American universities when they were still the privilege of a very small elite. It was then a real distinction to be a college man. Yet, even in the famous New England school where I first encountered American students, the spirit was already democratic and the Brahmin class a fossil. I have taught the Lost Generation, and smiled at them. They smiled happily in return, as young Existentialists would today: not even Calvinism, in whose eyes all generations are lost, could quell the ebullience of youth. At the end of my career, I have met the Veterans. I found many of them more eager as well as more mature than the average prewar undergraduate; less narrow in their outlook, less desiccated than the old-fashioned graduate. They improved the tone of the classroom; they did not create a revolution.

I shall not repeat wearily with the Preacher: "One generation passeth away, and another generation cometh: but the earth abideth for ever." I believe with Heraclitus that change is the only reality. I even admit the possibility, if not the desirability, of sudden change: love at first sight, conversion, crisis, revolution, catastrophe, adventure, miracle. There is an enormous realm uncharted by Taine's formula: race, environment, and time; or by Marx's: dialectic materialism. For all this I am duly prepared—as a man, not as a scholar. The student of history deals not with the fortuitous but with the essential; and what is essential, if not eternal, at any rate seems permanent. Within the paltry six thousand years of our civilization, fundamental experiences have remained stable. It matters little to the ordinary man whether he is killed by a stone ax or by an atomic bomb for the sins of his leaders. It matters even less to Daphnis whether Chloe's hair or her dress be long or short. The scholar is trained to take the long view, and the long view is monotonous. Unless, like Vico, Hegel, Comte, Spengler, Toynbee, he thinks in terms of aeons, not of men or even of nations.

The "long view" offers long-range dangers—besides the immediate peril of stumbling at the next step on an unphilosophical pebble. The worst of these is the conservative bias. From the truism (a truism need not always be a truth), "Essentials are permanent," we are easily tempted into the fallacy, "Whatever seems permanent must be essential." For centuries, the Chinese wore queues and bound their women's feet; therefore these quaint customs were of the very essence of Chinese culture. Americans also wear queues, according to God's holy ordinance; and woe to him who should dare to challenge the American way of life!

Thus the teacher might easily turn into an unreasoning upholder of tradition, a bulwark of prejudice. (How hard it is to discriminate between prejudice and principle!) He is apt to accept Matthew Arnold's definition of culture in its mutilated form: "getting to know the best that has been thought and said in the world," a proud, obstinate clinging to that which has been, a scholarly disdain for that which is. That is why, in the fine arts and in literature, the living forces are in constant rebellion against the schools. I was taught, in the nineties, to admire Victor de Laprade, an excellent educator who almost deserved to be a French Longfellow, while the names of Baudelaire and Rimbaud were not even whispered.

Conscious of this fundamental peril, I have made it my business as a teacher to challenge tradition. To challenge, not to destroy: I find no pleasure in sheer debunking. Charles Fox once asked the Speaker: "What would happen if (breaking a venerable tradition of the House) I were to mention a member by name?" The Speaker answered impressively: "God only knows." For all his radicalism, Fox was overawed. But I want to know. I am ready to test tradition experimentally, by attempting to break it. But it may also be checked through the historical spirit: for tradition is but crude, partial, uncritical history. The field of education is neither the ephemeral nor the fossilized.

For the scholar, the love of tradition is the most constant and most insidious temptation. There is, however, one aspect of conservative education which has almost faded away in my lifetime. In a caste-ridden society, the first aim of education is to impart fashionable prejudices. Polite learning is the Sesame into the goodly

Evening Thoughts of a Schoolmaster

company of gentlemen. You must have read the right books and pronounce *shibboleth* the right way. In good old England, a gentleman had a number of Greek and Latin tags at his command, and a member of Parliament had to be careful about his quantities. On that level, riding and dancing well, playing a good game of golf and bridge, drinking with discrimination, using the right tie, the right fork, and the right glass are infinitely more important than quoting Horace, Walter Pater, or T. S. Eliot. "Culture" in that highly artificial sense is dead; it has yielded to sophistication. Now, for the true sophisticate, the first and greatest of commandments is this: Thou shalt not be seen with an antiquated model, whether car, gown, art, or philosophy. By the time these lines appear, Sartre, Kafka, and even Kierkegaard may be as *vieux jeu* as Nietzsche, Ibsen, or Kipling. Keeping up with the elusive dictators of fashion is a pretty game. Educators are not very good at it.

Sganarelle, whose daughter is pining away, consults his neighbors. One of them, Monsieur Josse, advises: "Buy her diamonds, rubies, emeralds: when a girl is sick, these are infallible remedies." Sganarelle shrewdly replies: "You are a jeweler, Monsieur Josse."[1]

We educators must guard against the Monsieur Josse in our own hearts. We have a fine stock of jewelry to sell: but is it a panacea? I am persuaded that there is close kinship between the missionary spirit, propaganda, education, advertising: a cynic defined their common element as "inducing people to buy something they do not want." Propaganda we hate; we have misgivings about missions; I am too sane a man, of course, to question the value of advertising; but are we not tempted to exaggerate the importance of education?

The results of education seem beyond challenge in the sciences and the more complex techniques. It is not advisable that every child should have to rediscover calculus by his own unaided efforts. Even

[1] Molière, *L'Amour Médecin,* Act I, scene 1.

in that field, however, there may be a danger in over-organized teaching. England *teaches* far less than we do, and her scientists are second to none. But that subject is beyond my competence. If the question is to be raised, let it be done by a scientist.

In the trades and crafts, the common man has a better right to voice his opinion. I must confess that I am uncertain. Teaching and training there must be, but it is not proven that the schools are more effective than apprenticeship. In this century, innumerable courses are offered in journalism and the writing of drama, the short story, even poetry—God save the mark! These did not exist in my youth. Has the quality of the product been definitely improved? Only one advantage strikes me as certain: "going to school" betokens a certain degree of modesty. The novice, at any rate, confesses that he does not "know it all." And the best schools acknowledge experience as the only valid postgraduate course. Professor Baker took his class to *Abie's Irish Rose,* on the pragmatic plea—already advanced by Moliére—that "such popularity must be deserved." Be this as it may, we must recognize that there is a distinction between professional training and culture. It happens that I have received and transmitted very little training: this is not to be construed as a confession of incompetence or uselessness.

Patience: we are feeling our way. It must be evident by this time that by education we mean the aims and methods of a process which offers many different aspects. I am ready to admit that the most obvious definition of that process would be: the achievement of conformity, for the mutual benefit of the community and the individual. From the social point of view, conformity means, in the narrower sense, good breeding, in the wider sense, morality. From the political, it spells good citizenship. From the cosmic, it is philosophy, in so far as philosophy teaches resignation. This conception, which is not to be spurned, is purely negative. It emphasizes obedience to "one faith, one law, one king," as classical France had it. And obedience is a virtue only if we forget the original meaning of the word *virtue*, which is *power*.

Evening Thoughts of a Schoolmaster

The second definition, purely pragmatic, would be: the transmission of facts and skills, of knowledge and know-how (in French: *le savoir et le savoir-faire*).

The third is narrower still: we often limit education to schooling. A well-educated man is one who has gone through schools and won degrees. The Department or Board of Education operates the school system. Educators are schoolmasters. We forget that formal schooling is but one method of training among several: apprenticeship, independent study, experience, the expensive and overpraised University of Hard Knocks.

The fourth definition is Culture, as "the pursuit of our total perfection."

For our immediate discussion, I am thinking now of education in the narrowest and most definite sense: teaching and learning done in schools. It is in that magic instrument that democracy has had for ages, and preserves to this day, a touching, a pathetic faith. "After bread, education is the first need of the people," said Danton. Victor Hugo rang innumerable variations on the theme: "Open schools, and you will be able to close prisons." (Yves Simon, a professor of philosophy in a great American university, sneers at him for his simplicity.) "Not the Prussian drill sergeant, but the Prussian schoolmaster, conquered at Sedan": education pays, even in terms of artillery fire. Zapata, in the name of the Mexican masses, demanded first of all Land and Liberty: the Revolution, triumphant, gave them schools and more schools. The Soviets are attempting to stamp out illiteracy as though it were a bourgeois disease. And we all know that the Little Red Schoolhouse is the keystone of the Republic.

Be sure I have no desire to indulge in obscurantist paradoxes. I am convinced that what you study, how you study, under whom you study, are not matters of indifference. The mute inglorious genius, untaught, is hard to tell from the dumb. I am only attempting to trace limits and discern fine shades. Now it would be difficult to maintain honestly that schooling is a panacea. I have

Education of a Humanist

never met a Noble Savage, and I do not happen to have illiterates among my immediate friends. But I know there are criminals, crooks, and even morons with college degrees. There are limits to what a school can do: a school is not a scientifically run factory turning out perfect and interchangeable citizens.

The demonstration is not far to seek. The desire to impress an indelible stamp upon all pupils is strongest in Catholic institutions; and the means to that end, refined through long centuries, are marvelously efficient: yet Voltaire, Renan, Anatole France attended Church schools; they even were docile and grateful pupils. My mind was undoubtedly molded by my high school course at Chaptal, in Paris. I have lost track of my school fellows: but I could wager that they are scattered in the four corners of the political, social, cultural, and religious horizon. Our paths were already divergent when we were in the same classroom, and Chaptal could not force us into the one-and-only "French Way of Life."

On the other hand, it is possible for minds to converge without a common scholastic background. Once I had a twin, Werner Hegemann. We were of the same age, as is proper for twins. We had freely elected the same disciplines: city planning and unconventional history. We were agreed even in details: his book on Berlin is in close harmony with my book on Paris, and his Napoleon with my Napoleon. When we discovered each other, we corresponded with the warmth and freedom of old friends. The Spirit Ironic decided that we should never meet.

When we are concerned, not with individuals merely, but with nations, we are compelled to doubt whether universal schooling will suffice to curb our evil instincts and quell our anguish. The quality of our best sellers is no recommendation for our nearly perfect score in literacy. Germany was acknowledged to be the most highly educated country in the world: for three quarters of a century, she capitulated to barbaric tribalism, under the leadership of Bismarck ("Blood and iron") and of Hitler. Russia has been subjected for three decades to the most drastic educational processing: some

Evening Thoughts of a Schoolmaster

of us regret the good old *muzhik,* dumbly devoted to Church and Tsar. We have to accept the sobering and scandalous paradox that schooling is no guarantee of wisdom.[2]

We cannot be saved by education alone. This, of course, is but one instance of a law so trite that we blush to state it again, so constantly disregarded that we should have it broadcast every hour, along with the lyric praises of "the soap you will love." Education is no panacea, because there is no panacea. *Homo scholasticus* (not *sapiens*) is as dismal and fantastic a monster as *Homo œconomicus,* Manchesterian or Marxian. The eternal verities of our Constitution have failed to make us all wise and good. This Christian country is rife with lust, greed, and violence, as though it were not Christian. I am willing to work for "the more perfect state," the more equitable social order, the purer religion, the higher and deeper learning: again I am not a skeptic and I am not a pessimist. But not one of these agencies will suffice. More fundamental than democracy, social justice, or encyclopedic knowledge is the quest for bodily and mental health. *Mens sana in corpore sano* is probably the pithiest recipe for Utopia. (It might well lead to that dreariness which is the curse of most Utopias: imagine a world made up solidly of sane and sound men!) But I should dread a therapeutic autocracy, the iron rule of physiologists and psychologists, almost as much as a Marxian dictatorship.

The work of the most devoted men, at the service of the highest doctrines, is but an infinitesimal part of a whole which we cannot comprehend. It was over fifty years ago that I first listened to Tennyson's Victorian common sense:

---

[2] This may have definite consequences tomorrow, as we shall see in the last section of this book. We are not satisfied with the distribution of votes within the United Nations. It is proposed to amend the Charter by allotting votes according to population, economic development, education. In that event, education would inevitably be tested by schooling. As a result, a country in the same stage as the Russia of Tolstoy, Turgenev, Dostoevsky, would be pronounced irremediably inferior to the Russia of Stalin. The United States, of course, would rank very high; but, by that criterion, the Germany of Hitler would have been at the very summit.

Education of a Humanist

> Our little systems have their day,
> They have their day, and cease to be.

I found no discouragement in such a thought: our minds need "systems" from day to day, as our bodies need food, shelter, and clothing. I have sought the best, and struck a few bad bargains. In most general terms, I have believed in education, democracy, socialism, and free religion, and I see no cause to recant. But about any one or all of them, I refuse to the last to be Monsieur Josse.

SCHOLAR AND SCIENTIST

Every man's education should include a craft, an art, and a science. In my own case, this elementary wisdom was not completely ignored, but I deeply regret that it was followed so halfheartedly. If I had a second chance (but do I desire a second chance?), I should take a more thorough course in music and mathematics, the purest of the arts and the purest of the sciences. I envy those privileged mortals who can read the score of a symphony or pages of algebraic formulas with evident delight. As for the craft, I hesitate. My friends insist that deep within me there slumbers a culinary artist: for was I not born in France? Canon Ernest Dimnet, French of the French, who sold America the Art of Thinking (1928: the immediate result was the depression), is likewise an expert salad maker. But I have little faith in racial traits. Cooking is not in my blood. I have shown promises of talent as dishwasher and shoe polisher.

In the technical sense of the word, I am not even an amateur scientist, and I am fully aware of my loss. For the scientific method has at last come into its own: atomic research is only the most spectacular of its achievements. The rate of acceleration in scientific progress is breath-taking: discoveries are made every year which, in the past, would have graced a century. The gap between speculation and practical use is now a matter of months instead of decades. The scientific spirit is transforming the material world under our eyes. And it would be hard to deny that production, distribution, hygiene,

Evening Thoughts of a Schoolmaster

and housing are material problems, capable of a scientific solution. The haphazard methods of the political brawl, the clamorous market place, the gambling den, are now antiquated. By taking thought, man can do something far more intelligent than adding a cubit to his stature; he can lengthen his span of life, hold disease in check, reduce discomfort, abolish want. The business of America, as Calvin Coolidge sagely said, is Business; and serious business is not poker playing with mines or railroads as chips, but far-sighted planning and scientific management. If the word had not been copyrighted by a small group of enthusiasts, I should say that we are entering (backward and blindfolded, most of us) the age of Technocracy.

I fully expect the scientist to grow in stature and supersede, in many fields, the aristocrat, the soldier, the profiteer, the politician. And by the same token he will inevitably gain ground at the expense of the old-fashioned scholar, the custodian of ancient lore. Yet I for one am not ready to slink out of this new unfamiliar world, an indignant and bewildered ghost. For I refuse to admit that there is a gulf between scholar and scientist. The French and the Germans, who have some experience in these matters, ignore the distinction. A man may work in many different fields, from abstract numbers and inanimate nature to psychology and metaphysics, and be called a *savant* or a *Wissenschafter*.

I do not mean that one man should work in all fields, like Aristotle, Herbert Spencer, Gustave Le Bon, or H. G. Wells. We are tempted to smile at the universal genius, the modern Pico della Mirandola, ready to lay down the law "on all things knowable and a few others beside." It is not even necessary that the man who is an expert in letters or history should be, like Voltaire or Goethe, a gifted amateur in a totally different branch of learning. The case of Pascal is unique. He displayed the rigor of the mathematician and physicist, the acumen of the worldly-wise moralist, the imagination of the poet, the vision of the mystic. He possessed them all, but he could not bring them into full harmony. His tragic experience is the Calvary of the human mind.

Education of a Humanist

It is excellent, no doubt, that a philologist should have a good working knowledge of some totally different science, say chemistry; just as it is profitable for a mathematician to have some inkling of botany. It is highly desirable; it is not rigorously necessary. The unity—but I dread that word; let us say: the fellowship—of all the sciences lies deeper than in polite visiting from mansion to mansion. It is founded on a community of aim and method: to seek the truth without fear, and to test the truth without favor. The man who sets out to prove that Darwinism is right is no scientist, but an advocate. The man who studies a religion with the sole desire to understand is a scientist, even though his findings may be used by apologists or detractors. "Prove," that is, try and test, "all things," said the Apostle. This critical spirit should pervade the quest for truth, whatever path the seeker may choose. It should also guide the judge, if he be worthy of his calling; for the legal mind means something higher than an infinite capacity for quibbling.

When it comes to material means of investigation, the techniques are bound to differ. The mathematician, the astronomer, the physicist, the biologist, the historian, cannot use the same set of tools, material and mental. It is a ludicrous blunder to seek scientific rigor by borrowing the equipment of another discipline. A mathematician does not examine numbers with a microscope, does not distill them in a retort. Within the last hundred years, the humanities have suffered from this delusion in several different ways.

The first, and most egregious, was materialism in the crudest sense, the refusal to consider as a fact worthy of notice anything that was not of a physical nature. History and even literary criticism were thus systematically dehumanized. Texts and dates, instead of being properly collected and checked as indispensable raw material, were considered as ends in themselves. To seek the significance of a great personality or of a masterpiece was voted literary, that is to say, unscholarly and amateurish. The first step was to resolve the subject into elementary facts, each duly entered on a separate slip:

Evening Thoughts of a Schoolmaster

a legitimate procedure, if a whole order of facts had not been overlooked, to wit, simple and complex relations. The notion of quality was dismissed, because it had no place in chemistry. "Vice and virtue," said Taine (and hinted: poetry as well), "are products like sugar and vitriol."

If all facts are placed on the same level, it becomes possible to treat them statistically. The prosodical tricks of Shakespeare and Milton were thus tabulated; as though there were the slightest chance, by such a device, to reconstitute or even to understand the Shakespearean or Miltonic power! Intelligence, a term of extraordinary complexity, was reduced to a few simple elements, which were catalogued, classified, and finally summed up in the form of a quotient. When applied to school children or enlisted men, the method could have a rough-and-ready pragmatic value. When it was extended to the worthies of the past, the result was impressively learned and incredibly funny. Haphazard information, sheer guesswork, modified by an elaborate "coefficient of error," led to startling results. We were gravely informed that Marat rated I.Q. 170, Ali Wedi Zade, "Albanian robber chief," 155, and Napoleon 145. It was numerical, therefore it was scientific: figures do not lie. Psychology, in this case, impinged upon history and literature, and scholars had a right to raise quizzical brows. In aesthetics, the havoc was worse. The simplest form of the fallacy is the famous "golden rectangle," a proportion voted most pleasing by a substantial majority. But in such matters, the results of a poll are totally irrelevant: who is to assure us that the majority are not mostly fools? Not merely the village in Kipling's story, but a whole mighty nation could vote that the earth is flat: it would not invalidate the demonstration of a single competent scientist. Even if, in politics or in literature, we were to shift our ground from merit to success, from aesthetics to marketing, statistics might express a rough fact but not establish a reliable law. It is a plain fact that *The Egg and I* outsold the best work of Katherine Anne Porter and Janet Lewis a hundred to one. But we do not know whether it started an interminable procession of egg books and made the American public egg-minded; or whether, as we fervently hope, it proved to be the egg to end all eggs.

The numerical fallacy is only one form of pseudo science. More insidious is the organic fallacy. It was at its worst in the middle of the nineteenth century. It was partly due to a reaction against the rationalism of the Enlightenment, partly to the fear of radicalism— the disciples of Burke loved to emphasize slow unconscious growth in order to extol the wisdom of prejudice. But it was chiefly influenced by the brilliant development of the natural sciences, culminating with the work of Darwin. Again the technique of one discipline was ruthlessly applied to a widely different line of study. In sociology, in linguistics, the conscious creative power of man was dismissed as a delusion. Man could not write a Constitution; that of the United States was but a thin ideological veil over a living mass of customs. Man could not plan and create a city: Joseph de Maistre staked his reputation as a prophet on the proposition that our capital, Washington, would never be built. Man could not tamper with language, streamline the instrument, standardize its forms, reduce its absurdities: if Esperantists do understand one another, it is a curious freak that true scientists have a right to ignore.

This attitude is still traceable in the horror of many excellent minds for any kind of planning (bridges and tunnels, of course, should be allowed to grow by a slow unconscious process), and in the conception of "cultures" held by a belated school of anthropologists.[3] It happens that in the twentieth century the formidable alliance of mathematics, physics, and chemistry has assumed leadership. The sciences of unconscious growth no longer are the sole dictators of fashion. Indeed, they might in their turn imitate the pattern of the higher physics; control of the gene might follow the control of the atom, with results even more revolutionary.

[3] This philosophy has been defined as the Topsy school of thought; Voltaire might have called it Topsy Turvy.

Evening Thoughts of a Schoolmaster

Whatever his field may be, a man qualifies as a scientist if he be determined to find the truth. He does not have to serve the truth, which is independent of such service. He does not have to love the truth, which may be unlovely. But, in his professional capacity, he must refuse to place pleasure, profit, or prejudice above the object of his quest. The aim is the same in all branches of human knowledge. Honesty and diligence, as the conditions of accuracy, are equally required of all. A biased or careless scientist is a poor scientist. A certain allowance must be made for human frailty; but if his faults go beyond that narrow limit of tolerance, the man is debarred from the company of research workers.

The machine offers, in a superhuman degree, these basic virtues of impartiality and accuracy. I have seen at the FBI, in Washington, an instrument which picked out, among thousands of perforated cards, the one which referred to a given individual. By the standards prevailing in many schools, that peerless robot deserved a Ph.D., *summa cum laude*. But the contraption of levers, wheels, and wires must be built and must be fed. Its finding must be read. If the robot is superhuman, the man, on his part, must be pretermechanical. The human gifts required of scholar and scientist are the same in every domain. Three are outstanding: logic, imagination, synthetic power.

When scientists spurn logic, what they have in mind is a blind faith in abstract reasoning. The Aristotelian syllogism is but an instrument: logic is the art of conducting one's thought in an orderly fashion. Nature may be irrational: but the scientist cannot afford to indulge in fantasies, fallacies, and *non sequiturs*. Perhaps Descartes and Spinoza, who sought to model all science and all philosophy on the Euclidean pattern, emphasized unduly the element of rigid symmetry in the human mind: we have constantly to combat the tendency to arrogant oversimplification. But men in closer touch with the "natural" sciences, Bacon, Claude Bernard, were also great methodologists, that is to say, logicians. We are not bound to believe that the universe is governed according to the laws of Aristotle, Descartes, Carnap, or Korzybski; it may be that

Education of a Humanist

our world of orderly thought is but a small circle of light in the murky gulf of the absurd. All science is humanistic in the restrictive sense: it is only human, and cannot commit whatever Gods there be. But this microcosm of consistency is the only one that science can investigate. And consistency means logic. A scientific demonstration is a convincing piece of reasoning.

Imagination is needed for that leap in the dark that we call hypothesis. Research, which alone preserves science from desiccation and death, does not mean capricious wandering. The goal must be defined, even though, when attained, it may prove very different from what we anticipated. Of course, the process is dialectical: the hypothesis is the result of knowledge, as well as the path to knowledge unexplored. At every step, the scientist must "suppose the problem solved" (a good definition of Utopia), and proceed to verify whether the proposed solution actually works.

Scientific imagination is no mere flash. In order to formulate the hypothesis, and to test its validity, the searcher must possess the gift of conceiving a relation between events which, to the ordinary mind, would seem wholly disparate. The classical instance is that of Newton's apple: it took a unique power of synthesis to connect a commonplace incident with the stars in their courses. The scientist must be able to imagine not isolated facts merely, but a system.

Whoever attempts to ascertain the truth must be not simply a faithful observer and recorder, but a rationalist, a poet, and a philosopher as well. Perhaps "in spite of himself," for the words have fallen into disrepute. But the requirements will not be denied. The man at the miscroscope needs them no less than the one who is poring over an Etruscan inscription, a palimpsest, or a page from *Finnegans Wake*. These are human qualities, beyond the reach of the most perfect robot; and it is the task of the Humanities to refine and strengthen them.

I repeat that, in my mind, there is no hard and fast distinction between scholar and scientist. There are, obviously, convenient di-

Evening Thoughts of a Schoolmaster

visions within human knowledge, with fine intermediate shades and much overlapping. The dichotomy Sciences-Humanities, although rough, may be accepted pragmatically. But let us never forget that our pedagogical organization into schools and departments is no part of Holy Writ.

In world government, I once defined a region as "the largest area in which the free circulation of men, goods and ideas is at present possible." Intellectual disciplines form regions of that kind. We know, for instance, that mathematics, physics, chemistry, without fortfeiting their autonomy, have abolished customs barriers between them. Similarly, a "classical" scholar, that is, a student of "classical" antiquity, might be an archaeologist, a philologist, a historian of politics, art, literature, religion, an economist and sociologist, a philosopher. To a large extent, he has to use all these approaches. The man who should be exclusively an epigrapher or a numismatist, ignoring the multitudinous life of the Greeks, would not be a true master even of his own limited craft.

If we admit—grudgingly—the distinction between the Sciences and the Humanities, is there any reason to choose between the two lines? Buridan's ass would die at the parting of the ways, irresolute, or, as André Gide puts it, *disponible*. The encyclopedic answer, "Let us have them all!" will not avail: it cannot be done at the present stage. The eclectic answer, "Let us pick and choose here and there," is an evasion. What would be the reason of such a choice? To answer—let us be more modest: to discuss—such a question, we must return to the elementary distinction between education and schooling.

As a matter of schooling, in the technical sense of the term, I should unhesitatingly put the emphasis on the sciences. In the modern world, they have reached such a degree of complexity that common sense and a lively interest will not suffice. There must be rigorous and elaborate training, the guidance of experts, the help of a well-organized team, the use of expensive laboratories, all necessary keys to the enormous and recondite stores of scientific

Education of a Humanist

knowledge. The demands of scholarship, I know, are no less exacting: a man cannot improvise himself a Sanskrit scholar in a log cabin. Yet the final product, in most sciences,[4] depends absolutely on the equipment, although the equipment would be, and often is, dead lumber without the guiding hand. The achievements that scholarship investigates—language, poetry, art, philosophy, religion—exist apart from the investigator. So, you will say, does a scientific law: but the law has no standing in the human mind until it has been formulated, whereas the historical or linguistic fact is recognized (roughly) by the laity. Scientific discoveries are now made by professionals, to the exclusion of the untutored genius; masterpieces are not produced exclusively by the professors (indeed, it is often believed that, in the creative realm of culture, being a professor is something of a handicap). Scholars write theses about John Bunyan, Daniel Defoe, Jean Jacques Rousseau, who never attended a graduate school. A country without scientific institutes would simply have no modern science, and no amount of scholarship could compensate for the loss. A country without schools of arts and letters might very well possess arts and letters: these would be provided by the uneducated, and, in their leisure hours by the scientists. I do not know whether scholars should feel humiliated or exalted at the thought that they are not a necessity but a luxury.

The scene changes altogether if we turn from schooling, or the transmission and increase of knowledge, to education, or the pursuit of our total perfection. A learned fool is a fool still. By the standards of today, Socrates and Jesus were ignorant men; by any standard, they are still infinitely wise. This is true not only of isolated individuals but of society. Since I do not want to be *laudator temporis acti,* let me borrow my examples from the convenient future. A Utopia is a mental experiment: what would happen if this or that factor were added or removed? If consistent, a Utopia becomes, not

[4] This, of course, is not equally true of all the sciences. A mathematician might conceivably do excellent work in solitude; Mendel was a pioneer, with scant material facilities, and without the benefit of a team.

indeed a demonstration, but a plausible hypothesis. Now Ernest Renan in his *Philosophical Dialogues,* and Aldous Huxley in *Brave New World,* have offered us Utopias based on the unquestioned supremacy of science: both of them are nightmares. It may be said that Renan wrote in a fit of despondency after the disasters of 1870-1871, and that Huxley's book is a Swiftian satire. But H. G. Wells, scientifically trained, had a simple-hearted belief in science; his Utopias, in which the scientific element predominates, are dismal whenever they are not pessimistic. To return to actual history, the devilish inventions of the Nazis, and our own, presumably angelical, prove that science has no power to curb evil. It simply acts as a magnifier. To be sure, it could magnify the good as well as the brutal; but to admit that would be "unrealistic" and starry-eyed.

A Utopia founded on the ideal of the humanities, on the contrary, would offer a gracious picture. Our gadgets, of course, would not have been created. Our geographical range would be narrow: no telephone, no radio, no television. We would ride or walk to see friends a few miles away, instead of hurtling through the stratosphere over deserts and oceans. But, had we taken thought on humanistic lines, we could be decently governed, without war; our economy, on a modest scale, could be secure and just. We might not know vitamins under that name, but we could enjoy a frugal, well-balanced diet. We should not know that a table is a whirling mass of electrons; but our craftsmen would provide us with simple, commodious, durable objects. Our homes and cities would grow rich and mellow with the heirlooms of generations. We might not have a soap opera brought to us by turning a magic knob; but we might take part in communal dancing, listen to a ballad sung by a blind beggar, and perchance attend a performance of the *Oresteia.*

I am no disciple of Rousseau or Pope Pius IX, and no sworn enemy of "modern civilization and progress." To know the material world more accurately is a great adventure; and even the growth of industry through science is in itself a boon. I am simply pleading for a saner hierarchy of values. Materialistic knowledge could never, unaided, give us the Four Freedoms which are the conditions (necessary, not sufficient) of human happiness. Humanistic culture, seeking wisdom through clarity of thought, moral courage, temperance, justice, offers the more promising way.

We need education in the Humanities, but it cannot be imparted by the schools alone, and it does not depend upon any particular subject, such as classical languages or traditional philosophy. This education must pervade the whole of society: the home, the workshop, the market place, the press, the political arena. The schools can help only in so far as they seek to define and refine the common aim. For, I repeat, while the scientific spirit is the means, and scientific discovery the result, humanistic studies are only the means: the desired result is to foster the humanistic spirit. Science could be reserved for a minority: without participating in the effort, the masses would reap its benefit. Humanism is the heritage of the "common man."

This may seem a paradox. In our own age, because of their immediate applications to industry, agriculture, medicine, the investigations of the scientist appear practical, for the people if not of the people. It is the speculations of the scholar that seem abstruse and remote. We have been made to realize, with tragic immediacy, the impact of atomic research upon our daily life. We are not conscious in the same degree of the part played by history, philosophy, and even philology in shaping the course of men and nations.

Is this perspective true? We are struck with the influence of science just because science is alien to most of us. It thus acquires an impressive, a magical halo. The subjects that are the field of scholarship are with us all the time. Just as Monsieur Jourdain had talked prose all his life without knowing it, so John Doe has to be a philologist, for he has some command of language; a historian, for he remembers—vaguely—Washington's Farewell Address, the Versailles Treaty, Pearl Harbor, and Hiroshima; a philosopher, for he is likely to be a church member and to repeat a metaphysical creed. He may be all these things in the crudest fashion; he may be

Evening Thoughts of a Schoolmaster

unaware of his responsibilities; but he cannot evade them. He, very properly, leaves science to the scientist; but, when he picks up his morning paper or goes to the polling booth, he is immersed in problems which are the domain of the humanist. So the scientist can, and even must, isolate himself in his fortress of stainless steel. But for the scholar, the Ivory Tower, at times a necessary refuge, cannot be a permanent abode.

If this were granted, the reader might be tempted to say: "Then the humanist has no right to a separate existence; we are all humanists. The scholar should lose himself in our common humanity: *homo sum.*" But the process whereby mankind acquires consciousness—with all the perils, duties, and hopes that such consciousness entails—that process is by no means automatic. Mankind is different from a mere herd of bipeds because it is capable of taking thought; but though the mass can be swayed by thought, it cannot originate thought. There must be intelligent leadership; and there can be no leadership unless there is enlightened critical loyalty to leaders. When science is not indifferent, it is autocratic: it brings indisputable truths which the masses must accept even though they cannot understand. Humanism on the other hand is democratic: scholars are but an investigating committee reporting to the common man. If the experts fail to report, or if the masses fail to heed their findings, democracy suffers.

The Humanistic Schools are therefore intended to train experts, and also to prepare the common man to receive and appraise expert advice. I said *experts* rather than *leaders:* the investigator is not necessarily a man of action. I am not advocating a Mandarin system, clothing the scholar with actual power: it was probably a mistake to give Brain Trusters executive positions. But as specialists in the study of human affairs, the scholars have a right to be heard.

This conception of the Humanities requires a double reform. The scholar must frankly abandon the aloofness which is the proper attitude of the scientist. A dehumanized humanist is an absurdity. *Pari passu,* the public must give up the notion that students of art, history, poetry, philosophy, are quaint unearthly creatures buzzing in a vacuum. The man with the longer view, backward and forward, is a better guide than the "practical" man in his counting house. The scholar, then, must desire, and he must be allowed, to serve the people; never forgetting, however, that service is not subserviency. The expert, if he is to be worth his salt, must tell the people what they ought to know, not what they want to be told. He cannot be a politician. Perhaps there should be no politicians.

HUMANE LEARNING

So far, I have been talking of "the Humanities" with intentional vagueness. We all know loosely what is meant by the term. It has some official standing, which does not guarantee that it is intelligent. The time has come to stake our field more accurately.

The very name is embarrassing. We had to face that problem at Stanford, when the School of Letters was expanded into a School of Humanities. We had to challenge an old association of ideas which created misgivings and in some cases an adverse bias. Traditionally, the Humanities mean "classical," that is, Greek and Latin, scholarship. Anatole France boasts that, as a young boy, he was "a good little humanist," because he did well in his Latin classes.

To recapture forgotten learning, through the sacred texts of antiquity, was perhaps the most pressing task of the early Renaissance; it was not the final goal. Already, with Erasmus and Rabelais, the scholar looked forward, not back. In the seventeenth century, the most classical age of all, Molière could quietly affirm: "The Ancients are the Ancients, and we are the people of today." The classical tongues are of very great value, but they are not indispensable to a liberal education. We have heard of "Modern Humanities," in which the living languages take the place of the mighty dead. But is it true that proficiency in alien languages, ancient or modern, is the test of the true scholar? Plato and Aristotle remain the models of Humanism, although they had but their native Greek

Evening Thoughts of a Schoolmaster

at their command. Stewards on transatlantic liners, concierges in cosmopolitan hotels, shopkeepers all round the Mediterranean, are better linguists than many professors and than most of the creative writers. If Browning's Grammarian "settled *Hoti's* business . . . properly based *Oun,* gave us the doctrine of the enclitic *De,*" he did commendable spadework, but was not among the master builders. Semantics, named but not invented by Michel Bréal half a century ago, compels us to look beyond the mere form of words. To understand the shifts in their meanings, to catch their overtones, we have to be acquainted with the civilization of which they are the symbols. "What should they know of language, who only language know?"

Another ambiguity: the term *Humanities* is, etymologically at least, connected with the philosophy of Humanism. There are probably as many humanisms as there are romanticisms and existentialisms; essentially, Humanism should mean that man is the measure of all things.[5] Proudly—arrogantly, perhaps—it cuts off mankind from brute creation: it is the denial of deterministic materialism. But it also claims autonomy for man in his own sphere. It relegates the superhuman to the realm of the unknowable, a courteous substitute for outright denial. If this definition were accepted, Humanism would be a major heresy; Abbé Bremond and Jacques Maritain were flirting with a dangerous paradox when they spoke of "Christian Humanism." The plain "humanistic" attitude was the one assumed by Laplace when Napoleon asked him why he had not mentioned God in his treatise on Celestial Mechanics: "Sire, I had no need for that hypothesis."[6]

If this be Humanism, the Humanities may embrace it, but without being committed to its negations. For the study of man is not limited to his intelligence; it includes the subconscious, the uncon-

---

[5] Cf. Erich Kahler, *Man the Measure,* a great humanistic book.

[6] The Humanist Societies (or Ethical Culture Societies) are usually religious bodies denying the supernatural; or at any rate, denying that human conduct can or should be directed by thoughts of the supernatural; or, more obviously, denying as man-made and anthropomorphic the traditional conceptions of the supernatural.

scious, the physiological, and even the inorganic. Much in man is subhuman; he has not yet fully pawed himself out of the slime. And we cannot accept in advance any ceiling to man's endeavor. His spirit probes above and below, by all available means, some of them unthought of by classical scholars. Who knows but he may reach beyond the five paltry senses of today, and beyond that common sense which is but the sediment of the past? Like William James, I hate to see any door locked and barred before we have had a full chance to peer beyond. What is man's original sin, the cause of that anguish no humanist can deny? Is it the survival of the beast within us, or the denial of the angel? If this be romanticism and obscurantism, make the most of it. A humanism that would shut out these problems would be a self-made prison. A neat, orderly prison, no doubt, well lit with the equable light of classical rationalism, a fit bower to enjoy Alexander Pope. But I do not like prisons.

Now a mighty chorus is heard: "Least of all should the Humanities be confused with Humanitarianism!" Humanists are scholars and gentlemen: humanitarians are crude. They go beyond sentiment only to fall into materialism. They are the well-meaning but stodgy people who want to clear picturesque slums and build modern tenements. "Improvements," forsooth! Is not *improvement* a humbler synonym of *progress*? Scholars believe that material conditions are immaterial, and that man's nature, which alone is our concern, has not perceptibly changed throughout recorded time. This is not heavy irony: I have heard this lofty reasoning from many a lecture platform and from many a pulpit.

There are some, on the contrary, for whom the very core of humanism is sympathy. To be humane is not first of all to be learned, but to be kind. It does not suffice to shed an easy tear: kindness needs discipline and a scale of value difficult to master. Kindness to the wolf is cruelty to the lamb. After the First World War, America grew tenderhearted about those poor Germans left without any Poles to oppress. Kindness! We have yet to learn that

Evening Thoughts of a Schoolmaster

it is a crime to keep alive those who despair of life. I should be satisfied if the Schools of Humanities turned into Schools of Humanity. I should then engrave on their portals the lines of Keats.

> "None can usurp this height," return'd that shade,
> "But those to whom the miseries of the world
> Are misery, and will not let them rest."

From such schools would come forth not "social workers" only, and reformers of harsh or stupid laws, but historians also, romancers, and poets. Men who dared that dream—Saint-Simon, Lamennais, Michelet, Hugo—are my masters still. They were defeated a hundred years ago, but the whole world has been darkened by their defeat.

Incidentally, dropping the absurd plural *Humanities* would emphasize the oneness of mankind. This has been the firm belief of true humanists throughout the ages: Wendell Willkie, in his engaging artlessness, was heir to a noble tradition. Even when he studies and loves local color, the scholar seeks the universal, the catholic, the œcumenical, the City of Man. Tribalism is the mark of the barbarian, parochialism the brand of the uncouth. The aim of our schools might well be to prepare what George Washington aspired to be: citizens of the great republic of humanity at large.

Since this is not a treatise, but a confession, I must ask myself: "Am I a true humanist? Do I love my fellow man?" Frankly, I see no valid reason why I should cherish all featherless bipeds. Was not Alphonse Karr responsible for the cynical remark: "The more I know men, the better I like dogs"? One dog has been dearer to me than most humans. Shall we adduce that men are coöperators in the exploitation of the globe? But in that common enterprise there are degrees; masters and their human tools do not invariably love one another. On that level, a farmer should love his team of oxen better than he loves his competitor, or his enemy the tax-gatherer. The burden of a famous French song runs:

Education of a Humanist

> I love Jane, my wife; but I'd rather
> See her die than my oxen.[7]

If you try to silence me with the argument that man and man alone was created in God's image, I might answer with the Voltairian quip: "Surely man has returned the compliment." Many religions had gods in the shape of animals; and in the purest of all, we hear without a shock of the Lamb and of the Dove. But on this point, I am reassured by the Societies for the Prevention of Cruelty to Animals: man is never so humane as when he realizes his kinship with his humbler friends.

Since the Humanities are the sciences of man, Anthropology would seem a good synonym. But the term already has two meanings. The first, and in my opinion the more scientific, denotes the study of man as a species, and the classification of the various types within that species. As worthily represented, say, by the anatomist and surgeon Paul Broca, it is simply a branch of biology. The other conception, of which E. B. Tylor is an outstanding example, is the investigation of primitive communities, and a division of sociology. Vacher de Lapouge combined there two elements into a formidable mixture, *Anthroposociology*. The most famous disciple of that new science was named Adolf Hitler: we are a long way from the Humanities. No, Anthropology will not do. We should have to coin another word, Anthroponomy or Anthroposophy. But why insist on Greek? We are no longer in the days of Molière, when learned ladies offered—or threatened—to kiss a scholar "for the love of Greek." Latin is good enough for me; and even better, English: "The proper study of mankind is Man."

To escape from the purely classical connotation of the Humanities, I proposed to call our new division "School of Humane Learning." My colleagues smiled indulgently.[8] In the academic

---

[7] Pierre Dupont, *Les Bœufs*. I wonder if Dupont's farmer nowadays would transfer his affection to a tractor?

[8] When I think of the connection between *police* (material order), *policy* (immediate collective purpose), *polity* (over-all social system), *politeness* (facilitating

market, a well-known brand is supposed to be an asset; so the time-honored title "School of Humanities" was adopted. But names have consequences. The *belles-lettres* fragrance that clings to the Humanities repelled the Social Scientists, good earnest souls. And yet the Maginot Line within the sciences of man is as futile as it looks forbidding. I refuse to accept the economic interpretation of literature, or the literary interpretation of economics, as sheer confusion. But both meet under the sign of history, that all-embracing, integral history for which the sole purpose of man never was to wage war, sign scraps of paper, and overthrow governments. Their common method is historical, for their subject matter is historical, however brief the history: a scientific report on a strike, on a trust, on the TVA, is a case history. The manifold aspects of human life, however different, can never be absolutely separate. Not only do their frontiers merge, but the same cultural climate affects them in spite of all frontiers. In any age, there is an undeniable connection between the political, economic, and social regimes and the forms affected by art, literature, and even religion. No science of man can live in that abstraction, the eternal present; austerely naked as Truth may be, she is not unaffected by periods and styles. The social historians—we shall have to state repeatedly this essential truth—no less than other brands of historians, do recognize the Middle Ages, the Renaissance, the Classical period, the Enlightenment, Romanticism, Realism, as convenient divisions. The failure of the ill-concerted upheavals in all European countries in 1848 brought about or accelerated a shift from the romantic to the realistic in every field. After George Sand, Gustave Flaubert; after Delacroix, Courbet; after Lamartine, Morny; after the Frankfort democrats, Bismarck; after Fourier, Karl Marx; after Schelling and Hegel, Comte,

---

social intercourse), I feel tempted to propose "School of Polite Learning." The phrase has an old-fashioned flavor, but it ought to be timeless. It may be objected that to be polite is undemocratic, unrealistic, and unscholarly. I believe that the chief threat to peace at present is not the clash of interests or the conflict of ideologies, but simply bad manners.

Education of a Humanist

Haeckel, Spencer. And today, the same atmosphere prevails in all realms of human activity, economic, political, literary: the keyword might be—take your choice—Existentialism, Confusionism, or SNAFU.

This interrelation is so axiomatic in my mind that, in the course of this book, I shall rather insist on the necessary corrections and qualifications. I believe in interrelation and a common background, not in uniformity and unity. The various disciplines possess, and must preserve, a large measure of autonomy. If Karl Marx (in his minor works) and Proudhon both happen to be great writers, it does not follow that their economic theories are to be tested by the excellence of their style. If we propose to abolish tariff barriers between all the sciences of man, our ideal is not a unitary or centralized state, but a liberal federation.

No doubt special instruments are needed for special purposes; but this is not an insuperable obstacle between scholars whose common interest is Man. The necessity of using different techniques exists within the present conventional departments. An economist is not a student of religion (although he might be interested in the doctrine of the church on wealth and fair prices, and in the actual administration of church property); but an authority on Anglo-Saxon, a grammarian, a historian of literature, a critic, a teacher of creative writing, although all members of the English Department, do not need the same equipment, and their personalities are not interchangeable.

The defenders of the frontiers between departments claim that these divisions alone enable a man to specialize, and that without specialization no accurate knowledge is possible. (To be sure, it is open for a man to specialize in generalizations, and win the lofty title of philosopher.) I fully recognize the necessity of knowing more and more about less and less; this is not a jibe, but an accurate definition. It happened that my own field of research was for a long period limited to a single year in a single city, Paris in 1848. But in order to understand the full life of those stormy days,

Evening Thoughts of a Schoolmaster

I had to ignore the neat boundaries traced by the departments. An authority on Milton is of course a highly respectable scholar, no facile amateur or jack-of-all-trades. But, in order to know his Milton, a man like Allan Gilbert had to be grounded in geography, history, politics, theology, possibly medicine (to discuss the weird hypothesis that Milton's genius and his blindness were both caused by a congenital taint); he must have surveyed the literatures of Judea, Greece, ancient Rome, modern Italy, with a glimpse of France (Du Bartas), and perhaps even of the Netherlands (Vondel). Such a "specialist" must be a whole School of Humanities in one person.

I have been rambling, but not without a purpose. I have been feeling my way. A doctrinaire or a retained advocate would go straight to the point; my aim was to inquire: What is the point? I am repeating the homely and searching question of Marshal Foch: *De quoi s'agit-il?* Now I may attempt to call together the thoughts I have sent reconnoitering, and see whether their reports give a coherent picture of the situation.

The School of Humane Learning is concerned first of all with the study of social conditions. Its field is the Culture of certain anthropologists, although it is by no means committed to their doctrinaire rigidity; or the civilizations defined by Arnold J. Toynbee. Ultimately, the localized study expands into a world view; from cultures or group patterns, it rises to Culture in the Goethean and Arnoldian sense, the pursuit of our total perfection; from civilizations, or assemblies of prejudices, to Civilization, which is not the heaping up of gadgets but the attainment of freedom.

The School trains the individual for the sake of the individual, and does not sacrifice him to the Leviathan Society. But it is not prepared to consider the individual except within the framework of society. The individual in absolute isolation is not an object for science or philosophy. Without contact with his fellow men, past or present, without language, without law, he is not even a barbarian, a primitive, or an animal: he is an abstraction. Note that I am not denying the reality of the unique: only its availability for our study. Our human order may well be a fragile film over a dark flood. The unique breaks through from below, as insanity or crime; it soars beyond the common reach, as genius or mysticism. But even the explorers of the unconscious have to use consciousness as their instrument; insanity and crime are so named in relation to the social order; and the mystic who does not attempt to convey his vision is lost to the world. The subject of science and scholarship is not man as a particle of the Universal Soul, but man as a "sociable animal." In human terms, the individual cannot manifest himself except within the all-embracing community. The proper study of man is Mankind.

The tie which binds men together, through space and time, is language. Our first task is to master that essential instrument; then to appraise it, to note its flaws and "aberrations," and, by exploring its utmost possibilities, to get intimations, at any rate, of what it is as yet unable to convey. The School of Humane Learning is first of all a language school; in this respect, the ancient tradition of the Humanities is fully justified. The study of our mother tongue must come first; from the kindergarten to the graduate seminar, we must seek to understand ourselves and others. I remember with gratitude the thorough drill in grammatical analysis, the grouping of words into etymological families, the discrimination between synonyms, which were part of my elementary schooling in Paris. Children should be taught "the meaning of meaning": semantics begins in the nursery. Grammar, even when unconscious and full of inconsistencies, is a logical scheme; the parts of speech imply a philosophical framework. The distinction between an individual name and a common noun is taught in the grades; but it leads to the problem: What is the validity of a common noun? Does it stand for a pragmatic classification, for an "essence," for an eternal idea? A science is a code of consistent symbols, that is to say, to borrow

Evening Thoughts of a Schoolmaster

Condillac's phrase, a well-made language. A mass of facts not connected by some "grammar" cannot form a science.

The study of foreign languages, ancient or modern, is justified when it clears away obscurities or exposes absurdities in our own, or when it brings to us depths and refinements of which our native tongue is not yet capable. This is also the value of literature, considered as a discipline, not as a source of enjoyment. (Enjoyment, I believe, cannot be taught and certainly should not be enforced; literary study at its best only removes obstacles.) To master an author is to learn a new language. A great poem is a thought revealed, refined, made new, by adequate expression—a verbal symbol which was lacking before.

Finally, the School of Humane Learning is essentially historical. Not that it clings to the dead past: it seeks to understand life. But it recognizes that life cannot be seized except in the time-flow. The instantaneous, each event a glimpse and gone forever, is not capable of scientific interpretation. Humane learning is concerned with irreversible processes (again, I am more than willing to eschew the controversial term *progress*). In this respect, it is a biological science. It is not a mere branch of zoology, because it introduces new elements: the consciousness of growth, and, through that consciousness, the possibility of deflecting its course or altering its rate.

In thus making the historical spirit one of the major keys to Humane Learning, I am challenging the upholders of the Eternal Verities in politics, economics, art, literature, philosophy. I never was among those who maintained that the Gold Standard was an unrepealable natural law, or that the number of Justices in the Supreme Court was as fixed as the constellations. (But the constellations themselves are changing with majestic deliberation.) Economics and government are historical, not experimental, sciences: experiments belong to practical politics and can never be repeated under exactly the same conditions. The philosophers themselves, who revel in the Absolute, cannot deny that there is a history of

Education of a Humanist

philosophy, not a single truth compelling universal assent, not a series of discrete illuminations, each more perfect and more eternal than the rest. Even religion has to accept the historical framework: the Eternal Will manifests itself through time. Bossuet rightly denounced the "variations" of the Protestant churches; but Newman took pride in the thought that the Church was the living instrument of progressive revelation. Grant Allen could write an intelligent book on the evolution of the idea of God. With strict literalness, in our domain, "time is of the essence." The timeless in its two forms, the instantaneous and the everlasting, is beyond the scope of Humane Learning.

My definition of our field therefore is: the collective, conscious, cumulative activity of man. Here we have to guard against three misconceptions. First of all, the word *cumulative* might raise again our old bugbear Progress, or fatalistic optimism. There may be a Rake's Progress: errors and diseases are cumulative too. A war never is the result of a mere accident, but the consequence of wrong choices. Some may be long forgotten; some may seem innocent enough when they are taken. President Truman started us on the path to World War III when, after giving his blessing to the United Nations in San Francisco, he hastened to Potsdam to play secret diplomacy and power politics. In the second place, the historical process is not deterministic. It does not bar out the possibility of chance, indeterminacy, choice. The factors involved are so innumerable and so constantly changing that their combinations remain beyond the range of prediction, within the time-scale of our planetary life. Finally, although the historical process, as it appears to man, is continuous, it certainly is extremely uneven. If it be a stream, that stream divides itself, stagnates, loses itself apparently in dead arms, rushes through rapids, tumbles into cataracts, widens into a placid lake, like the Rhone from glacier to delta.

Humane Learning is therefore History in all its branches, as it affects our present and our future. The main divisions, although never hard and fast, are clear enough: language, art, literature, politics, economics, sociology, psychology, philosophy. At almost every point there is some fruitful interchange with a neighboring science. Politics and economics, for instance, are to a large extent conditioned by geography, which in its turn is linked with geology.[9] (There is a slender but undeniable thread between the Neo-Thomism of the University of Chicago and the oil fields.) Language is connected with logic, and logic with the highest achievement of pure reasoning, mathematics. It is no mere accident that mathematicians and logicians, Descartes, Couturat, Peano, Richards, should take interest in language as an instrument. On the other hand, language, the condition of thought, takes us into psychology, which inquires how we think; and modern psychology is inseparable from physiology.

Of the professions, engineering is the farthest removed from the humanities; yet it has close contacts with economics, which, in spite of its vigorous denial, is a humanistic science. Under the banner of functionalism, engineering is absorbing architecture, which through the ages has been classed among the arts. Above all, it takes a leading part in planning, which is the very test of Humanism. A society which cannot plan, that is, which cannot exercise an activity that is collective, conscious, cumulative, will be incapable of establishing order, liberty, prosperity, and will not long endure; it is bound to dissolve into subhuman chaos. Medicine, a practical branch of the natural sciences, is associated at every turn with the humanities. Many doctors are fine humanists even in the narrower meaning of the term; and not a few of them have a touch—realists would say, a taint—of the humanitarian.[10] Law is evidently humanism in action. The connection is so close that in France the study of law is often taken up not for professional purposes exclusively but as a foundation for general culture.

---

[9] And with biology as well: cf. Maximilien Sorre, *Les Fondements biologiques de la géographie humaine*.

[10] Cf. Dr. Alfred E. Cohn, *Minerva's Progress* and *No Retreat from Reason*, two books which are eminently humanistic.

Education of a Humanist

Within our School of Humane Learning, we must see to it that the traditional departmental divisions, if they survive at all, are a convenience and not an obstacle. They must not hinder the comparative method, which is an indispensable instrument. A philologist cannot confine himself to a single language; nor a folklorist, if he is to be more than a mere collector, to a single country. We should be ready to recognize fields of study which ignore conventional boundaries. I shall not attempt to draw up an exhaustive program, but shall limit myself to a few examples. The major subject might be a period. This is already recognized to a large extent in the case of Classical Antiquity and the Middle Ages; and the same approach might be profitable in the case of the Renaissance, the Enlightenment, or, a narrower and more doubtful case, the Baroque. Paul Hazard's masterly work, *La Crise de la conscience européenne*, deals with a single generation, but explores those few decades in all countries and under every possible aspect. The unit might be geographic: not history, art, literature, economics in themselves and separately, but France or Germany.[11] This is the method of the anthropologists, who note everything they can observe about a culture. Alexis de Tocqueville, James Bryce, André Siegfried, Harold Laski did for the United States what Malinowski had done for the Trobriand Islands; the monograph of the Lynds on Middletown is in the same spirit as Robert Redfield's on Tepotzlan. Finally, the theme may be a thought, an ideal, traced through space and time. Lecky's *History of the Rise and Influence of the Spirit of Rationalism in Europe* is a case in point; or Andrew D. White's *History of the Warfare of Science with Theology in Christendom;* or again Denis de Rougemont's *L'Amour et l'Occident,* and Grant Allen's *Evolution of the Idea of God.*

Philosophy is the keystone of "humane learning." It goes far beyond the highly technical department, which, in a cryptic language of its own, records for our confusion the history of doctrines

---

[11] Cf. André Siegfried's tantalizingly brief but substantial study, *The Mediterranean,* an epitome of the humanistic sciences and not excluding poetry.

Evening Thoughts of a Schoolmaster

and systems. No man has a right to call himself a humanist unless he be a philosopher. But philosophy does not belong exclusively to our school. The old term "Natural Philosophy" had its justification. All branches of learning (as distinguished from practical training) could equally be called "scientific" and "philosophical." Of this deeper unity there is at least one symbol: the highest degree granted by the universities is that of Doctor of Philosophy. Philosophy is the common summit to which all paths aspire: wisdom and learning fused into one.

II. French Civilization

THE TEACHING OF FRENCH

For many years, although my chief interests were in literature and civilization, I taught elementary language courses. I never felt in the least humiliated by this kind of work, which might have been given in high school, or indeed in the grades. It is an important subject, and a craft difficult to master. Not everyone who knows French is qualified to teach it. I found also, in my long experience, that no one could be a good language teacher unless he were something more.

Elementary teaching is exacting, but it has its rewards. For one thing, the results of your efforts are at once apparent. In an advanced course, your students come to you with very different preparations: it is a blessing to start from scratch. In literature, can you ever swear that members of your class are going forward or backward? But with beginners, after a few lessons, you know for certain that they have left their native shore. What they speak may not yet be recognizable French; at any rate, it no longer is American. Many of them, especially the girls, treat a new language as though it were a game, that is to say, with great seriousness. Incidentally, the teacher gathers, as a small perquisite, a priceless collection of boners; and he chuckles silently at the thought that his young charges will never know what enormities they have been uttering.

Herbert Spencer, who took great pride in his skill at billiards, once was thoroughly trounced, and remarked: "To play a good game is the sign of a liberal education. To play too good a game is the sign of a misspent youth." This truly philosophical remark might be extended from billiards to languages. I do believe indeed that to know foreign languages is an indispensable part of a humanistic education; even the Greeks might have been better Greeks if they had known Persian, Sanskrit, or Hebrew. But the moment comes when excessive concern with languages becomes a waste.

There is no substitute for language study as a cure for tribalism. I admit it is not an infallible cure: a polyglot may be narrow minded. But the universalism of science and religion, the catholicity of art, the world-wide outlook of big business are all curiously impotent to dispel the delusion that the ways of our province are the only wise ways. Actual travel, per se, will not cure us: the tourist, unlike Danton, carries his country under the sole of his shoes. All he brings back from a world tour is the assurance that the Taj Mahal looks very much like its postcard pictures. Travel books and histories written in English will do some good. I have no prejudice against reading foreign masterpieces in translation: I am grateful that I was not deprived of Ibsen and Tolstoy. There are more great books in acceptable English translation than the average man could read in a lifetime; and I'd rather have him know Proust and Gide in English than *L'Abbé Constantin* in French. Granted that a translation can never be absolutely true to the original, the loss is not so great as when groping one's painful way through an imperfectly mastered idiom. Still, the realization that there are other cultures, very different from ours, and not wholly contemptible, comes best when we leave our own language behind.

It is tremendously difficult to get out of our own skins and try other people's for a change, especially when our skins are so smooth, aseptic, and comfortable. I have been repeatedly impressed with this truism when meeting American men (and women) of good will. They are in sooth the salt of the earth, aye, and the pepper too: generous, sensible, energetic, well-informed, with true charity embracing all mankind. Yet they seem incapable of realizing that the obvious American truth might not be the whole truth. This was very striking in their advocacy of disarmament without a well-knit organization for international justice. "We have no defense on the Canadian border, and therefore no fear of war," said a lady to Ambassador Jusserand. "Ah! Madam," the veteran diplomat answered, "if only we could swap neighbors!" The Hughes program for the Washington Naval Conference, the Hoover Moratorium, and the Truman Doctrine were suddenly placed before the world, and imposed upon the world, because, in their authors' eyes, they were self-evident. This is parochialism on a global scale.

The well-meaning persons whom I like, admire, and criticize, had, I doubt not, studied languages, possibly many. They could probably still parse a page of Caesar, or quote a telling phrase from Fraser and Squair. We had an ambassador of good will who could spout *Amigo* and *Tovarich* with the best of them. But mentally they never could avert their eyes from the Stars and Stripes; they could not lose themselves in another people's soul. They could never understand why a cosmopolitan like Roussy de Sales was so skeptical, and even so resentful, about their evangelical activities.

To break down these prejudices, hostile or smug, we need a better knowledge of languages. But the price is high: such knowledge demands more time than most of us can afford; and if carried too far, it would lead not to humanism, but to the desiccation of the sheer linguist. There is no magic way out of this difficulty, not even the streamlined, speeded-up methods evolved during the war by our armed forces. My own suggestions are simple and submitted with due modesty. I am convinced they would improve the situation; I am aware they would not lightly remove every obstacle.

First of all, we do not need many languages: Cardinal Mezzofanti, who knew sixty, was a prodigy not an example. One is enough for the majority of high school students; two for most college undergraduates; three or more only for those who desire to become professional scholars. The fewer they are, the greater the care that should be exercised in selecting these languages. I am sorry to find myself

Education of a Humanist

on the wrong side of the scholarly fence, but I cannot satisfy myself that Latin should preserve its present preëminence. Very few indeed are the high school students who can give it the time and care that alone would justify the effort. A superficial acquaintance with Latin is useless. The time of Latin tags is gone, although I find it difficult to break myself of the habit. Etymology, so often invoked, is a delusion and a snare. We do not need to know Greek to use the *telephone,* or to understand that an *automobile* is a self-propelled vehicle. For more subtle terms, like *virtue, charity, humanity, classic,* the original meaning is no sure guide to the present usage. If I need my Latin Lexicon to use properly *nugatory, impecunious, supererogatory, sesquipedalian, pediculous,* or *eleemosynary,* I had better not use them at all. From the artistic point of view, I am sensitive to the majesty of the Latin tongue; still, the great creative literature, delicate and profound, was not the Latin but the Greek. The best of Latin thought has long passed into our blood stream.[1]

Now I find the irrepressible Monsieur Josse asserting himself again. I was for half my career in the French line of business, and I believe that I had a fine assortment of goods to sell. Smile at my sales talk if you will, but listen with an open mind. French is the European language with the longest continuous literature: for nearly a thousand years there have been in every generation French works that Europe could not afford to ignore. The plea on behalf of French is particularly strong with people of English speech. Throughout the ages, the two cultures have been intertwined. If Chaucer is perhaps the best example of the medieval Gallic spirit, Voltaire has justly been called England's best gift to France. French is different enough in form, thought, and charm to be a challenge; at the same time, its vocabulary and syntax offer enough points in common with ours to make the language accessible, if not easy.

---

[1] I shall explain in my last chapter why I advocate "Basic Anglo-Latin" *(Latino sine flexione* or *Interlingua)* as an auxiliary language: an Esperanto which would at the same time be an introduction to classical Latin. But that is a totally different problem.

French Civilization

I am stating the case for French as simply as I can. I never believed that French was in a class by itself. Intrinsically, it is not supremely beautiful. It is a bad instrument in clumsy hands. The saying "Whatever is not clear is not French" is nonsense. It is possible to be vague, ambiguous, and cryptic in French. There are *équivoques* and *mots à double entente* even in plain conversation; and in Mallarmé or Valéry, the meaning may be so refined as to pass all understanding. I always thought that Rivarol's *Discourse on the Universality of the French Language* was elegant twaddle. If Rivarol spoke of the "inherent probity" of French, a character in Goethe called it *une langue perfide,* and there is truth in both assertions. I am fully aware of the arguments which can be adduced in favor of German, Spanish, and Russian.[2] I have no desire that French should enjoy an exclusive privilege. My point is that, as a language in the contemporary world, French has claims which cannot be lightly dismissed; and that in addition it ought to be for us, because of its historical importance, something of a classical language, a worthy substitute for Latin.

Let us learn a few languages then, and learn them well: a smattering is a frittering. I am now coming to a point upon which I find myself again at variance with many of my learned colleagues: in my opinion, it is possible to acquire a thorough reading knowledge of a language without being able to speak it fluently or write it correctly. To limit one's field is not unscholarly; the important thing is to choose the field wisely. My contention is that a reading knowledge, the easiest part of language study, is also by far the most rewarding.

I am writing for Americans, not for the Swiss or Czechoslovaks. Most of us will never go abroad at all (except perhaps on army transports). When we do, it is likely to be for a short vacation and along the time-honored routes. This is sensible enough: if you have a few weeks only to spend in France, you will want to see Paris, the

---

[2] Do not count on a knowledge of Russian to clear up the misunderstandings between the two countries. The most bitter enemies of the U.S.S.R. in America know Russia and the Russians; its most ardent supporters do not.

great cathedrals, and the *châteaux* of the Loire, rather than the textile works of Tourcoing or the bicycle factories of Saint-Etienne. On the beaten track, you need not limit yourself to the shops that bear the familiar sign, "English Spoken, American Understood" (for H. L. Mencken's fame has reached distant shores). A few weeks before the trip, you will be able to master the magic phrases that will enable you to order a *bifteck* and to buy postcards.

I spoke of a reading knowledge: I should have said a passive, or better still, a receptive knowledge. For reading plus phonetics—we shall soon return to that—will enable you to understand even though you can neither speak nor write. In a recent extensive tour of Mexico, I never was allowed to use my Spanish (perhaps my interlocutors loved Spanish too well to run the risk); but no one could prevent my listening to Spanish in the lecture room, the meeting hall, the theater, and even the lowly second-class autobus. Unless you are a missionary, it is not essential that you should speak; it is far more important that you should listen.

This applies not to the tourist merely but to the businessman as well. We have a brisk and expanding trade with Latin America, but very few of us will ever have direct contact with the ultimate customer. I noticed in Guadalajara, the second city in Mexico, that while the shops were stocked with United States goods, the American colony was extremely small. The agencies of American firms are naturally in the hands of native Mexicans, who are better acquainted with local conditions and are satisfied with lower salaries. Americans as a rule are found only in the higher managerial positions, although we discovered one in the local jail.

There is no reason, therefore, why millions of young Americans should spend five or six years acquiring a command of French or Spanish in the hope that they may take a few weeks' trip, for business or for pleasure, across the Atlantic or south of the Rio Grande. The disparity between the effort and the result is too great.

On the contrary, in two years of normal high school work, in a single year of an intense college course, it is possible to acquire a

French Civilization

thorough receptive knowledge of French, Spanish, Portuguese, or Italian. (German is a harder nut to crack; I have not tried Russian.) And this knowledge is not good intermittently, a few weeks every ten years perhaps, maybe once in a lifetime: it stays with you always. For a couple of dollars, you can buy your paper-bound bit of France, and, in Keokuk or Milpitas, spend happy hours with Colette, Mauriac, or Bernanos.

Note that beginning with a receptive knowledge does not in the least preclude the possibility of acquiring later an active command of the language. Of course, there will always be a minority who will desire, or who will need, to speak and write French, Spanish, German, Russian, as perfectly as possible. But we should teach first to the many what is of greatest value to the many. The time of the few will not be wasted.

There is one strong objection to a mere reading knowledge when it totally neglects the spoken language. There are few people who do not read orally, at least to some extent; even when their lips do not move, they imagine faintly the sound of the words they read. If the right pronunciation were not taught from the first, bad habits would be formed; and if a man wanted to acquire an active mastery of the spoken language, he would be under a heavy handicap.

So I am convinced that students should be well grounded in phonetics from the first: the sounds should be properly analyzed, described, and made definite through the use of scientific symbols. Many young people object to the unfamiliar signs, although they are fewer and simpler than the rules of most card games. In my early twenties, I too was averse to phonetic script, as willfully creating an unnatural obstacle. I was converted by Paul Passy, a great apostle, and, like not a few apostles, something of a fanatic. One episode is still fresh in my memory. Passy had explained to us why French had a rich variety of oral vowels and only four nasal vowels, *an, in, on, un* (four too many, if you ask me). "We can change at will the shape and capacity of the oral cavity, but not of the nasal cavity. Ah! If only we had a trunk like the elephants!" This phonetician's dream was expressed with such wistfulness that the whole class was convulsed with friendly laughter.[3]

GERMANY AND MEDIEVAL PHILOLOGY

In 1906, three months after my arrival in America, I attended the annual meeting of the Modern Language Association at New Haven. I happened to have a chat with the president of that learned body, an august personage in the profession, who treated the fledgling instructor with the utmost kindness. Casually, he asked me: "Where did you study in Germany?" Somewhat taken aback, I answered that I had visited Germany, but never had studied there. In a courteous, encouraging tone, he proceeded: "Oh well, you will have a chance in high schools and private academies."

I am not vindictive, but that rankled. Seven years later, fate played a neat trick on me. Rutger Jewett, of Appleton's, showed

[3] The best way to improve your reading knowledge is to read abundantly. Pick up a long, easy, entertaining tale: for that purpose, nothing compares with the romances of old Dumas (I first read *The Three Musketeers* in English). In a short time, you will be floating on the pleasant stream and forget your native speech. I toyed with the idea of a reader on the dissolving picture principle. The narrative was to start in English. On every page, five new French words were to be introduced. Long before the middle of the book, thanks to the large element common to both languages, the text would be more than half French, and wholly French at the end: *French Without Tears;* but it would be wise not to read aloud such an *entente cordiale* monstrosity.

Since I am shedding a tear on the grave of stillborn ideas, I was tempted (by the financial success of Messrs. Fraser and Squair) to write a French grammar. I went so far as to borrow a title from that great Christian apologist, Mr. Bruce Barton, then at the height of his fame as a latter-day Athanasius: *The Grammar Nobody Knows.* I did not proceed. I have, by the way, quite a collection of books thus written "by title only." Here are a few samples: *Casual Remarks of a Casual Officer, a War Diary; The Live Wire Meets a Deadline: A Romance of Journalism; The Ghost Writer and the Skeleton Crew: A Gothick Tale;* and in French, a story oozing with irony and pity: *L'Homme de Peine et la Fille de Joie.* Perhaps happy titles are all the happier for not having heavy books tagged on to them; like those charming little angels in old Italian paintings—just a head and a pair of wings—they cannot be spanked by the critics.

me the glowing report from his reader which had induced him to publish my first book, *French Prophets of Yesterday,* aptly described as a congenital worst seller. I asked him who was my providential benefactor. It was the very man whom, for seven years, I had been hating with mild, scholarly, but unextinguishable hatred.

This personal experience revealed to me the stranglehold that, for two generations at least, Germany had on American higher education. Our universities were loyal colonies of the *Vaterland.* Our men of learning felt that Oxford, Cambridge, the Sorbonne, even though they could still turn out a good piece of work once in a while, were hopelessly outmoded. Those fanes of ancient lore were loved by a few for their odor of refined decay; they were the delightful haunts of erudite shades, with the nostalgic charm of Versailles. If you craved for profundity and vigor, it was in Germany that they had to be sought.

I soon realized that Germanophilism had deep and healthy roots in American soil. There have been sturdy German settlers in this country from the earliest days of its independence. In the nineteenth century, they came in their millions and proved able, honest, law-abiding citizens. No wonder that, by 1900, we had half-consciously adopted the dream of Cecil Rhodes: a world governed by the virile Saxon, with scant regard for the lesser breeds. Our policy never was admittedly pro-German, but it worked exactly as though it had been. This bias reappeared, actually undiminished, after the storm of the First World War. We adopted immigration quotas intended to preserve the Nordic character of our population. We accepted blindfolded the quaint notion that the Versailles Treaty was a tissue of iniquities. We insisted that it was foolish and criminal for the Allies to expect reparations from the Germans, while it was wise and righteous for us to exact repayment from the Allies. Even today . . . but let us return to our pedagogical pastures.

Now I have no thought of denouncing America's inveterate pro-Germanism as a foolish delusion. I have been a Germanophile myself all my life, and at times under very difficult circumstances. I am a Germanophile still. I never denied that, for over a century, the material output of the German universities had been most impressive in bulk and most highly finished in details. Only when in the name of science I was asked to fall down and worship German infallibility, I could not give up the essential instrument of all science, the critical spirit. Arrogance is the mark not of the scholar but of the pedant.

I could not help noticing that, in peace-loving America, the prestige of German science was so closely linked with that of German arms that it seemed almost a by-product of victory. Granted, as we were constantly told, that it was the Prussian schoolmaster who triumphed at Sedan: conversely, and perhaps with greater truth, it could be said that Moltke and Roon were lending their authority to the philologist in his professorial chair. Bismarck—deceit and brutality at the service of a medieval dream—remained unchallenged, a massive rough-hewn idol. The learned world, either in Germany or on this side, utterly failed to question the vital lies of the Hohenzollern Empire. No wonder that the shoddy second Reich was so promptly followed by a third. I have been outspoken enough in my criticism of Napoleon-worship to be just as fearless in my denunciation of other demigods.

I do not know to what extent the overwhelming prestige of Germany was justified in philosophy and in the sciences. But in the field of Romance Languages, and particularly of French, the situation, in 1906, was appalling. In the key positions, at the head of departments, Frenchmen were heavily outnumbered by Germans. More striking still was the disparity between the number of Americans who had taken advanced studies in France and in Germany.[4] Note that individually those Teutonic interpreters of France were

[4] For this there was a technical reason; in those days, the German Ph.D. was easier than ours, while the French *Doctorat ès Lettres* was almost inaccessible to foreigners. The French have since established a competitive Doctor's degree, chiefly for the export trade.

not only competent but eminently fair. They were not a Fifth Column; there was no conspiracy on their part to traduce or belittle their chosen subject. My Stanford chief, John Ernst Matzke, born in Breslau, resented as a personal insult any attack on France. Their bias was manifested in a more insidious way.

They were honestly persuaded, and they had contrived to convince the academic world in this country, that the one essential thing in the study of Romance languages was medieval philology. Modern French was taught, condescendingly, to the undergraduates; but in the graduate schools, where the masters were formed, philology reigned supreme. In one of our best Eastern universities, the six graduate courses offered were all in Old French; in a prominent center of the Middle West, out of seven courses, only one was in Modern French; in a great institution of the Pacific Coast, out of four courses, three were in the medieval field. At Harvard, Columbia, Chicago, the disproportion was not so glaring; but on the whole, the ratio was four to one in favor of medieval philology.

When I glanced at the theses, those "masterpieces" which qualified a man as an expert in his craft, for one thorough and discriminating study like Carrington Lancaster's *The Tragi-Comedy in France,* how many belonged to the type *Dialektische Eigentümlichkeiten in der Entwickelung des mouillierten L im Alt-Französischen!*[5] At that time, among the honorary members of the Modern Language Association were found medievalists and phoneticians, but not a single literary critic. France was represented, not unworthily, by Paul Meyer and Antoine Thomas. But Ferdinand Brunetière, Emile Faguet, and Gustave Lanson were ignored. Linguistics stifled literature, and the Middle Ages eclipsed modern times.

Now Romance Philology is an unimpeachable branch of learning, and the pre-Romantic contempt of the Middle Ages as "Gothic," that is, uncouth, denoted a flaw in the classical mind. The centuries

---

[5] J. E. Matzke. Since *dialektisch* means both "dialectal" and "dialectic," a friend of mine, to whom I mentioned this impressive title, thought it was inspired by the method of Hegel and Marx.

of the cathedrals and the great scholastic philosophers were highly civilized. Indeed, their fault, not in reasoning merely but in the arts as well, was not naïveté, but excessive refinement; not rude monolithic unity, but too great a wealth of conflicting impulses and principles. And it would be ludicrous to assert that the medieval synthesis could safely be ignored because it has left no trace in the modern world: there are thirteenth-century minds among the most vigorous thinkers and poets of the present day. For that reason, I believe it is legitimate to build, in this age, Gothic cathedrals for Gothic worshipers; a modernistic temple would be a painful anachronism. And the architecture of Yale, Princeton, and Chicago is justified, if these great seats of learning do intend to be fortresses of medieval thought.

The issue is a matter not of exclusion but of proportion. The excessive emphasis placed on medieval studies distorts the perspective of French culture. I for one would gladly grant that Gothic architecture is second to none; and—a willfully ambiguous admission—that Thomistic philosophy is at least as good as any. But this is not true of medieval French literature. Frankly, that half-millennium, although not barren, is mediocre. It started well, with the *Song of Roland,* an epic of faith and fighting, stark in thought and feeling, spare, swift, unerring in its simple craftsmanship. It ended magnificently with François Villon, a narrow but supreme poet, a weird luminous shaft in the anguished twilight between two worlds. And I am familiar with many a delightful work of art in the interval, farce or fabliau, chronicle and song. But after all, the *Romance of the Rose* is dusty, *Reynard the Fox* has a very limited range, and, for all its miraculous freshness, *Aucassin and Nicolette* is but a charming miniature. There is nothing in all this to be compared, even remotely, with the *Divine Comedy.* Boileau was wrong when he swept contemptuously aside everything before Villon, but not altogether wrong: twenty years under Louis XIV outweighed the five hundred that preceded the Renaissance. The true greatness of the Middle Ages did not express itself in the vernacular. It found its symbols in the great Bibles of stone, and its highest thought used

French Civilization

Latin for its instrument. Medieval France had but a decapitated literature.

Shall we say that the study of origins is indispensable for the understanding of later ages, down to our own? I agree; but the limits of this excellent principle can soon be reached. It would be a waste, if we were to trace the stormy careers of David Lloyd George and Winston Churchill, to spend too much time investigating the Saxon witenagemot. The trouble with our Romance scholars is that they never went beyond the equivalent of the witenagemot. The great writers of later ages took their Old French heritage for granted; they were infinitely more interested in the Greco-Roman tradition and in the usage of polite society. Philology, in the narrower sense, accounts for, but never explains, a number of quaint survivals. It tells us, for instance, the reason (which is not reasonable) why the adjective immediately preceding *gens* is feminine, while the others are masculine (*Instruits par l'expérience, les vieilles gens sont soupçonneux*). Oddities of this kind, and irregular spellings, plurals, or conjugations never could give a deeper insight into meaning or beauty. And the medievalists knew it full well. But they were "scientists": sense and charm had no standing in their eyes.

I know I am giving offense to friends and colleagues, survivors or epigones of the philological dictatorship. I must repeat that I recognize the value of linguistics as a great science in its own right and a most helpful element in humane learning. I know that linguistics must delve into the past, and that we must have devoted specialists to explore even the most minute and most recondite crannies of the universe. My quarrel was with those who actually sought to subordinate the humanistic study of literature to that of a single contributory branch. Yes, we need experts in every field, but what we need even more is a sense of proportion. And that sense, forty years ago, was woefully deficient. When I came to Stanford, the university, then one of the richest in the world, had been operating for fifteen years. The library was well equipped for Romance philology; but there was not on our shelves a single book by Agrippa

Education of a Humanist

d'Aubigné, Régnier, Bossuet, Montesquieu, Michelet, Taine, or Renan. We had, it is true, the Anglo-Norman poems of Simon de Freine: surely a strange revaluation of all values.

It would have greatly incensed our Romance scholars to tell them that their unbridled medievalism was a survival of the Romantic era. During the classical age, the Germans suffered from an inferiority complex. They were aware of their own worth, yet they had had to accept as the protagonists of European culture first the Italians, then the French. In their quest for *Gleichberechtigung* or equality of status, they rediscovered the great days in which the Holy Roman Empire of the German Nation was the very core of Christendom. They lived themselves nostalgically into the times of Barbarossa. They have not quite awakened from that dream.

It must be said, however, that they were too realistic to deny the greatness of modern Germany. If they went back, joyously, to Gothic, it did not cause them to neglect Goethe. Similarly, in the English field, Anglo-Saxon never eclipsed the study of Shakespeare or Milton. France was singled out as the sufferer. Unconscious bias and unconfessed self-interest combined most efficiently. The German and Germanized Romance scholars, even when they were perfectly correct in their attitude, had no deep love for modern France; and they were shrewd enough to know that in the domain of literary criticism they would be hopelessly outclassed. "Let no one enter unless he be a philologist": this scientific wall efficiently defended their preserves.

So, without malice prepense, the medieval bias contributed to spread and strengthen a prejudice which, as we shall see, was all too prevalent in the American mind: that the greatness of France was entirely a thing of the past. If the best authorities failed to study modern French literature, it proved conclusively that French literature was not worth studying; it was only worth enjoying, with an apologetic smile. And could there be a more damning evidence of France's decay than the fact that her own language could best be taught by Germans and through German books; that if you wanted

French Civilization

a "well of French undefiled," you had to go to F. C. Diez and Meyer-Lübke?

The philological fallacy had another unfortunate result, which, in many cases, has not yet been corrected. The common Latin origin of French, Spanish, and Italian led to their being grouped into a single department. From the strictly linguistic point of view, this arrangement is above reproach. It has at least two drawbacks, however, one of a practical, the other of a cultural nature. When a university wanted to be most scrupulously fair, it established a parity between the Germanic and the Romance (or, more logically, Romanic) languages. Now, in most cases "Germanic Languages" meant purely and simply German: the Scandinavian tongues and Dutch seldom were included in the curriculum. But there were three major Romanic languages, without counting Provençal, Portuguese, Catalan, and Rumanian. As a result, Italian was almost completely sacrificed, with the sole exception of Dante. French and Spanish had to divide the appropriations. Moreover, the head of the department could hardly be expected to be a first-class authority in all three languages; many of his staff felt that in their own field they were far more competent than he, and his intellectual authority suffered in consequence.[6]

The cultural consequences were far worse. The standard grouping, legitimate on a linguistic basis, distorted history and literature. France does not disown what she received from Rome; but she is not exclusively, or even predominantly, a Latin nation. The Mediterranean race in France is but a minority. Roman law survived only in the South; until the Revolution, in the richer and more populous North, custom law prevailed. Between France and her Latin "sisters" stand the highest mountains in Europe; between France and northern Germany, through the Low Countries, the way is freely—all too

---

[6] Spanish, in many instances, was then treated as a poor relation. Now the situation is reversed. Spanish enjoys a great and legitimate vogue, but French in its turn occupies a subordinate position, out of keeping with its historical and cultural importance. Separation is the obvious remedy.

Education of a Humanist

freely—open. These physical facts are translated into terms of culture. France was profoundly influenced by Italy at the time of the Renaissance, but so was the rest of civilized Europe. The vogue of all things Spanish was more superficial and lasted at most two generations. On the other hand, for the last three centuries, it is with England and Germany that France has kept up the most active intercourse. Innumerable factors have decreed that Paris, not Toulouse or Marseilles, should be the focal point of French cultural life; and Paris is in closer touch with London, Brussels, or Cologne than with Rome or Madrid.

All large universities should therefore have a separate department of French; smaller institutions might, for purely administrative purposes, have a department of Modern Languages. But the division Romanic-Germanic should be condemned unhesitatingly. Philology deserves to have an organization of its own, on an Indo-European basis. It ought to be frankly severed from literature, for the two require different types of mind and different methods. This autonomy would not preclude, of course, frequent and friendly relations. It is not impossible for a man to be at the same time a philologist and a student of literature, just as it is possible for another to be interested in graphic arts, jurisprudence, or religion, and to be also a literary critic. There is no *Sinn Fein* in the Humanities.

I had planned to make my career in America; I was discreet enough not to seek to impose my French habits of thought upon my new countrymen. So I did my honest best to fill the gaps of my education in medieval philology. For two full years I took a stiff course, seven hours a week, under John E. Matzke, a fine scholar, a very able teacher, and a true friend. His enthusiasm was contagious, and I enjoyed the work. Forty years have gone by: I can state candidly that this great effort was an almost total waste. It simply postponed by two years my starting on my real work. My advice to my successors is this: Do not take up Romance philology unless you want to specialize in it. It is a legitimate field, but a nar-

French Civilization

row one. As a background for your French studies, take up geography, the history of institutions, and that of the arts. If your interest lies in the France of the Renaissance and the Classical Age, by all means master Greek, Latin, and Italian; if you choose modern France, from the Enlightenment to the present day, you will need English, German, philosophy, economics. Above all, do not be fooled by the claim that philology alone is "scholarly." Philology is a card game, and you may bluff at it as (I am told) you bluff at poker. On the other hand, there may be scholarship of the most exacting type in an investigation of Alfred de Musset.

So, a foreign beginner, I found it wise not to rebel. I served faithfully my term of apprenticeship and kept my counsel. Fortunately, there were at that moment other men, older than I, and infinitely better qualified to lead the good fight for liberation. To them, and particularly to Barrett Wendell and to Irving Babbitt, I owe a debt of gratitude: they made the academic atmosphere respirable for me.

Barrett Wendell went to the Sorbonne as Exchange Professor. He brought back a book, *The France of Today,* which, to many Americans, was a revelation. Instead of the conventional *Trilby* picture of the Latin Quarter, it revealed a France that was hard-working to a fault, fearless, intellectually austere. The outstanding defect of the French as I knew them, and as Barrett Wendell saw them, was not frivolity but excessive strenuousness. I found the more easy-going pace of American college life decidedly more to my taste.

Irving Babbitt was a doughty champion indeed. His very bulk, his New England conscience, his appalling erudition, his relentless logic, his massive self-confidence, inspired profound respect, not without a tinge of awe. With this formidable equipment, he attacked "the Philological Ring." He could perform the miracle of routing the supercilious by turning upon them the Higher Superciliousness. His early controversial books were victories in the war for freedom. His *Masters of Modern French Criticism* was more than a campaign document. With it Babbitt proved his mettle: no one could consider such work as amateurish. And he revealed to America a collective achievement—a half-century of French criticism—which, in a secondary field, was of unique value. The book was both a manifesto and a demonstration.[7]

Not seldom is the hero of Resistance and Liberation tempted to turn into a dictator. But if he does, then, regretfully, respectfully, a loyal follower may withdraw his allegiance. With most of Babbitt's opinions in his later books, I disagreed *in toto*. But it was the healthiest, the most stimulating kind of disagreement, the kind I should have liked to rouse in my own students. Babbitt was a dogmatist who, in spite of his courage and his clearness of thought, never was able to formulate his dogma. A native shrewdness prevented him from adopting outright the reactionary code of Brunetière and T. S. Eliot. He was a humanist in the noblest sense, even though his "armor of elastic steel," as he liked to call it, was too unyielding and threatened to choke him. We corresponded as early as 1910, but I never knew him personally, and I deeply regret it.

There was an ironical twist in this austerely dignified career. Babbitt—and Norman Foerster as his energetic lieutenant—managed at one time to "sell" Humanism to the Great American Public. Humanism was not exactly front-page news, but it got into the papers. It had its flutter of popularity, like Technocracy, Keyserling, Pareto, and Existentialism. It must have been infinitely embarrassing for the Harvard Brahmin to find himself in the gaudy Paradise of the Sunday supplement, with Babe Ruth, Jack Dempsey, Jimmy Walker, and "Peaches" Browning. To cap it all, Sinclair Lewis (unwittingly, I presume) selected that honored name for the very antipodes of scholarly humanism. For a while, we had a Babbitt at the zenith of American thought, and a Babbitt at the nadir. For remote historians, this coincidence may prove bewildering.

[7] I have no thought of minimizing the influence of Paul Elmer More and Joel Spingarn; but Babbitt was more of a fighter than either, and his special field happened to be my own.

French Civilization

TRIBULATIONS OF AN INTERPRETER

My intention was to be in America a modest and faithful French interpreter. Not an apologist, not an advocate: the interpreter is neutral. To serve equally both his clients is the first article of his professional code: I have not consciously transgressed the duties of my office. My objectivity, which was resented by many Frenchmen, can be explained without any lofty claim to scholarly detachment. It would have been impossible for me to follow "the national line" and defend everything French: I knew France too well for that. I had gone through the Dreyfus crisis; then our enemies had been the Nationalists with their war cry: "France, right or wrong!" France, obviously, was the Flag, and the Flag was the Army that bore it and defended it, and the Army was the General Staff to which passive obedience was due: a faultless logical chain against which I had rebelled. I could explain but I could not preach in the same breath the France of Rabelais and that of Calvin; the France of Bossuet and that of Voltaire; the France of Hugo and that of Claudel; the France of Maurras and that of Jaurès. If we admit the existence of an entity or deity called France, it could not be defined and demonstrated as if it were a religious dogma; it could only be evoked through a multitude of details, which might at first seem inconsistent. My faith in France was robust enough not to rely upon evasions and distortions. My sole business was to say: "Here, to the best of my knowledge, is what the French are. If you like them better upon closer acquaintance, well and good. They crave appreciation, for they are human; but they do not want to be admired through some false glamour."

I soon realized, however, that even the most modest interpreter, if he be afflicted with a conscience, may have to go beyond a mere literal translation. The interpreter has to protect his client against misinterpretation. Paul Mantoux, in 1919, occasionally softened the snarls of the Tiger; and Clemenceau, who had a good command of English, told him with a friendly growl: "You'll lose your job if you make me bleat like that." In 1918, I received the order: "See what those d---d Frogs are doing, and tell them not to." I knew that the French officer to whom I was to convey this message had no sense of American humor; so I translated, with what may be called the deeper faithfulness: "Colonel X's compliments; and he desires to know what is your pleasure in the matter of . . ." In many cases, to interpret means to explain.

I expected the task of explaining France to be not easy by any means, but direct and pleasant. And so it was, to a very large extent. Most of my students came to my classes with a genuine desire to learn, that is to say, with a definite awareness of their ignorance. Ignorance, per se, is a friendly enemy; it puts up a stubborn fight, but recedes with a smile, and is glad to acknowledge its defeat. I found, however, even among the young, something far more discouraging than ignorance: a heavy mass of prejudice, witless, amorphous, cohesive. What made it so hard to sweep away this tenacious, viscous mass was a thin protective coating of friendliness: "Of course, every American loves France."

In a crisis, when all ambiguities melt away in a crude and violent flame, our feeling toward France is unpredictably ambivalent. It may turn to fanatical Gallomania, as in the days of the Marne and Verdun, when the French could do no wrong. It may lead to a no less fierce and unreasoning Gallophobia, as when Oswald Garrison Villard, a true American of the old school, a genuine liberal, a gentle and fearless soul, proclaimed France "the enemy of mankind."

In normal times (for, believe it or not, there were normal times once, or at any rate, times that did not disturb the delusion of normalcy), our sentiments toward France are not so sharply polarized. There is a small cultured minority for whom France is indeed, as she was for Jefferson, a second country. There is no corresponding group of consistent French haters and baiters to match the raving *Franzosenfresser* of nineteenth-century Germany. The vast majority of the American people have the vaguest ideas on the subject, as indeed on every other; for there is nothing quite so stupid as the col-

French Civilization

lective mind, and it would be more charitable to deny its existence altogether. Our publicists, echoes of bemused Uncle Sam, heap up contradictions. France is our earliest, our most constant friend, our sister Republic, the frontier of liberty; France is realistic, unscrupulous, nationalistic through and through, always ready to grab at a selfish advantage and welsh on an obligation. France is a nation of heroes, from Roland to De Gaulle; France is a nation of cowards, who fled at Waterloo, surrendered at Sedan, and collaborated with their victors. France is ever the intellectual vanguard; France is congenitally antiquated, all facile elegance and conformity to familiar patterns. France is the home of all the bourgeois virtues and likewise of all the Bohemian vices. The French are faultless craftsmen; the French are deplorably slack and incompetent. Out of this whirl there emerges an equivocal composite picture: the France we love for the wrong reasons, with a solid background of contempt.

I feel deeply embarrassed to use *The Last Time I Saw Paris,* by Elliot Paul, as the text of my homily. I have never met Paul, but men whom I greatly respect speak of him with genuine regard and glowing affection. His *Life and Death of a Spanish Town* was obviously sincere, and touching without mawkishness. Few books gave me keener delight than his Homer Evans murder mysteries; and his political opinions happen to coincide, *grosso modo,* with mine. The best writers are not free from literary sin: I should be glad to write *Requiescat* on a misbegotten work which does even less justice to its author than to its subject. But the book was a symptom, and its success was a portent.

I do not doubt that Paul knows something about France, in his own unconventional fashion, and that he is sincere when he professes to love the country and its people. It is this distorted knowledge and this perverted love that made *The Last Time I Saw Paris* both so typical and so dangerous; as Paul's friend Mireille would say after entertaining a learned judge: *Corruptio optimi pessima.* But in spite of distant personal sympathy, and gratitude for many hours of excel-

Education of a Humanist

lent fooling, I must voice my protest. We paid a heavy price, in the form of a second world war, for two decades of misunderstanding; and a great responsibility rests on the professional purveyors of misinformation. A sophisticated *bon vivant* attitude and the facile charm of a *Vie de Bohême* atmosphere are not valid excuses.

Elliot Paul's main thesis is that the squalid Rue de la Huchette is an authentic symbol of Paris and of France; that if it "could be resurrected, there would be enough of France alive today to stir a spark of hope in the hearts of men." My contention is that Rue de la Huchette is a slum justly condemned by the city. But for the war, it would have been razed as an *îlôt insalubre,* or unsanitary area. We may feel a kind of pitying tenderness for the slums in the material world and in the spiritual: we do not want them resurrected.

The danger of accepting a slum as the symbol of a nation is that even if you are full of indulgence for the local squalor, you are bound to condemn the nation that breeds it and tolerates it. Elliot Paul has a profound New England love for cleanliness and decency; he chose to live in a quarter where these virtues had but a subordinate place; the result is that he speaks of France and everything French in terms which Nazi propaganda at its worst would have hesitated to use. Everything about the country is rotten: housing, health, business, bureaucracy, politics. Science, art, poetry are stricken with the same incurable blight. French literature—including, I suppose, Claudel and Valéry—has for its "one and only theme the *cocu.*" If the picture were true, then welcome the Führer and his rod of iron! The hands are Elliot Paul's, but the voice is Goebbels'. At times it is Mussolini's: we are informed that the Corsicans "after all, are practically pure Italians."

This book would take its place among the Homer Evans extravaganzas if only it were amusing. It might be described as *Mayhem in B Flat* against the French language; a *Mysterious Mickey Finn* for the student of French affairs; and *Hugger Mugger* not in the Louvre only, but all over the place. It is a double-barrelled mystery story: how can a man live so long in Paris and know so much about it that

French Civilization

is hopelessly not so? How can a man pose as a friend, believe himself a friend, with a muzzy, three-o'clock-in-the-morning expansiveness, and in his sober hours be so systematically blind and unfair?

It is certainly not a good sign for an authority on France, who has dwelt in the Rue de la Huchette off and on for some eighteen years, to show such perfect imperviousness to the language of Clément Vautel and Racine. His pages are sprinkled with French expressions: when they happen to be right, it is such a miracle that we feel we ought to light a candle to St. Anthony of Padua or St. Christopher. Elliot Paul's French has a solid New England foundation, relieved with bits of Croatian Serb and demotic Greek; only such a combination would account for such gems as "Vous valez également à deux fois rien." But that quaint *lingua franca* only reveals inexhaustible depths of delusions. Laden barges drift where they have no business to be; trains get into unexpected stations; St. Sulpice is mixed up with St. Germain des Prés; the Halles are on the wrong side of the Rue de Rivoli. For the uninitiated, it sounds as impressive as Mark Twain's magnificent description of the desert: "Far in the empty sky a solitary œsophagus slept upon motionless wing."

There is one side of Elliot Paul's fabulous erudition that I am unable to check: I take it for granted that he was, as he claims, intimate with the business staff of *Le Panier Fleuri*. As for Hyacinthe Berthelot, the supreme flower, the exquisite symbol of a dying civilization, she may be authentic, but that does not make her credible. I never came across a more unconvincing heroine. If he produces for my confusion the originals of her letters, my interpretation would be that the young lady was vigorously pulling his leg.

Of course, if Hemingway accurately describes the life of American correspondents in Paris, this nightmarish chronic befuddlement is easily accounted for. But their misdeeds are not limited to jumbling French grammar, Parisian topography, and the Ten Commandments. Elliot Paul, who is by no means the most misinformative, has one of his heroes married at church *before* the civil ceremony, does not know who were the members of the Little Entente, mistakes

Education of a Humanist

President Poincaré for the mathematician, states that Daladier had Parliament adjourned for two years, believes that the *Croix-de-Feu* were Léon Daudet's youth organization, and gives a wholly perverted account of the debt problem. Madariaga was right: the press is too powerful to remain irresponsible. Democracy is founded on opinion, and opinion is fed by the press. We cannot afford to have as our guides men who follow no principle but picturesqueness: if it makes a vivid picture or brings out an epigram, it must be true. Journalists and professors live on the same planet and are engaged in the same task of education. The men who are addressing a handful of youngsters are required to have a rigorous preparation and to obey a rigid honor code; those who sway the minds of millions can get by with a certain degree of unscrupulous smartness.

My guess is that the Elliott Paul mystery—symbol of many others—can be explained by the pathetic quest for superiority. The Rue de la Huchette admirably satisfies such a craving. The man from New England loves to live among the "natives," because their penury and squalor confirm his sense of indomitable rightness. The same feeling works beautifully in reverse. The friend of Mariette and Mary the Greek feels superior not only to Paris but also to Dorchester, Massachusetts, because he has consciously risen above its prejudices. This is some compensation for the fact that he does not understand Racine.

I know that French writers of great talent—Aragon, Céline, Sartre—have given us an even more damaging picture of French society than Elliot Paul's. I shall certainly not accuse Paul of being a discourteous guest, who exposes the sordid secrets of his hosts. Such "nice" scruples would kill honest reporting, and, by extension, honest history and honest literature. If those who know were too polite to tell, how could the truth ever break out? The gentlemanly code, by the way, would condemn French writers even more severely than foreign witnesses. They know that their books will be read abroad. If it is bounderish to traduce one's host, it is an even worse breach of etiquette to sully one's own nest. Our Master Napoleon said, "We

French Civilization

must wash our dirty linen in the family": an admirable advertisement for home-laundering machines.

Even Céline, however, has an excuse. Confession and self-satire are free from smugness and may have a tonic value. French writers know the worth of the French heritage; many would blush to dwell upon it, but it is implicit in their work. They reveal, in their ruthless self-criticism, the artistic courage which is not the least glorious of their traditions. They are the heirs of the cynical writers of farce and fabliau, of La Rochefoucauld, Molière, La Fontaine, La Bruyère, Voltaire, as well as of Balzac, Flaubert, Zola, and Maupassant: a lineage which is not the whole of the French past, but which is not devoid of morose grandeur.

Other foreigners have borrowed from the French their dark *palette*. Ilya Ehrenburg and Erich Remarque, for instance, have achieved notoriety. I refrain from expressing an opinion about their art. Considered as sociological studies, their somber pictures are woefully one-sided. But, if they distort the perspective, they do not confuse the issues. They note much that is rotten in France, but they do not grow sentimental over it. If they wade in filth, it is not to the tune of a nostalgic song. Inaccuracies and lopsidedness might be forgiven; it is the utter and willful confusion of all values that must be considered an aesthetic and ethical crime. That it proved a recipe for popular success is an aggravating circumstance.

I must say that our latent Gallophobia is no exception. As a people, we do not like foreigners. Who does? Xenophobia is a universal disease. The very existence of foreigners, unashamed of their differences, is a challenge to our cherished idol: the American (or Chinese, or Hindu, or Liechtenstein) Way-of-Life. But if differences are irritating, they may also have a fascination. If we like best what is most familiar, we also grow weary of our own folkways. It is hard to predict, in any particular instance, which of the two forces will prevail. Naturally, the completely foreign, the frankly exotic, has unqualified appeal. We fall in love with Bali, which enriches our experience without any threat to our own pattern of life. We have no objection to pleasant, harmless, small countries like Switzerland, the Netherlands, Denmark, Uruguay, because "they are not in our class." At one time we exalted Finland into the home of all the sturdy virtues, because Nurmi could walk marvelously fast, and because the Finns did not default on a purely commercial debt. The Russians, as a people, are still remote enough and poor enough to enlist our blurred sympathy, however barbarous may be the various regimes inflicted upon them. Few Americans went to Germany as tourists unless they were of German origin or thoroughly Germanized through our universities. With France, with England, with Italy, the case is altogether different.

When we consider these countries, we cannot ignore the greatness of their cultural wealth; we admire their ancient cities, their monuments, their old masters in art and literature. But we need to believe that all this splendor belongs irremediably to the past. If those nations were as good as we in terms of today, and in addition so rich in artistic heirlooms, it would turn us, if not into paupers, at least into mere *parvenus*. For our self-respect, in order to maintain the dogma of our superiority, we must be convinced of their decadence. So we love the magnificence of old England, of old France, of old Italy. We love it better than they do themselves: when it comes to preserving their past, we are thoroughgoing Tories. We love their annals, because they deal with the dead. And we also love their "little people," as Southerners love their Negro retainers; we love them, that is, so long as they know their place. We have no love whatever for those intellectuals or statesmen who are thinking of their countries not as historical museums but as living and growing concerns. Quite obviously, they have no love for us. We treat them as recalcitrant ghosts; in their eyes, we are upstarts and purse-proud.[8]

[8] Exactly the same conditions prevail in our relations with Mexico. We love all the monuments of departed colonial splendor, and even the pathetic gaudiness of the Maximilian interlude: we have genuine sympathy for the humble, the common people, the *peones,* the little street vendors, the deft handicraftsmen. But we resent the presumption of those educated Mexicans who think they are as good as we.

French Civilization

In all this there lingers faintly a trace of the colonial inferiority complex. We are still abnormally sensitive, as James Russell Lowell was three generations ago, to "a certain condescension in foreigners." But our special brand of xenophobia has another cause: we are biased against foreigners because all of us, except (perhaps) the Indians, are of foreign origin. The immigrants who came in such enormous waves until four decades ago remained socially and economically inferior so long as they were patently immigrants. They had to be Americanized before they were treated as equals. Pride in your native country had to be surrendered at Ellis Island. For anyone who wanted to rise, Europeanism was the original sin; it had to be washed away by the American baptism.

I found in my long years of teaching that genuine love for France, with most Americans, ends with the Ancient Regime. We have never quite forgiven the Revolution for beheading its most stubborn enemy, Marie Antoinette. The epic of the Revolutionary wars is a dead letter to us; we do not thrill to the name of Lazare Carnot. The prestige of Napoleon is personal, not national; aesthetic, not political. What does it matter that he abandoned his armies in Egypt and in Russia? He provided for us the grandest story of individual success; he is the Self-Made Man *in excelsis*. For the France of the nineteenth and twentieth centuries, most of us have a feeling that hovers between amused tolerance and irritation. That blend determined the attitude of Franklin Roosevelt toward De Gaulle. The President—the greatest prima donna in our times, far more so than either Churchill or Stalin—was irked by a man who believed that France still had "greatness," not in the vaults of the Bank but in her soul.

(It is difficult to be the Chosen People and love the rest of mankind; Ego worship is too absorbing to tolerate universal philanthrophy. It is radically impossible to love those who also claim that they are the Chosen: for that is rank blasphemy. Our conflict with the Soviets (I shall repeatedly insist upon this fact, which dominates the present world situation) is not due primarily to our hatred of their system; we hate them because they refuse to acknowledge the superiority of our own way of life. If Communism were practiced by a small, quaint, remote body of men, say in Tibet or in the Trobriand Islands, we would study it sympathetically, perhaps enthusiastically, as a fascinating experiment. But every great nation is a Messiah in its own eyes, a menace in the eyes of its rivals. Such competition for the good of the world engenders not love but hatred.

Happy is the architect who is given a clear area to build upon, with solid ground for his foundations! The teacher of French Civilization found his assigned lot cluttered with ramshackle constructions that had first to be cleared away; and when he tested the soil, he found it treacherous, a quagmire filled with loose debris. So a great deal of the work was, apparently, destructive: it consisted in blasting away prejudices. Naturally, those who cherished these prejudices as God-given, self-evident verities, thought the effort willfully paradoxical and futile; the word "chauvinistic" provided at the same time a condemnation, an explanation, and to some extent an excuse. If I denied, for instance, that according to French law an accused man was held to be guilty until he had proved his innocence; if I suggested that a Folies-Bergère revue or a Palais-Royal bedroom farce did not truly depict the home life of an average French family, the argument was stopped short by an understanding smile: "Of course, that is what you are bound to say as a retained advocate."

Explaining France was to the very end a dubious battle. My testament on the subject, *France: A Short History,* was on the whole accepted as an honest and carefully balanced statement. I did not conceal my sympathy with the subject. When sympathy is either fanatical or superficial, it distorts; but, when it is deep and calm enough, it is indispensable to understanding. But, in the case of two or three critics, the old accusation of chauvinism, "France, right or wrong!" reappeared, at least as a minor accompaniment. Perhaps the next section will dispel this misconception.

French Civilization

FOR ALL THE GODS OF THE NATIONS ARE IDOLS...

Before 1900, I had reached the conclusion that nationalism was the outstanding evil in the modern world. The dark experience of half a century has confirmed my conviction. Religious fanaticism has greatly abated. In civilized countries, religious wars have ceased. In Mexico, strenuous efforts were made to goad the Indians into rebellion against the anticlerical measures of the government; but, ardent Catholics though they were, the Indians refused to rise. Even Mohammedanism no longer seeks to conquer by the sword. The phantom of a Holy War has been exorcized: on the contrary, we have seen the Arabs unite with the Infidels against the Turks. Arabs and Jews tolerated each other's presence throughout the Mediterranean area: if Zionism is causing strife, it is because the Jews, abandoning the purely religious bonds of fellowship, are attempting to create a new nation in a land which the Arabs, for a thousand years, have considered their own. The struggle between Pakistan and Hindustan is an anachronism: three hundred years of tutelage have arrested the development of India, and the conflict, being evil, assumes a nationalistic form. Anti-semitism in Europe is not a racial, a religious, and least of all an economic hysteria: it is nationalistic. The Jews everywhere were accused of remaining a foreign element in the body politic. Hitler believed—like Ludwig Lewisohn—that they were inassimilable. Pure economics, purged from the nationalistic virus, would work for free trade and peace, the gospel of the Manchesterians. Even the clash of social ideologies could be kept within the bounds of reason. If we are in a state of "cold war" with the Soviets, it is not because they share the economic views of the early Christians and of the Catholic religious orders: it is because we accuse the Communists of attempting to disrupt our national unity at the behest of a foreign national power. We oppose the sweep of Muscovite conquest exactly for the same reason that England resisted the advance of Napoleon, or that we fought against the imperialism of the Nazis, the Fascists, and the Japanese.

Education of a Humanist

Nationalism is evil because it boasts of being above reason, and because its professed unreason has a monopoly of the power to destroy. Unreason in itself is harmless; pathetic at times, it may also be amusing. We have strange cliques in art and literature, fantastic sects in Southern California, weird crazes in the most fashionable circles: this is not altogether a sane world. After all, sanity and morality are but the average: let us deal tenderly with the lunatic fringe, for it may contain saints, poets, and pioneers. Force is not evil in itself. It is needed to curb unreason, to repress disorder, and, ideally, to ensure justice. But force without stint at the service of unreason without check is a combination so deadly that our civilization may not be able to survive its impact.

I must quote again the profound definition of *la Patrie* which I heard during my year of military service in France. Asked by an officer, "What is *la Patrie?*" a half-witted Norman peasant answered: *"La Patrie,* c'est les Prussiens." We roared. But his subhuman intuition had cut through the tangle of subtleties, paradoxes, and fallacies and grasped the essential truth more firmly than Barrès, Maurras, or Péguy: nationalism is hatred and fear. Abolish these and you will not love your country and your countrymen any the less, in so far as they are lovable; but you will not deny justice, admiration, sympathy, to your fellow men across the border. You will be the better citizen; you will have ceased to be a nationalist.

What we worship as the Nation is the epitome and sublimation of everything that, in an individual, we would condemn as mean and coarse. This may sound like a hard saying, but check dispassionately the following points. By its very nature, a nation—any nation—is bound to be (a) *Selfish:* "Myself first and last!" *Sacro Egoismo! Sinn Fein!* (b) *Smug:* "God's own country"; *Gott mit uns;* Holy Russia. (c) *Brutal:* absolute independence, above any law, can be maintained only by the sword. (d) *Cowardly:* the nationalist is forever trembling; he never has armor or weapons enough; he bullies the weak and is considerate of the strong—what an improvement there would be in our manners if we knew for certain that Russia has started the mass production of atomic bombs! And how our "realists" despised our old friend France when they thought she was down and out! (e) *Treacherous:* diplomats "lie for their country"; military attachés forswear espionage and practice it; we boast that we kept on good terms with Vichy in order to undermine Vichy. (f) *Hypocritical:* all nations profess the purest idealism and behave with the most cynical realism; Professor William L. Langer tells us proudly that the Atlantic Charter, the Four Freedoms, the Declaration of the United Nations were sheer camouflage for practical American interests: "considerations of a sentimental or ideological character are dangerous if they are made the basis for foreign policy." (g) *Indifferent to justice:* "Myself right or wrong!" *Raison d'état.* (h) *Confused* to the point of imbecility, for no nation ever has a single mind. Every term of the arraignment is from the mouth of the nationalists themselves. Granted that the Germans are a good people and a bad nation: theirs is only an extreme instance, and we are all tarred with the same brush. There is no such thing as a bad people or a good nation. "The Myth of a Guilty Nation" is delusive only when it is applied to a single example, for guilt is inherent in the very idea of nation.

This was clear in my mind, as I said above, before 1900. I expressed my conviction, without reticence, in the thick of the First World War. When all were admiring the heroic patriotism of the French, I exposed the nationalism of their great theorist, Maurice Barrès.[9] I was not "above the strife"; but if the strife had been merely one between two nationalisms, my reaction would have been "A plague on both your houses!" The enemy was not German nationalism, but nationalism wherever it could be found. Isolation and neutrality would have been fully justified, if the purpose of our intervention had not been to strike at the very root of the conflict; to shape a world in which nations would no longer be a law unto themselves; to proclaim with Nurse Edith Cavell that nationalism—even in its purest form, patriotism—was not enough.

[9] In *Five Masters of French Romance* (London and New York, 1916).

Education of a Humanist

So ardent was my belief that I saw the need of guarding against it. There is nothing so dangerous as a self-evident truth: self-evidence may be a thick carapace for the protection of prejudice. Whenever you meet a postulate, challenge it. Descartes admitted the rule of self-evidence, but only after the critical spirit had done its ruthless work. "Doubt till you can doubt no more" does not imply that when you stop doubting you have reached the ultimate and eternal truth. It only means, "This is the present limit of my endeavor." The most valuable lesson of Cartesianism is not "I think, therefore I am," but "I doubt, therefore I think." Stones, I surmise, are not tormented with doubt; neither are nationalists, who try their best to be "monolithic."

So I have constantly submitted my antinationalism to the severest tests. I did not want to be a fanatical negativist. One form of bias I found it easy to eliminate: I was free from personal animus. I did not hate or despise individual nationalists. I had (a very general experience) an indulgent affection for Paul Déroulède, a little boy who played soldiers and never grew up, the last obstinate apostle of a martial *Revanche,* the artless bard of Chauvinism, who could only play the bugle and had reduced the notes of his instrument from four to one. I admired Maurice Barrès, a sensitive artist, and generous even when I found him perverse. I deeply appreciated Abbé Ernest Dimnet's *France Herself Again,* a nationalistic book, but free from the least trace of stupidity or meanness. I wished I had written that book—reversing the terms of the equation. It marked the origin of a friendship which I have treasured for three decades. I could feel the unostentatious glow of Marshal Foch's personality, and, within his own field, the lightning penetration of his mind. I was not repelled by the stodginess, the frigidity, even the surliness of Raymond Poincaré: there was rugged, homely honesty in the man, and his vigorous intellect cast, a few feet ahead, a very clear light on a very straight and very narrow path. Clemenceau was one of my heroes, in spite of the manifest blemishes in his intellect and in his temper. Many years later, I recognized at once the miraculous virtue in De Gaulle's patriotism, as well as in Churchill's, although I might easily find myself on the other side of the barricades.

On the other hand, I never liked, admired, or trusted a man simply because he shared my antinationalist convictions. Pierre Laval was a sincere antinationalist throughout his career. It may be the only belief that he ever held with any degree of earnestness and fervor. He held it during the First World War, when it required some moral courage. Back of his collaboration policy, back of his unreserved acceptance of the New Order, there was at any rate the sense that nationalistic hatreds must cease. Yet, with his cleverly legal grafting and profiteering, with his low backstairs cunning, with his greasy good nature, with his parvenu snobbishness, he ever was one of my *bêtes noires;* more accurately, one of my *bêtes puantes.* There are saints and rascals in every camp. Patriotism may be "the last refuge of the scoundrel," but this could be said also of socialism or religion. A great cause offers sanctuary to the criminal, and a point of vantage to the hypocrite. But even a host of Tartuffes could not disprove or sully the sincere faith of millions.

The second temptation of antinationalism is to see nothing but evil in the annals of a country. It is true that in France "royalism is integral nationalism": the dynasty grew with the people, and molded the people. The feeling of jealous proprietorship, the quest for prestige, the "honor" of infinite sensitiveness which must be vindicated by the arbitrament of the sword, all these traits of modern nationalism were inherited by the masses from their former masters, and in the democratic era, history is still concerned primarily with war, the sport of kings. So the whole past appears to us as a bloody battlefield. How senseless, in our eyes, are the Italian expeditions of Francis I, how futile and ultimately disastrous the showy adventures of Louis XIV! Because he loved the people, Michelet, the greatest poet among historians, saw the whole classical age as a long nightmare. The painter Courbet directed those who, in 1871, pulled

Education of a Humanist

down the Vendôme column, a monument to martial glory. Gustave Hervé, who was to go through bewildering avatars, won early fame —or infamy—by declaring that the flag of Austerlitz and Wagram should be flung upon a dunghill. Hatred of the past is natural among those who want to build a city of justice; all ardent reformers are iconoclasts, and the early Protestants affirmed the purity of their faith by defacing cathedrals.

It is an easy trap to fall into. Radicals would have it that everything was cruelty and corruption under the Ancient Regime—the thesis of *A Tale of Two Cities,* probably the worst historical novel ever penned, and certainly the most cheaply melodramatic. Reactionaries like Maurras and Daudet sought to prove that, since the Revolution, stupidity had held undisputed sway. Combine the two schools and you will be persuaded that all was ever for the worst in the worst possible France. It requires no little effort to recognize the unrivaled freedom of thought, the charm of manners, the brilliant prosperity, the stately public works under one of the most thoroughly despised of the French rulers, Louis XV the Well-Beloved. It takes perhaps even more of an effort, against the Royalists and the innumerable herd of their American followers, to discover that the nineteenth century in France was far from stupid; that, under every one of its many regimes, there was a great deal of quiet, honest, slow-moving but efficient administration; that health, comfort, education steadily improved; and that the times of Balzac or Pasteur could hardly be called a new age of darkness.[10]

The third temptation is, in order to condemn the nationalism of one's own people, to condone and even to extol the nationalism of other countries and particularly of the enemy. This is a temptation which pure souls find hard to resist. In their eagerness to hear the

---

[10] I took to heart—*cum grano*—such books as Louis Dimier, *Les Préjugés hostiles à l'histoire de France;* F. Funck-Brentano, *L'Ancien Régime;* and even Pierre Gaxotte, *Le Siècle de Louis XV.* In the same way, Julián Juderías *(La leyenda negra)* and José Vasconcelos *(Breve historia de México)* protest against the systematic defaming of the Spanish past.

French Civilization

other side, they hear nothing but the other side and accept it uncritically. During the First World War, sincere pacifists, with the highest motives, spoke and acted as though they were the agents of the Kaiser. Between the two wars, "liberals" carried on a revisionist campaign which was strictly in line with Hitler's propaganda. Thus they ruined the chances of those German republicans who had accepted the treaty of Versailles as harsh perhaps, foolish in some details, but not altogether iniquitous.

I was in England soon after the Fashoda crisis and during the Boer War: if I did not unquestioningly accept the views of the most extreme jingoes, I was accused of French chauvinism. Yet everyone knows that all was not sweetness and light in British imperialism. I loved to look at leisure through old volumes of *Punch*, as good an encyclopedia of social history as one could desire. I remember a cartoon relating to the Anglo-Portuguese dispute in South Africa. A big irate John Bull was kicking a diminutive Portuguese, "half-monkey and half-child," with the words: "Look here, my little fellow; I don't want to hurt your little feelings; but you get off that map." I saw no reason why my antinationalism should work against France alone and commit me to an even more outrageous brand under an alien flag.

Liberals have often been described as the friends of every country except their own. This bias is the result of honorable scruples; still, it must be resisted. I have not the slightest love or respect for dollar diplomacy, and no belief in the inerrancy of our Secretaries of State; still, I cannot accept it as a dogma that Uncle Sam is infallibly wrong. I have the greatest sympathy with the Russian people, trying desperately to overcome the ignorance and poverty in which they had lived for centuries. But if, in the name of international brotherhood and social justice, they revert to the methods of Ivan the Terrible, I refuse to say: "Holy Russia, right or wrong."

Scientists use extremely delicate scales. A "scruple," I was told, weighed one twenty-fourth of an ounce. It is not easy, and it is not popular, to be "scrupulous." Take the case of the countries still

Education of a Humanist

under tutelage. If the natives are struggling for human rights, for emancipation, for liberty and equality, and if the Dutch or the French are attempting to maintain their imperial supremacy, that is, privileges for their own nationality, then I stand unreservedly with the natives. If on the contrary they are seeking to establish, in the name of "independence," a narrow, jealous, totalitarian *Sinn Fein,* and if the Dutch or the French have understood at last the need of a free association of free peoples, then I am with those who support the more generous policy. Two "ifs" on either side, with many intermediate shades, create a situation of the utmost complexity. I cannot promise that I shall commit myself to "Viet-Nam, right or wrong!" any more than to "France, right or wrong!" The presumptions, of course, are heavily in favor of the natives.

After taking these elaborate precautions against my antinationalistic bias, I could honestly use it as a working hypothesis. And it worked. All those things which, according to nationalistic historians, had made for the grandeur of France suffered a radical change when they were considered without the glow of patriotic fervor. In the cool light of common sense and morality, they were seen to have done the country and the people irreparable harm. "Glory" had to be paid for in terms of impoverishment and suffering; worse still, it brought about a coarsening of the nation's intellectual and moral fiber. A military epic has been justly described as "a most costly entertainment of the cheapest kind." The average citizen, the French John Doe, who when reading his own history struts and frowns like Louis XIV or Napoleon (*bzw.* Frederick the Great or Bismarck), is tainted with endemic vulgarity. A touch of the ludicrous is added when the would-be heroic soul is clothed in a soft, comfort-loving body, when Don Quixote and Sancho Panza are inextricably mixed, when, as Doudan put it, the good bourgeois wants at the same time to "bestrew with his corpse" all the battlefields of Europe and to toast his toes by his cozy fireside.

French Civilization

But, although no longer funny, the delusion or delirium of grandeur is more dangerous still if the man is ready to live and to die, like Hitler, for his unholy dream. I think highly enough of General de Gaulle's intelligence to imagine that, when he speaks of *grandeur,* he has something deeper in view than martial glory. Grandeur may be a call to greatness, the spurning of all that is mean. But I must admit that many honest minds have reasonable misgivings. What tragic irony if the secret of the Sphinx were but the bugle call of old Déroulède!

So I felt free to examine, without fear or favor, "the men who had made France great." To the nationalistic mind, four names stand out at once: Francis I, Richelieu, Louis XIV, Napoleon. Richelieu is a character apart; the three sovereigns had much in common, in spite of their widely different abilities. All three assumed power amid universal hopes: France felt rejuvenated under youthful leaders. They gave the country, weary with the strife of factions, a sense of inner peace and collective endeavor. In the deeper sense, all three stood for a "New Deal." 1515, 1661, and 1800 had the promise of a summer dawn. How soon were those aspirations frustrated! The new masters grabbed the resources of a hardworking people, to squander them in the reckless gamble of war. They turned the splendor of the young Renaissance, the calm radiance of the classical spirit, the blending effulgence of the age of reason and of romanticism, into a limelight trained upon their histrionic persons. And their adventure ended in ruin and defeat.

Richelieu never was loved; he was hated and feared. Although he did wage war, his great work was at home. He trampled out the last remnants of feudal misrule, a more ruthless destroyer of the past than those Jacobins denounced by Burke. But he created nothing except unmitigated tyranny. As an economic administrator, he failed: France suffered bitter hardships under his iron hand. More conscious of his goal than the pleasure-loving Francis I or the commonplace Louis XIV, it was he who focused the terrible leveling ideal of enforced conformity: one faith, one law, one king. And, on the European stage, it was he who turned the nefarious game of high politics into a national way of life. In my childhood, the maxims of Richelieu were still taught with admiration: Humble your rivals; divide in order to rule; bribe when you can, fight when you must, but, through force or deceit, *dominate*. For domination alone brings prestige *(la gloire),* and prestige is god.

Richelieu, with his implacable will-to-power, was only yesterday the avowed pattern and exemplar of French diplomats: Hanotaux, Delcassé, Paléologue, Barthou. Even at present, we can detect traces of his influence. France, monarchy or republic, must remain one and indivisible. The least desire for autonomy, in Alsace or Brittany, is treated as a crime against the nation. But Napoleon III was a fool for having favored the unity of Italy, and for not having opposed in time, and vigorously enough, the unity of Germany. Such Machiavellism is so cynical that it appears naïve.

If Hitler—against the best traditions and the best interests of Germany—favored the rigorous unification of the Reich, he was only following the example of France. Of course I condemned the nauseating combination of brutality and deceit in Frederick II and Bismarck: but in this also Germany had French models. The Electors of Brandenburg played the sedulous apes: because the Grand Monarch had his magnificent Montespan, the third-rater in Berlin had to parade a Royal Mistress. Frederick II, so much keener and more energetic than the Bourbons, wanted his Potsdam to be a Versailles. If Bismarck harked back to the medieval glories of Otto the Great and Barbarossa, the European supremacy of Louis XIV and Napoleon I served as his immediate pattern.

We think of the Germans as hopelessly addicted to war. It is their national sin; they carry the taint in their blood. Whoever has met actual Germans in free and friendly intercourse knows that this monstrous charge is untrue; and whoever reads French history is aware that the Rhine does not separate spotless lambs from ravenous wolves. In all countries the martial spirit is a collective de-

French Civilization

lusion superimposed upon the sanity and peaceableness of most individuals. The Odinic idol "Germany" is the concentration of all the primitive and perverse impulses that sensible men easily repress in their private lives. It is true that, in popular mythology, France is a drawing room or a formal garden, England a hunting ground for red-coated squires, Germany a camp filled with the clangor of arms. But if you look at the record, as it was my business to do, you will find that the sociable French have been warriors ever since the dawn of their history. For centuries they fought interminably on German territory. Down to 1813, they always managed to have Germans fighting against Germans, for the greatest glory of the French king or emperor.

Have the Germans invented and cornered *Schrecklichkeit?* At no time was war ever conducted by means of gentle persuasion. What is victory? The proof that you have tortured the enemy into submission. The court of Louis XIV might be noted for elaborate etiquette; but the behavior of his armies was not invariably urbane, and for two hundred years the ravaging of the Palatinate remained a lurid memory in the German mind. Napoleon's senseless Spanish war, from 1808 to 1814, was conducted with unforgettable ferocity.

In the story of all countries, truculence had its seamy side. The hands that flashed the sword knew also how to line capacious pockets. The great Elizabethan heroes were splendid pirates, and the conquerors of India had not forgotten the tradition. Young Bonaparte, in a fervent address to his ragged troops, told them: "Soldiers! You are destitute: I am going to lead you into the richest plains in Europe," the practical eloquence of a gang leader. Marshal Masséna was rebuked, not for plundering, but for taking more than his share. The Louvre was bursting with glorious loot. The most patriotic French historians and novelists relate scenes of arson, pillage, and rape with stoical equanimity: *C'est la guerre!* In their eyes, it does not tarnish the luster of Napoleon's victories.[11]

---

[11] Our callousness to gold-braided misdemeanor is appalling. Honest and virtuous Britain long took it for granted that a Colonel in the Indian service should come

Education of a Humanist

So the annals of France did not fill me with pride. Neither did those of any other country. The smaller states, if you give them a chance, are as treacherous and as ferocious as the great empires: insects fight as mercilessly as tigers. The Swedes were the terror of the North until they "degenerated" into decency. Poland and the Balkan countries never evinced the purest Franciscan spirit. Even the Belgians had peccadilloes on their conscience in the Congo of Leopold II, and the neat and thrifty Dutch in the Achin peninsula. Wholesome American homes talk calmly of dropping atomic bombs on teeming European cities.

There is an essential episode in French history which remains an enigma to me: the miracle of Joan of Arc. It causes the anti-nationalist to pause and ponder.

It would be tempting to consider Joan as a daughter of the people, who felt "the great distress of the kingdom" and yearned to restore peace. But her protest against the horrors of war did not assume a democratic, pacifist, or religious form: she took part, decisively, in the great and cruel game of armed politics. One of my Chaptal teachers, Camille Guy, maintained calmly that she had picked out the wrong side. The quarrel was between two claimants who belonged to the same royal house; had the King of Paris prevailed, instead of the King of Bourges, his rule would have been French, not English, for of his twin dominions, England at that time was the lesser. The connection might have lasted for centuries, until England at last should win independence. Churchill's great

---

home a nabob. Field-Marshal Lord Roberts of Kandahar, the Victorian hero, complained to native Indian authorities that the prostitutes pressed into the service of Tommy Atkins were not attractive enough. The looting of Peking by the European Allies in 1900 was pronounced "excessive" even by men who were not squeamish. Of similar episodes in the late global unpleasantness we have but sketchy knowledge. They do not reach the courts unless they are far beyond the limits of good taste. Even when they create a scandal, they are hushed as much as possible, so as not to offend chaste ears and rejoice malicious ones. Enough has transpired, however, to make us feel that modern officers and soldiers are not unworthy of Napoleon's marshals and of his *grognards*.

proposal in 1940 for the merging of the two countries was a belated attempt to correct Joan's fateful error. A paradox, no doubt; like not a few others, it is at the same time outrageous and disconcertingly sensible.

One might imagine that the splendid legendary figure of the Warrior Maid was "invented," that is, picked out and deliberately made use of by shrewd realistic manipulators.[12] But there is no shred of convincing evidence to support such a hypothesis. It would have been a masterly move: the counselors of Charles VII showed themselves utterly incapable of such imaginative statesmanship, both before and after the Maid dashed like a meteor through the murk, the confusion, the frivolous apathy of royal politics.

I find it difficult to accept the idea of supernatural intervention. Not that I rule out a priori the possibility of a miracle: science is the quest of actual truth, not the defense of a purely rationalistic philosophy. But miracles cannot be accepted without close examination. One of Renan's masters, Etienne Quatremère, used a quaint criterion: he rejected those miracles which were "too difficult of performance." I am inclined to reverse the argument. I am skeptical about miracles when the issue is not of sufficient importance: *de minimis non curat praetor*. It might be vital that the sun should stand still so that Joshua could put all his enemies to the sword. But no such emergency existed in 1429. The issue was whether the succession law of the Salian Franks applied to the French crown. It was a matter to be settled by jurists; it did not justify the dispatching of angels and saints to an adolescent shepherdess. To have God Himself tip the scales in favor of Charles VII and against Henry VI implied first that the weakling of Bourges was "France," and second, as Friedrich Sieburg put it (but with a question mark), that God was a Frenchman. I know that the Church, reversing herself after five hundred years, has made Joan of Arc a saint. But the Church is eternal, and historical perspective is constantly changing; another half-millennium might bring another reversal.

[12] Cf. Jehanne d'Orliac, *Joan of Arc and her Companions* (Philadelphia, 1934).

Education of a Humanist

Any free discussion of a sacred subject is offensive to delicate souls. The orthodox affect to believe that, if you try to understand, you are going over at once to the witless scurrility of Voltaire's poem. Nothing of the kind. It is perfectly possible to examine a strange phenomenon with deep respect and ardent sympathy, and confess that it remains strange. Joan is appealing, not merely because she was young, and a girl, and a martyr; the world is full of young girls, and the worst causes have their martyrs. But she showed humanity even on the field of battle; and, in her trial, she revealed a shrewdness and a robust sense of humor hardly less miraculous than her victories. Her case proves that history cannot explain all that it is bound to register. We feel that Shakespeare, Voltaire, Schiller, Anatole France, Andrew Lang, Bernard Shaw, shone in their several ways at the expense of Joan of Arc, but failed to understand her. And if we can read Michelet without the same inner protest, it is because he gave us the facts, with a richer glow of love than any other historian, and with the least admixture of theory. His narrative is a gospel, not a treatise: Heaven knows that there is an abysmal difference. Even if it were a fairy tale, Michelet's brief treatment of the Maid would remain a masterpiece. It entrances, but it does not explain.

I repeat that to admit the miraculous character of Joan's mission —miraculous in the literal sense, not in the merely rhetorical—is to proclaim the divine claims of the French monarchy and the special election of France among the nations.[13] I know that this state of mind—shall I say, this state of grace?—has not disappeared. Charles

---

[13] Clovis was anointed with Holy Chrism, which a dove brought down from Heaven. The same vial, miraculously renewed, was used even for his remote successors. The Revolution attempted to destroy it; but it was found again for the coronation of Charles X, last of the legitimate kings, in 1825: the sons of Voltaire tittered. The coronation rite was almost an ordination; it conferred upon the sovereign a sacred character. As a result, the Lord's Anointed had the healing touch; he could cure a certain kind of scrofula. The Stuarts claimed the wondrous gift, as kings of France *in partibus*.

French Civilization

Péguy, once the advocate of the Universal Socialist Republic, became increasingly a mystic nationalist and made himself not the poet merely, but the devoted servant of Saint Joan. And Péguy is still offered to us as an inspired prophet. People—none too kindly—have diagnosed in De Gaulle a Joan of Arc complex. Because I am a son, and a lover, and a student of France, I cannot believe that the French are God's own people. The title was for a while in dispute between the Jews and the Germans. The Russians and ourselves are the next claimants. God forbid! For in this world at any rate such a promise has proved a heavy curse.

The miraculous call, the Messianic mission, turns nationalism into virtuous imperialism. It is a benefit to the lesser breeds to be ruled by the chosen, a greater benefit still to be adopted. There are many brands of imperialism, from the apostolic and cultural to the economic. Not one is free from brutality, for it is righteous to use force in order to make the will of God prevail. The resistance of the inferior is a rebellion against the spirit. It is not quite certain that the Filipinos wanted to be under American tutelage in 1898; one may doubt that the Lithuanians craved to fall within the Russian orbit in 1939.

Empire need not be considered crudely as military government first of all. It may be interpreted as a natural desire to protect and defend our way of life, not at home merely, but everywhere in the world. Culturally, the French are avowed imperialists. They find it hard not to divide the world into three zones: the Parisian, the provincial, and the barbaric. They believe that their language ought to have remained universal. Of course, with our realistic common sense, we know for certain that such primacy belongs to ours.

Great scholars, G. A. Borgese, Hans Kohn, Arnold J. Toynbee, and Sir John Maynard among others, have discovered that Russia, under whatever regime she may be suffering, is in her own eyes the Third Rome, destined to inherit the earth. A monstrous delusion, no doubt, but as commonplace as it is monstrous. Austria once tactfully adopted the device A E I O U, which, in Latin and in German, meant that the whole world was to come under her sway. The Japanese, the Germans, the British, the French, the Spaniards, all at one time entertained the same dream and have nostalgic memories of its promise. In China, it was a placid, massive conviction, unchallenged until the middle years of the nineteenth century. Three generations before Mussolini, Italy boasted of the primacy which by right should be hers.

Etymology is sensible once in a while. *Prestige* is the key word of nationalism, and *praestigium* meant originally a delusion, a juggler's trick. The prestigious, the glorious rulers, the reckless spenders of gold and blood, were not the makers of France; they were magnificent parasites. French history, however, has one point in its favor: repeatedly, the proud have been chastened in their own persons for their manifest sins, so that the lesson was clear for all eyes to see. Francis I, Louis XIV, Napoleon, lived to taste humiliation and defeat. The curse of German history is that its demigods, Frederick II and Bismarck, "got away with it." Even at present, Germans who courageously defied Hitler refuse to see that the root of the evil was not in Nazism itself, but in the Prussian tradition; and well-meaning friends of Germany in this country insist that not a particle of Bismarck's work be undone. Frederick II was literally a "monster" in an age which, with Fleury and Walpole, had been honestly striving to be humane; the gratuitous invasion of Silesia was a relapse into barbarism. The Utopians of the Frankfort Parliament were in the right against Bismarck, who sneered at them; the Liberals who fought Bismarck in the Prussian Diet were right until they too capitulated to the prestige of victory. The policy of blood and iron was a disease which, for decades, was concealed under a show of force and prosperity: it broke out cancerously in 1914 and again in 1939. French history is a well-made play, in which retribution is swift. Great achievements and fantastic dreams jostle one another in the dark confusion of German history. Germany still has to fight her War of Liberation, not against her neighbors but against oppressive ghosts.[14]

IS THERE A FRENCH "CULTURE"?

The essential part of my work, for the first twenty years of my teaching career, was to introduce American students to French literature. Before we could get into actual criticism or appreciation, we had first of all to understand the texts. This required, as a prerequisite, learning the language; and, as a condition hardly less necessary, forming some idea of the historical background. To use again a familiar example, it is not sufficient to know that *roi* means *king;* we must also understand what *king* stood for, say, in the days of Bossuet. To appreciate the *Song of Roland,* one had to study Old French accidence and syntax; to appreciate Hugo's *Legend of the Centuries,* one had to master not merely his enormous vocabulary but also—a more delicate task—the Romantic syntax of thought.

The reader knows what I feel about diplomatic, military, and Court history. I could not dismiss it altogether, much as I despised it. It existed, not so essential as it appeared in its own conceit, still not without influence. The writers whom I wanted to interpret accepted it, although it played but a minor part in their thought. Obviously, the first fire pumps of Newcomen and Calley, about 1705, were far more important in the annals of mankind than the Battle of Blenheim the year before. But no one was aware of it at the time. As a matter of fact, Mr. Winston Churchill does not know it even yet.

At a later stage, in my discussion of literature, I shall try to trace the limits of the "sociological approach" in criticism. "Race, environment, and time," to use Taine's convenient formula, explain surprisingly little in the realm of art and poetry. It is possible, for

---

[14] Werner Hegemann attempted it in his *Entlarvte Geschichte* (new edition, Leipzig, 1934); but he was not a "professional" historian, and he had humor. So his influence was not commensurate with the vigor of his thought.

Education of a Humanist

instance, to pick up the Book of Job and the Book of Jonah and enjoy them as though they had been written yesterday by an author from Woonsocket, Rhode Island. Especially, the historical background has nothing to do with permanent aesthetic values. Granted that Shakespeare was an Elizabethan, not all Elizabethans were Shakespeares. But to define the boundaries of a subject is not to deny its validity. So I took up the social history of France as a clue to some features in French literature.

For this study, I adopted the then accepted term, History of Civilization.[15] The history of civilization was at that time looked askance by the experts. In their opinion, it denoted either the popular presentation of quaint customs, Walter Scott without the thread of romance, or sweeping generalizations about the destiny of mankind. At present, the term has almost disappeared; the "history of civilization" has been swallowed up by its own victory. All history today is the history of civilization. Such is the key to the activities, say, of Arnold J. Toynbee, or of the excellent team of scholars who, under the direction of William L. Langer, are presenting to us the series, *The Rise of Modern Europe.*

Civilization and Culture have innumerable meanings, some of which seem to me indefensible. For practical purposes, I took the two words in the plainest, least controversial sense. By Civilization, I meant the collective material achievements of man, from the first concerted hunt to the elaborate social security system of the Hohenzollern Empire.[16] By Culture, I understood those achievements which, in order to be recorded at all, had to be also collective and material, but in which the material element was merely a condition. From the point of view of civilization, culture is a luxury. From the

---

[15] Cf. my *History of French Civilization:* vol. I, From its Origins to the Close of the Middle Ages; vol II, The Life and Death of an Ideal (The Classical Age); vol. III, The Nineteenth Century. Volume IV, The Twentieth Century, is inchoate in *The France of Tomorrow* and in a number of essays written for encyclopedias and magazines.

[16] This definition was offered in 1912.

French Civilization

point of view of culture, civilization is an indispensable servant, but a mere servant.

This distinction, which I still believe to be convenient, denies the Marxian fallacy that culture is not merely conditioned, but actually determined, by civilization. This is true only in a minor degree. Civilization, by ensuring (precariously) a modicum of comfort and security, makes culture possible. But it does not matter overmuch by what means such leisure and freedom have been attained. The effect of any efficient regime (and it would not be a regime unless it had some rough measure of efficiency) is to enable a few men at least to forget the regime for a while: then they can enjoy life and ponder the mystery of fate. For the artist or the mystic, feudalism, capitalism, and communism are simply modes of release. That regime is best which can most easily be left behind. This may be achieved through determined simplicity—the heroic method of the anchorites and of Thoreau—or it may be sought through a highly perfected technique. The aim of Utopia, that is, a perfectly adjusted, smooth-working civilization, is to free us from worldly care. What we do with our freedom belongs to the realm of culture. It includes jazz, cocktails, Plato, Dante, and Einstein.[17]

The first thing that struck me when I started expounding French Civilization was that it did not exist. Toynbee made a similar discovery: he found that not one of the great influences which molded England's life was special to England, or exclusively of English origin. If we wanted, as some appear to desire, to have "pure" American history, we should have to eliminate the classic heritage, the Bible, the English language, the Renaissance, the Reformation,

---

[17] Needless to say that I am not denying the constant interaction of the two. Commercial art and applied science occupy a middle ground. The State, which is the highest manifestation of "Civilization," may be affected by ideologies and even by ideals which belong to the cultural sphere. As a matter of fact, the sentimental and aesthetic element is strong in politics. When the ruling of men is turned into a game, a drama, a pageant, it is a form of art. As we shall see, History, as it lives in the public mind, transmutes drab or chaotic reality into legends.

and the Enlightenment—all "foreign -isms." It would be necessary to ignore the fact that the growth of science, the Industrial Revolution, the competing economic and social doctrines, without which American life today would be meaningless, all originated on the other side of the Atlantic. There is a larger unit which is necessary and almost sufficient to account for the development of any country.

In the case of France, that unit is Europe. I cannot say Western Europe, for French civilization implies the Greek heritage. I am reluctant to exclude Russia: the great Russian novelists have become an integral part of Western experience, and the Soviets claim to be guided by the thought of Karl Marx, who was a Westerner. Even "Europe" is ambiguous: Egypt, and above all Judea, are among our wellsprings. I do not want to substitute "the Mediterranean area" for Europe. For a thousand years, the nerve center of France has been Paris, and Paris belongs to the Northern world. French Civilization is European, or Western, Civilization, studied in one of its arbitrary fragments. Between the various members of that group, the fundamental unity is far greater than any of the divergences.

Not that I deny local differences: in Europe, when you pass from one country to another, you actually cross a frontier. But Europe is not a mosaic of sharply contrasted pieces, every one of them homogeneous. A more intimate knowledge reveals a much greater diversity and much subtler shades than appear on the crude political map. France is an epitome of the whole continent. Quite obviously, Flemings, Alsatians, Bretons, Basques, Corsicans, although they all bear the stamp of France and feel themselves French, are further apart than, say, a man from Sarrebrück and a man from Sarreguemines.

I am ready to grant that a national way of life, through a long centralizing tradition, does become a reality. But it is not the only reality; it is not even the most essential. The class, economic or social, has a deeper existence. A miner leads a miner's life on either side of the political border. A priest, a teacher, a banker, are

French Civilization

molded in the details of their daily activities by their professional duties and interests. Nothing is so striking, in this connection, as the bonds between the members of the military caste throughout Europe, even though their first principle is to fight and to die for absolute, exclusive nationalism. They are conscious of forming a freemasonry. At the time of the Dreyfus crisis, the German Ambassador Münster wrote to the former military attaché Schwartzkoppen: "Do not forget that the liberty and the future of an officer are at stake—an officer whom, whether he be French or German, you must always consider as a comrade." The aristocracy, in spite of all patriotic professions, places caste above country. A nobleman will marry his daughter to a foreigner with a title rather than to a plebeian hero of his own nation. Royal families, the symbols of national unity and continuity, are of course the least national of all. The Bourbons have German, Polish, Italian, and Spanish blood in their veins. The future Prince Consort of England is German and Greek as well as British.

Religion is undoubtedly a part of a nation's culture. In France, nine tenths of the population are Catholics, that is to say, internationalists, with a leader residing abroad. The last traces of religious autonomy, or Gallicanism, have been effaced. The periods, vague and debatable though they be, are actually more substantial than the nations. No doubt a Frenchman of the eighteenth century and a Frenchman of today are both French. But if you take a historical painting or a portrait, you will first of all be struck by its eighteenth-century or contemporary character before you are able, on closer examination, to discern whether it is French, English, or German.

It might be said that, if we want to catch the spirit of France, we must seek it in the depths of the people, not in the cosmopolitan privileged orders, nobility and higher clergy, not in those aristocrats of the spirit whose sole country is art. Joan of Arc, not the king's court or the bishops, was "France." This romantic theory of the people's soul is that of Herder and Hitler, and at the time of the

Education of a Humanist

French Revolution, it was the common folk who were truly the nation: *patriot* and *democrat* were almost synonymous. But we must not forget that many peasants fought against the Revolution. Today, the industrial masses, polling nearly 50 per cent of the votes, proclaim their allegiance either to the Second International or to the Third.

No doubt there is a thin veneer of Frenchness imposed even upon the physical features of all the provinces. In the flat plain of the Beauce, in the grand mountains of Dauphiné, you know you are in France, for roads and signposts are of the same type, Dubonnet and Chocolat Menier are recommended everywhere, and all modern public buildings offer a deplorable uniformity. Exactly in the same way, there is a Frenchness, at times even a Frenchiness, about most Frenchmen. In many cases, that family likeness is purely sartorial and tonsorial. When I returned to France, clean-shaven, with American clothes and Harold Lloyd goggles, I was immediately accepted as a "Yankee." It is a fact that there are in France more short, stocky, brown-eyed people than in England: but a tall blond Frenchman is as legitimately French as a small dark one. I would cast no slur on the patriotism of Generals Henri Giraud and Charles de Gaulle because both are over six feet tall, like Charlemagne, while Marshal Foch and Napoleon were as short as King Pepin. Of two most "typical" Frenchmen, one, Voltaire, was a bag of bones; the other, Renan, was a ball of fat. The stage Frenchman—more or less Tartarin of Tarascon—is a caricature of the Mediterreanean type. He might be a Greek or an Italian: certainly not a Lorrainer or an Angevin. He is conspicuous because he gesticulates, and seems ubiquitous because he is voluble. I have spent winter months with Burgundian peasants, my relatives: they had—let us be courteous—inexhaustible reserves of silence.

National psychology is a morass, even though such men as Fouillée, Boutroux, Brownell, Madariaga, have ventured into it and brought back not a few shrewd observations. Everything that has been said, and can be said, in praise or blame of the French is true;

French Civilization

it is true likewise of every other people on earth; and the reverse is just as true. I am a Parisian, and I know that not all Parisians are witty, or loose, or gay; I cannot forget that the most perfect flowers of Parisian life at its most "Parisian," under the Second Empire, were Jacques Offenbach from Cologne and Princess Pauline Metternich from Vienna. I am not such an optimist as to believe that every *midinette* is a dream of elegance; and bitter experience has taught me that not every *bistro* is a culinary genius.

France is Europe. She rejoices in such worthies as Macdonald, Clarke, MacMahon, Hennessy, Thomson, Archdeacon; as Zola, Gambetta, Monticelli, Giovanninelli, Gallieni; as Kleber, Schrader, Hirschauer, Zurlinden, Peyerimhoff, Koenig, Herzog; as Strowski, Zyromski, Kostrowitzki, Schrameck, Lazareff, Bibesco, Popesco; as Heredia, Fernandez, Zamacois; as Carcopino and Papadiamantopoulos.[18] The psychological range is even more extensive than the ethnical. When I read of French logic, I think at once of Paul Claudel; the praises of French lucidity evoke many painful hours wrestling with *L'Etre et le néant* by Jean-Paul Sartre; the infallibility of French taste brings irresistibly to mind the masterpieces of Louis Céline.

On the other hand, there is no quality or fault so French that it cannot be found everywhere in the world, from Peru to Cathay. Mankind is human, the world is one, and not merely by virtue of the robot plane and the atomic bomb. Collective traits of race, caste, or country are but special manifestations of universal passions and delusions. A great prophet of reaction, sneering at the humanism of the Enlightenment, said: "I have met Frenchmen, Germans, Italians, but never *Man*." My experience is just the reverse: under every flag, I have met Man under the guise of men. In every clime, individuals fell into innumerable, shifting, interpenetrating groups, without ceasing to be unique, and without ceasing to be human.

---

[18] Emil Herzog, Kostrowitzki, and Papadiamantopoulos are better known as André Maurois, Guillaume Apollinaire, and Jean Moréas.

Education of a Humanist

But out of that welter, we are told, there emerged vast organic entities, the national souls; they formed habits which in the course of centuries became a second nature; their inner conflicts were resolved into a permanent equilibrium. This cohesive system of prejudices a profound instinct urged them to maintain, for they knew that disruption or inharmonious change would cause a weakening of their structure, a disease, or perhaps death. This equilibrium, foreshadowed by Herder and Burke, constitutes what the disciples of Barrès call a *nation;* in ancient or primitive communities, it creates a *culture;*[19] on a larger scale, it appears as the *civilizations* defined by Arnold Toynbee.

The "national souls" and the "cultures" which are their raiments seem to me immense and vague romantic myths, oddly belated in an age which believes itself to be realistic and scientific. We need Occam's razor: "Do not multiply essences or abstractions unnecessarily." In my opinion, it is the forces in conflict that are real; their mutual checkmating is provisional; their reconciliation little more than nominal and as a rule illusory. Not static balance, but strife and change, are the laws of life.

I had not merely studied in books or observed from without that entity called French culture; it had been the atmosphere in which I had spent most of my formative years; and my acquaintance with England should have made my consciousness of France all the keener. But, as a result of knowledge and experience, I could calmly affirm that French "civilization" or "culture" (here the two terms overlap and almost coincide) was a delusion.

I might be told that the trees kept me from seeing the forest. The perspective of history brings out the majestic unity which is lost in the din and dust of strife. But I could not be impressed by

---

[19] *Culture* in this sense is altogether a deplorable term, apart from the fact that the word had been preëmpted, with a much more definite meaning, by Goethe and Matthew Arnold. *Culture,* etymologically, implies a conscious effort toward a preconceived perfection; whereas the culture of certain anthropologists is unconscious, mere inertia. It is not too late to correct this ambiguity. The words *communities, societies,* or *groups* would not be open to the same objection.

that "unity" which Henry Adams so greatly admired in the Middle Ages. Obscure primitive mythologies, the Greek ideal of reason, the Roman ideal of law, the Odinic ideal of prowess, the Christian ideal of mansuetude, all existed in the thirteenth century, unreconciled, and indeed irreconcilable. I admit that Christianity colored everything, the monarchy, feudalism, even the guilds, even the scant and rude living of the serfs, just as Business colors everything in present-day America. But it was a mere coloring. It did not affect the nature of the institutions. Had the Middle Ages been Christian through and through, they would have been a pacific socialistic theocracy, and they were nothing of the kind.

Even the splendid Christian glow, when analyzed, turned to be confusion. It embraced rank superstitions, a teeming idolatrous polytheism, an elaborate hierarchy, a contest, fierce at times, between the regular and secular clergies, between the centralizing Papacy and the local churches, a curious undercurrent of anticlericalism and even skepticism, a vast political and economic power, a dogma at the same time rigid and mysterious, a philosophy or rather philosophies of infinite subtlety in a running fight with free thought, saintliness in its most exquisite purity, flight from the world, action upon the world, gross materialism, and mystic ecstasy. Medieval Christianity was a spiritual world constantly at war with itself.

The brief moment of classical harmony under Louis XIV—we shall discuss it at greater length in the chapter on History—was a miraculous meeting of forces moving at different rates in different directions. Hardly was the picture in focus when it became blurred again. From that time to the present year of grace or disgrace, no one who is not a self-blinded doctrinaire can entertain any delusion about French unity. This is why we find the great traditionalist Charles Maurras fighting so hard against two centuries and more of French tradition.

To the "realistic" or unconventional observer, it is evident that France, in the political, social, intellectual, and spiritual domains has been for ages in a state of civil strife. Peace, in France, never is

Education of a Humanist

unity but a weary truce, or a convention not to use certain weapons which are at the same time murderous and ineffective. France is evolving toward the democratic ideal, which is not unity, but diversity made harmless: elections are bloodless battles; it is better to count heads than to break them. There may have been a flash of national communion in August 1789, in February 1848: we know that these rays of fraternal hope left the night stormier and darker. There was once, and once only, a "Sacred Union" reconciling, before a common danger, what Barrès called "the different spiritual families of France." *(La Patrie, c'est les Prussiens.)* It was in 1914; it was a union exactly of the same kind as the whole-hearted coöperation between Roosevelt, Churchill, and Stalin; it did not last so long. By 1917, Clemenceau had to impose unity by dictatorial methods.

In every crisis, the division is so profound that both sides welcome foreign aid against their compatriots. The Rightists were following a French tradition when they said: "Rather Hitler than Blum!"—and they had their wish. Their ancestors had said: "Rather Alexander of Russia than Napoleon!" Earlier still: "Rather the Duke of Brunswick and his Prussian troops than the Revolutionists!" Or, two centuries further back: "Rather Philip of Spain than Henry of Navarre!"

This attitude is not special to the Rightist, and it is not the sad privilege of France. It is universal among all parties and all nations. The Resistance heroes said, in deeds if not in words: "Rather Churchill than Laval!" And in 1948, while every party was making stirring appeals to national unity, deeper rumblings could be heard: "Rather Marshall than Thorez!" "Rather Stalin than De Gaulle!" Let us look beyond the French frontier. In 1823, Ferdinand VII of Spain was restored to absolute power by French arms. In 1849, Francis Joseph welcomed the assistance of Russia in putting down the Hungarian Revolution; in 1921, in Hungary again, it was the Rumanian army that drove out the Communist government of Béla Kun and made the long "Regency" of Horthy possible. In the

French Civilization

Finnish Civil War of 1918, General Mannerheim defeated his leftist compatriots thanks to the Germans of von der Golz. The classic example is that of Franco (¡España arriba!), who gladly used Moors, Italians, and Germans to kill half a million Spaniards. Yet excellent judges tell us that Nationalism is the greatest spiritual force today. No: Nationalism is so dangerous because it is spiritually so feeble, and in sole control of the army. Perhaps it refuses to think just because it has the power to kill? More accurately, it refuses to think because thinking would be suicidal. Fanaticism is not the fruit of deep-rooted faith, but the refuge of doubt and despair.[20]

The passionate watchword, "France one and indivisible!" is a battle cry against reality. And so, by the same token, is our hundred-percentism, our defense of the American way of life. The American way of life—this cannot be reiterated too frequently—consists simply in the right to differ unmolested. Are we rugged individualists, or are we not? Americanism means liberty: therefore it is antitotalitarian, antiunitarian, pluralistic. All creeds, all thoughts, all dreams, all "ways of life," from the monk's to the nightclub addict's, are accepted, provided they do not disturb the peace. It is not dissent, but the forcible suppression of dissent, that is an un-American activity.

As a result of this pluralism, we were told by German critics—and by a few Americans as well—that we had no "culture." Each of us is a rich unclassified ethnographic and historical museum; all centuries, all countries, are represented in our minds. We are a hundred and fifty million blurs blending into the one glorious blur called America. So be it. If by culture is meant the unconscious acceptance of a pattern, let us return thanks that we have none. If we had, our first duty would be to challenge it. America, I am proud to say, recognizes no orthodoxy, only traffic rules. I could

---

[20] Paul Déroulède expressed the truth with childlike candor: "Dans la France que tout divise/Qui donc a pris pour devise:/Chacun pour tous, tous pour l'Etat?/Le Soldat" (In our France *divided on every issue*/Who has adopted the rule:/One for all, all for the State?/The Soldier). Yes, intelligent France is profoundly divided. The soldier alone is a true nationalist, because he does not think ("Theirs not to reason why") and because he is ready to fight.

easily conceive of an America without the present political parties, without our familiar sects, without the all-pervading profit motive. If it remained free, it would be still, in a new garb, the America of the Founders, the America I sought forty years ago. If a pattern, any pattern, were imposed, then let *Ichabod* be written across the face of the land.

Do I deny the "civilizations" of Arnold Toynbee as well as the national cultures? My business is not to deny but to question, in order to understand. When I sought to define the Napoleonic Legend, I was not trying to prove that Napoleon had never existed. Cultures and civilizations were methods for seeking culture and civilization. From the moment they hardened into patterns they became fossils, since culture and civilization are dynamic. They turned into attempts to dam the flow of history. Toynbee himself tells us that the world has at last become one. All traditions must now merge, not into a single over-all pattern, but into a common quest for peace. And the plain fact is that peace, liberty, diversity, are one. Prophets, poets, philosophers, and simple homely minds too, throughout the ages, were conscious of such a goal. It came into clear focus in the eighteenth century, the century of Kant and Washington: *Que chacun, dans sa foi, cherche en paix la lumière!* [21] What an effort is needed today to recapture that serene light!

Whenever I could check up on this ideal of cultural pattern, in my own experience, in my environment, in the history of the countries I knew, I found that it was a romantic metaphor at the service of a despotic dream: "Be free according to the approved standard, or you will be purged!" This made me skeptical about the "cultures" I did not know. I did not question the information gathered by the anthropologists: I took it for granted that it was accurate as well as entertaining. I questioned—as they did not—their fundamental assumption. The most gifted among them could

---

[21] "Let every one, under his own law, seek the light in peace!" (Voltaire, *Les Guèbres*).

not turn themselves into American Indians or South Sea Islanders. They observed from without. They noted the superficial conformities: were they aware of the complexity that might be lurking in the obscure origins of ritual and myth? Did they gauge what proportion of implicit faith, indifference, reluctant obedience, frustrated revolt, there was under the apparent uniformity? They accepted the cultures as static, that is to say, fossilized: were they conscious that such immobility might conceal inner strains; that certain forces, still presenting a bold front, might be decaying; that others, modest in appearance, were gathering strength? What curious notions—André Maurois has toyed agreeably with the idea—an "anthropologist" from Mars would form if, by such objective methods, he were to study the "patterns" of our terrestrial anthill!

There would be no harm in presenting cultural patterns for what they are: in good old-fashioned parlance, superstitions. But nationalists and anthropologists revert invincibly to the attitude of Burke: they try to impress us with "the wisdom of prejudice." A "culture" is not simply an obstacle to free thought, it is a norm to be followed; in the words of Maurice Barrès, a determinism to be accepted. It is wrong to bring Christianity to the natives, for it upsets them. It is wrong to have them give up cannibalism, for it is part of the immemorial equilibrium of their folkways. Even Eboué, the great Negro Governor General of French Equatorial Africa, one of the first leaders among the Free French, yielded to that reactionary tendency.[22] His own example proved how completely tribal customs could be left behind.

When I questioned the validity of the "culture" hypothesis (in the Tylorian, not in the Goethean, sense), certain anthropologists haughtily answered: "Are you, a layman, accusing us of teaching nonsense?" The reproof would not close the debate. Learned men, in ancient days, have taught things which to us seem wholly erroneous:

[22] In his remarkable circular, *French Colonial Policy in Africa* (1942). The Brazzaville (January 1944) and Dakar (February 1944) Conferences paid tribute to Eboué's doctrine, but wisely amended it beyond recognition.

say the chronology of Bishop Ussher. Yet, even though mistaken, such men were scientists if they tried to ascertain facts and to organize them intelligently. I no longer need to be polite—blessed release! But I can earnestly assure my learned friends that I do not accuse them of expounding a pseudo-science, like astrology and chiromancy. I see at least two great virtues in the "culture" idea.

The first is the interaction of all social phenomena, even though the interaction be loose, even though there be no single ruling principle of unity, even though no state of equilibrium is either inevitable or permanent. You cannot alter one of the major factors in the life of a people and expect all the others to remain unchanged. You cannot promote scientific free thought and hope to preserve a dogmatic authoritarian religion. You cannot preach political democracy and trust that racial, social, economic privileges will never be challenged. Between the various elements of a culture there may be an extensive lag. But a rough balance is bound to be restored.

The second point is the extreme difficulty of grafting certain slips from a particular culture into a different one. In its time and country, the Anglican compromise was admirable, although not fully sufficient: we can hardly hope that it will prove the salvation of India or China. The Parliamentary system has ripened in England over the centuries: it is very doubtful that it is applicable anywhere else. Constitutional monarchy has become innocuous in the North of Europe: it might lead to virulent conflicts in the South. The value of any instrument—and churches, philosophies, political and economic regimes are but instruments—is strictly relative to the cultural group. We can preach universal principles: culture, not a culture. We cannot impose our own methods of applying these principles:

Que chacun, dans sa foi, cherche en paix la lumière!

This is what the teaching of French Civilization has taught me. Many Frenchmen have been, many remain, among the most nationalistic, that is, among the most tribal, people in the world.

French Civilization

I have not spared their idols. On the other hand, I could sincerely and proudly claim that the humanistic strain has always been strong in the French tradition. Old Clemenceau never was a better "nationalist" than when he told Pershing: "Above Paris is France, and above France civilization." [23]

[23] Gen. John J. Pershing, *My Experiences in the World War* (2 vols.; New York: J. B. Lippincott Co., 1931), II, 93.

III. Literature

RESEARCH AND CRITICISM

From the first and to the last, the center of my teaching was literature. The study of language and that of social history were only approaches. My desire was to understand and to appreciate the great books of the past, and through that knowledge to derive the greatest possible benefit, in delight or wisdom, from the works of today.

So literary history was for me but a pathway to criticism. Any fact not relevant to appreciation does not exist in my eyes. It has often been said, and we are in constant danger of forgetting, that nothing is quite so stupid as a fact. Herbert Spencer remarked: "My neighbor's cat just had kittens. It is a fact, it is not science." In the same way, Anne-Honoré-Joseph Mélesville, Baron Duveyrier, brought out *The Burgomaster of Saardam* in 1818. It is a fact. It is not literature. The first words that should be taught our students should be the scholarly equivalent of "So what?" Research for its own sake is but a quaint and harmless pastime. It is on a level, as we may read in *The Crime of Sylvestre Bonnard* and *Brideshead Revisited,* with collecting matchboxes.

But, if I never saw any use for uncritical research, I firmly believed that the critical spirit demanded first-hand information. Erudition, even about recondite subjects, has its major and its minor uses. A third-rate book, by illustrating the taste of its time, may throw a great deal of light on a masterpiece. We say glibly that Shakespeare was an Elizabethan. The statement is meaningless unless we know in what way he resembled other Elizabethans and in what way he differed from them. Incidentally, erudition, for all the dusty drudgery it involves, is not without its sedate delights. The tourist who in Paris knows only the grand vistas and the architectural masterpieces has his generous reward. If he explores the less obvious, he is soon impressed with the law of diminishing returns. But if he goes deeper still, he will discover the charm of intimate acquaintance with every stone and every face in a particular neighborhood. The majestic edifices will lose none of their stateliness; they will acquire a subtler meaning from familiar associations. Among the secondary writers, you may come across unexpected friends, eccentric or unobtrusive, humorously flamboyant or pathetically incomplete. These, however, are but the trifling gratuities collected by scholarship, not its justification.

Original research is the prime condition of honest criticism. Every philosopher must begin with systematic doubt. If a man is persuaded from the very start that Plato (or Spinoza, or Hegel) is in possession of the whole truth, he abdicates his freedom of thought and ceases to be a philosopher. He has no right to call himself a Platonist unless he has challenged Plato. A scientist is not merely permitted, he is urged to question Aristotle, Hippocrates, and Galen. The decisive medieval argument: *Magister dixit* is a *Requiescat*. When I came to America, I encountered a man who had chopped up René Doumic's textbook on French literature into three hundred questions. If a student had the three hundred answers pat, he knew French literature. Whoso would save his artistic soul must first smash up all such prayer wheels.

It is not easy. The prayer wheel is a convenient device; I have seen it revolve smoothly in examinations for the doctor's degree. It is obviously far easier for teacher and pupil alike to learn neat, ready-made judgments than to rely upon their own taste. Constantly I found students noting down what seemed to them useful

Literature

formulas and repeating them with adolescent gravity. Once I happened to mention Victor Hugo's picturesque and vigorous line,

Sur le Racine mort, le Campistron pullule,

which means that in a pseudo-classical age, worthless imitators swarm about the remains of genius like flies on a dead lion. This came back to me in the form: "There was a campistron once who was pullulating."—"What do you mean, pullulating?"—"I don't know; but that is what you told us campistrons did."

Blatant ignorance and assertive parrot-knowledge are of equal deadliness in literature. There should be some point—a period perhaps, or a kind, or a writer, or even a single work—about which you will not be tempted to bluff, and about which you cannot be bluffed, because you know. I developed, when I was still in high school, a depraved taste for the classical tragedy of the eighteenth century: I saw with my own eyes Campistrons pullulate. I studied with actual eagerness those bloodless automata, proceeding stiffly, inexorably, on their eighteen hundred alexandrines. I cannot recapture this queer fascination. It taught me at least one great lesson: that a fanatical devotion to "standards" could result only in standardized products. I found later, fortunately, a less questionable field. I became deeply interested in the Second Empire. I had known for years Flaubert and Baudelaire, Taine and Renan, and not a few other writers of high merit. But I became acquainted with hundreds of lesser celebrities. I read newspapers, memoirs, private correspondences; I did not spurn cartoons and popular songs. I was familiar with the architecture, the interior decoration, the fashion in dress and food of that age so close to ours, and yet now one with Nineveh and Tyre. I was more at home in the Paris of 1860 than in the San Francisco of my own days. It is not in the least essential that one should understand the Second Empire rather than a number of other periods. But firsthand knowledge about something is an excellent protection against all snap judgments and plausible generalities. Research, in the humanities, is the nearest equivalent to experiment in the physical sciences. On a chosen sample, you are able to test both the conventional version of the truth and your own hypothesis.

I am more impressed with the value of research as a contribution to training than as a contribution to knowledge. It is extremely important to acquire new facts; it is more vital still to use intelligently the facts already at our command. There is no need to declare a moratorium on discovery, as Georges Duhamel proposed; but Nazi Germany showed the perils of technical information outrunning wisdom. The investigator who does not have a critical mind is a mere journeyman; his labor will be wasted unless the result is used, as raw material, by someone who can think. On the other hand, research might bring no new fact, no new idea, and yet be profitable. What if all our efforts should simply confirm the accepted view? It makes a great difference whether a thing is believed merely on hearsay or established after a thorough inquiry. Renan confessed ruefully that after a lifetime of labor he had reached the same conclusions as the man in the street. But it is more difficult to sneer at Renan than at John Doe.

It is impossible to know everything at first hand, and the unphilosophical specialist may be a fool in every field not his own. We are saved from this danger if we consider critical training as inseparable from research. The combination of the two will enable us, when we have to work on secondary or tertiary sources, to appraise the efforts of others. Working at second hand, as we all must, is the most exacting of all techniques. Many scholars are careful never to mention a fact or an idea without a proper reference; but they seem to think that a correct bibliographical indication confers the same authority on anyone who ever wrote a line. The trained man, if a new problem should become vital in his eyes, will have at his disposal not a vast store of irrelevant facts but a set of efficient tools. Jaurès was, to begin with, no "authority" on the Dreyfus affair. He knew less about artillery, the espionage system, the organization of the General Staff, than dozens of other men.

Literature

But his philosophical and historical education enabled him to discover and demonstrate the truth, even though many important documents were kept hidden from him.

It is therefore absurd to consider Research as a single entity, august and frowning. Of two books which scrupulously follow the same scholarly pattern, equally painstaking, equally accurate, equally recondite and inaccessible to the general reader, one may have life and the other be a mere lump. Much research I have seen in a long academic life could be described as "the blind led by the blind into a blind alley." Much, even though its findings were soon to be forgotten, has contributed to the growth of a man or an idea. Learning, without the critical spirit, is stillborn; but the critical spirit, if it merely challenges or denies and never pauses to investigate, is a mere gadfly.

The philosopher, the judge, the scientist, the scholar, are all men who refuse to accept anything on hearsay.[1] The study of literature is not the reverent transmission of respectable prejudices, but the brushing away of cobwebs. For cobwebs are no argument. The bottles to which they lend the prestige of high vintage may contain poor stuff, or even be empty. The critic cannot take conventional fame at its face value. As a social historian, he cannot dismiss it; it is a recorded fact that Béranger, the song writer, was universally admired, even by Goethe, and that fact may have a meaning. But popularity is an equivocal crown. Perhaps we should say of him who wears it, "It serves him right."

The first thing that the investigator discovers is the utter capriciousness of literary opinion. His task would be easy if the public were infallibly wrong. Some good judges felt quite sure that *The Bridge of San Luis Rey* and *The Last Puritan* must be spurious literature when they turned into best sellers. (André Gide, unaware

---

[1] To these must be added their folklore compeer, "the Man from Missouri." Missouri has made four outstanding contributions to American culture: the homespun critical mind, who "has to be shown"; Mr. T. S. Eliot; Mark Twain; and President Harry Truman. There must be something in the soil and in the air.

Education of a Humanist

of that damning fact, took *The Bridge* very seriously.) But there is no such easy rule. The public took at once to *Le Cid,* by Corneille, to the great plays of Molière, to *Les Misérables,* as eagerly as to *Les Deux Orphelines, Les Deux Gosses,* and *Clochemerle.*

Ah! But that is the "general," the profane herd! Apart—consciously, willfully apart—from the common reader, there is an elite, an enlightened circle, the educated and discriminating, what the French used to call *les honnêtes gens,* the gentle, the well-bred. They still exist, although, alas! not so formally recognized in a democracy, and their opinion alone counts. But it counts for surprisingly little, for they are the cultural element of "Society," and Society, far more than the heavier masses, is swayed by vogues. Society takes pride in its own fickleness. You do not have to wait for the next generation: the very next season Society jeers at the craze of yesteryear. The list of books about which Society once raved reads like a necrology. And, like the masses, Society is not unerring in perversity. It may hail, cherish, and even preserve a truly great book as well as an obvious fake or a confessed potboiler. Praise, disdain, and oblivion are so unaccountable that the man in quest of the truth must disregard them equally.

As for the "constituted authorities," the Academies, the Universities, they have long been laughed or yawned out of court. The French Academy, the most illustrious, the most influential of all, harbored from the first a majority of nonentities. Rostand, in *Cyrano de Bergerac,* enumerates ironically the deeply forgotten names of the early Immortals: Bardin, Habert, Foncemagne, Cordemoy, Vatout, Porchères, Colomby, Bourseys, Bourdon, Arbaud. The list compares not unfavorably with that of our own days, except that Marshal Pétain and General Weygand are not likely to be forgotten so soon. At any rate, any Parisian taxi driver could name offhand a few members of the French Academy; the American Academy has not impressed itself so deeply upon our national consciousness. The professors are manifestly at sea when they attempt to appraise positions not yet fully "established." That is why I am so doubtful

Literature

about the "teaching" of contemporary literature: who will first teach the teachers?

Why, the authors themselves. It is their craft, and they ought to know. But they do not. They cannot be trusted to judge sanely of their own genius or of the merits of their friends. Each author worthy of the name brings forth his own note, unique and by definition incomparable. Of course, they have an instrument in common, language, and at times certain refinements of technique which define a school or a group. This creates a freemasonry: within the charmed circle, members may quarrel; but they will present a united front against the Bœotians. Now their mutual recognition offers absolutely no guarantee of excellence. The French poets assembled in their hundreds and elected a Prince: first Léon Dierx, then Paul Fort. Admirable bards both of them; but the Academy, the professors, or even Chance, could have made as wise a selection. Of the Symbolists, two or three names have survived: we forget the many who were once considered—by one another—as the very marrow of French literature. So it went with the *Parnasse* a generation before: by reciprocal verdict, they were all poets; and now their place knows them no more. So it was with the various romantic *Cénacles* about 1830: Arvers, Barbier, Brizeux, Hégésippe Moreau have at any rate one or two little flowers in hospitable anthologies; but what of Evariste Boulet-Paty, Coran, Fontaney, Lefèvre-Deumier le Parricide, Dovalle, Ulrich Guttinguer, Gaspard de Pons, Jules de Saint-Félix, and many others? Literature may be, like the House of Commons of better days, a most exclusive club; but mediocrity is evidently no absolute disqualification. Ronsard's *Pléiade* has a better record. Of the seven, the glorious chief and Joachim du Bellay have been confirmed by posterity; we still hear faintly the thin merry tinkle of Belleau's *April;* and who could forget such a euphonious name as Pontus de Tyard?

No: neither the masses nor the classes, neither the officials nor the writers themselves have the words of eternal life. We must turn for instruction to the professional judges, the critics. By whom elected? By the classes, and the academies, and—more reluctantly—by the authors, whose authority we have questioned. But the blunders of critics are notorious. They have been repeatedly noted for the edification of the reading public. Jeffrey's dictatorial "This will never do" should be an everlasting lesson to the cocksure.

Henri Peyre in his searching book, *Writers and their Critics,* has given us a choice collection of critical misdeeds, culled from the literary annals of England, America, Germany, and France. Two examples will suffice: Sainte-Beuve and Boileau—both French, because criticism is one of France's undisputed glories. The two men, in widely different epochs and schools, were supreme masters of their craft.

Sainte-Beuve is often considered, and not unjustly, as the Critic par excellence. He had keen interest, diligence, a penetrating mind. He gave us marvelous series of psychological portraits. But, when he had to appraise his own contemporaries, he fumbled most pitifully. He never fully understood the greatness of Balzac; he overlooked altogether the later and more profound poems of Alfred de Vigny; he knew Stendhal, and was blind to his unique power.

Boileau is the god of classical criticism. He had an all-absorbing devotion to literature, unconquerable sanity, and quiet courage. Even Louis XIV bowed before his authority. He supported the greatest, Molière and Racine, who happened to be his personal friends, against jealous cabals. He forgot to find a niche in his *Poetical Art* for his other friend, La Fontaine. With *The Divine Comedy* towering in the past, and *Paradise Lost* arising in his own day, he calmly asserted that a Christian poem was an absurdity. He did not condemn Shakespeare because he had never heard of him; but he condemned the Spanish dramatists for using a technique resembling Shakespeare's. He believed French literature began with Villon. All this is sheer ignorance, and it might be pleaded that ignorance is no crime. But when he did know, his stately critical wig was often awry. He saw nothing but pedantry and confusion in Ronsard; he rejoiced because the downfall of that "pretentious" poet enabled Des-

Literature

portes and Bertaut to write more acceptably. He hailed with a cry of joy the advent of Malherbe. And when he wanted to bestow the utmost praise, he selected as his standards of perfect prose D'Ablancourt and Patru.

Time has dealt kindly with Desportes and Bertaut, D'Ablancourt and Patru: it has buried them deep. Our last resort then is Posterity. "Time will tell" and "You can't fool all of the people all the time" are most comfortable platitudes. But the superficial resemblance between a platitude and a truth may be deceptive. Time tells, but does not invariably give the right answer. Has Time settled for us any of the major problems in history—the rise of Christianity, the downfall of Rome, the validity of the Reformation, the beneficence of the French Revolution? And if you can fool all the people some of the time, what guarantee have we that, abandoning one error, they will not rush blindly into another? I have known people who jumped straight from isolationism into imperialism.

In literature, works of very little worth, if they be melodramatic or sentimental enough, may survive almost indefinitely. A lady expressed astonishment that Saint Denis was able to walk so many miles with his severed head in his hands. She was told: "Oh! After the first step, the rest is easy." Certain reputations, properly decapitated, still proceed undisturbed. It was for Casimir Delavigne, the middle-road dramatist, that the famous line was penned: *Il est des morts qu'il faut qu'on tue,* there are corpses that demand to be killed anew. Fifty years after Delavigne's death, Gustave Lanson deplored that it was still necessary to mention him. Fifty years after Lanson's marvelous epitome of French literature, Casimir Delavigne is still with us. Perhaps the critics will get tired of beheading him and acknowledge his right to bore posterity.

There was a symposium in *The Nation* a few years ago about "Great Books I have never read." The admissions were startling, perhaps willfully and boastfully so. But someone still found it necessary to brag that he had not read *Paul and Virginia.* I thought those deplorable young people had been under ground for a hundred

Education of a Humanist

years. *The Lady with the Camellias* (vulgo *Camille,* one of the worst near-puns in any language) simply will not stay in her dishonored grave. The result is that she has killed the other and much better plays of Dumas *fils,* a great dramatist in spite of his insufferable cleverness, without whom the rise of Ibsen and Shaw would be inexplicable. *L'Abbé Constantin* still appears on the stage, and, until recently at least, on the list of our "educational" publishers. Perhaps the outstanding case of an interminable twilight is the *Romance of the Rose*. For nearly three hundred years it was a European classic. Skelton and Marot, in the Renaissance dawn, were still clutching that medieval wraith. To be sure, scholarship considers the *Romance of the Rose* an incomparable document; there was a new and monumental edition some thirty years ago. But as a work of art it has long ceased to command respect. It "fooled all the people" for about as long as we have been admiring Milton or Racine.

Time is but a slow poison for spurious masterpieces. Does Time rehabilitate the unjustly neglected? Once in a long while. Stendhal, as he had prophesied, was read and understood fifty years, a hundred years, after he wrote and failed. Kierkegaard was rediscovered. Melville had a splendid aftermath. A very uncertain gamble. There is a character in a story by Max Beerbohm who sells his soul for the privilege of jumping a hundred years ahead of time and finding himself famous when his blatantly successful contemporaries are dust. His anticipatory ghost does explore the British Museum, and after a painful search, he discovers a single reference to himself as "a fictitious character in a story by Max Beerbohm." From the French sixteenth century, Maurice Scève and Louise Labé have been exhumed, but not restored to life. Even textbook writers know that Agrippa d'Aubigné is immeasurably greater than Malherbe; yet this truth, coolly acknowledged, has not made D'Aubigné a familiar, beloved, and revered name. The crucial example is that of Salluste du Bartas, like D'Aubigné a Huguenot poet. His *La Semaine* (an epic of the Creation) has unmistakable greatness and was admired

Literature

by Goethe. But both his religious party and his literary school were defeated. Had they lived, his fame would have not merely survived but grown. Through patient exegesis, his obscurities would have become profundities; through pious imitation, his oddities would have turned into standards. Fame feeds on incense. If the altar fire grows dim, it may yet blaze anew. If it dies, through unjust neglect, it remains dead.

So, in any generation, the men whom fame has passed by may well be greater than the Casimir Delavignes; and the chances are slight that indifferent Time will bring about their vindication. The seed that fell by the wayside, upon stony ground, or among thorns, was not inferior to the one that brought forth fruit an hundredfold. But there is no way by which the injustice can ever be repaired. Even to be mentioned as a failure demands a certain degree of luck. What of those who never had a glimmer of success, those who were never acknowledged, never noticed, never published at all? My Darwinism is not of the optimistic kind. The fittest to survive (so proved by the fact that they have survived) are not necessarily the best. There are war dead whom the world could ill spare. There are millions of Nazis alive today, while Hitler's victims are irretrievably gone. There must be mute inglorious Miltons who never were given even the opportunity to fail.

Impartial, omniscient posterity is a delusion. Molière's Alceste said of a sonnet: *Le temps ne fait rien à l'affaire,* Time is not of the essence. He had in mind the time consumed in travail: effort is not the measure of perfection. But we may apply the phrase to the judgment of future generations: Time, in this case also, is irrelevant. When you read a poem fresh from the author's mind, Time has passed no verdict: but you must, be it only in the form of a yawn. Do not say that your favorable response is a prophecy that the book will endure: such a prophecy would be too wild a venture. You can only voice the conviction that it deserves to live, the hope that it may live. But even that hesitant intrusion of the Time element is not

Education of a Humanist

essential to enjoyment. The aesthetic response may be called forth by the evanescent: a bird's note, a chance ray of sunshine, a fleeting smile. A flash may reveal an abyss of tenderness or awe. What does it matter if it can never be recaptured by the same means? The experience was an enrichment. There are books which I have enjoyed deeply, without caring whether the world and I would remember them on the morrow. Greater than Time is the timeless: an instant may afford a shuddering glimpse of the eternal which will not be gained by the plodding reverent study of the very old.

The critic who will not receive his opinions ready-made, the "research scholar" in the deeper sense, soon finds that there is no inevitable connection between merit and success. The one belongs to the aesthetic sphere, the other to the social. Their meeting is perhaps more than a coincidence; it certainly is far less than a law. The opinions of others—masses, classes, Academies, universities, cliques, critics, and old Chronos himself—carry with them no obligation. Your own responsibility—this is the keynote of all Humanism—remains entire. It is your own palate that must be pleased, and your own soul that has to be saved.

Yet critics, undaunted, still nurse the unconquerable hope that they will at last discover the infallible touchstone. They are still hankering for the Law in a domain which lies beyond the Law. They still want to rig up the perfect selective machine, into which perforated cards will be fed, instead of helping individualities to fuller self-realization. Men can be "taught," that is, assisted; but can we teach literature? [2]

[2] It was properly asked: "Why care for posterity? What has posterity done for us?" The intentions of the author, at any rate, are not invariably respected by posterity. Many have echoed Horace's boast, *Exegi monumentum—Aere perennius*, not seldom with ludicrous effect. Ronsard and Chapelain wrote ponderous national epics, destined to live through the ages; they sank at once into deepest oblivion. Piron wrote tragedies more slowly than Voltaire, because, he said modestly, *Moi, je coule en bronze!* (Mine are cast in bronze); and he is remembered for a few epigrams. On the other hand, Aristophanes was literally a "journalist": he handled with scurrilous wit the men and the issues of the day, without a thought for the opinion of remote barbarians in the dim future; and the strange poetic satiric medleys still have life.

Literature

LITERATURE AND LANGUAGE

From the time I was sixteen, my attention was not divided between English and French literature: it was devoted jointly to both. It seemed to me as natural a condition as having two eyes and two ears. Without a thought, I had realized on the cultural plane that complete merger of the two Empires that Winston Churchill was to offer so dramatically in the darkest hour of 1940. After I received my first degrees from Chaptal[3] and Saint-Cloud, I had to concentrate on my English studies. I had four years of graduate work in that field, two in London, two at the Sorbonne. When I came to America, I taught French, but I lived in an English-speaking country, and with a Scotch-Irish-American wife. My interest in the two languages remained inseparable. So it gave me no shock when in mid-career I went over from the French Department to the English. In a sense, I was returning home.

I am a "man of letters": language is my tool, and words are my raw material. I love and curse them. Perhaps the fact that I acquired a second set, deliberately, in my adolescence, made me more conscious of their power and of their perversity. I am bilingual to the extent of dreaming and cursing in two languages. And this has forced upon me the problem, which arises in the case of all word-craftsmen from the mighty poet to the lowly professor: to what extent are their art and thought conditioned by their instrument? A soul cannot express itself in the same way on the flute, the cymbals, the snare drum, and the trombone. If we transform this truism into terms of Swahili, Greek, English, or Volapük, will it retain its validity? In my own case, is there a change in my personality when I shift from French to English? Or am I the same average person, wearing (for a little too

---

Beaumarchais, with more than Shavian insolence, said: "I know my *Figaro* is but froth; in two or three hundred years, people will stop talking about it." *Habent sua fata libelli.* . . .

[3] Technically, it is not the *collège* or *lycée* that grants the bachelor's degree, but all the preparation is done there.

Education of a Humanist

long) medium-weight, medium-priced, neutral-colored suits, some signed Hart Schaffner and Marx and others Belle Jardinière?

This personal problem, in its turn, raises a much more complex one. Is language an unconscious collective growth, with a life of its own, beyond individual control? Or is it a tool, which we are using consciously, which we are free to sharpen, to alter, even to discard for a better one? At one extreme, our ideal would be the spontaneous, untutored language of the folk, racy of the soil, the natural symbol of the ethos. At the other, it would be the dream of Bertrand Russell and of all the logicians: a scientific instrument, spare, aseptic, rigorously objective, so accurate that it would automatically expose ambiguities and reject fallacies.

The conflict is an ancient one. It was focused in the eighteenth century. The *Philosophes,* Condillac and Volney among them, defined science as a "well-made language," and conversely wanted to turn language into an infallible thinking-machine. Rivarol claimed —rashly—that the ideal of absolute probity had already been achieved in French, which thereby had deserved to become universal. The French Revolution made "General Grammar," inseparable from logical analysis, a basic study in its Central Schools. But Obscurantism (the term here is a definition, and implies no blame) had declared war on the Enlightenment even before the Enlightenment had received its name. Vico, Hamann, and Herder extolled the Dark Forces, and Burke the wisdom of prejudice. In many fields, and particularly in the linguistic, historical romanticism won the day. Oddly enough, it finally appeared in unromantic professorial garb. Generations of Dryasdusts, through the nineteenth century and well into the twentieth, fought hard for the primitive, the folklike, the unconscious. As we all know, the latest notable avatar of Obscurantism, the apostle of the mystic *Volkseele,* was Adolf Hitler.

I never was an eclecticist; but I never believed that in the complexity—and perhaps the chaos—of our pluriverse any human institution, any human being, ever conformed to a single and rigid formula. It stands to reason (to my reason, at any rate) that there

Literature

are in language elements of the unconscious and of the enlightened, of logic and of chance, of imitation, automatic or deliberate, and of creation, spontaneous or willful. There are many levels in language, and each plane is subject to its own law. The total may be a monstrosity. But it exists, and it works, after a fashion. So did our Democratic Party at the time when it embraced both Henry Wallace and Senator Bilbo.

1. At the lowest level, below consciousness, we find language as sheer reflex: the cry, the call, the groan, the sigh. This links mankind with the higher animals. It survives in articulate speech as the interjection, as the mimetic onomatopoeia. Habit may cause the willful and the sophisticated to sink into the unconscious. A scholar, hitting his fingers with a hammer, might very well substitute "Zounds!" for the conventional "Ouch!" or for the yelp of the wounded dog.

2. On a second level, we find subconscious speech: unformed sentences, deformed words, chance perceptions, distinct or mingling, evanescent thoughts, inchoate feelings, rushing helter-skelter like debris in a flood. This occurs when the artificial dictatorship of the conscious Ego is relaxed: in dreams, in drowsiness, in certain forms of lunacy, and also (I am told) at certain stages of intoxication. There you have the substratum, not the deepest self, but the chaotic stuff upon which the self imposes its pattern. However confused, it is expression, and therefore it is language. It is attempting to force its way into literature: the use of that method is closely akin to psychoanalysis, and its masterpiece is *Ulysses*. It may be noted that even in Joyce's most elaborate efforts, the many streams, separate or blending, are suggested rather than actually reproduced. Language, especially in printed form, is but a thin single line of expression. It cannot do justice to the welter of our innermost. A musical notation, on a symphonic scale, would be needed. It is a fact also that by definition you cannot catch your subconscious alive. As soon as you bring it to light and clothe it in definite words, it loses its mystery. Joyce cannot give us even glimpses, but only hints, of the sunken world. Not that such hints are not valuable as well as fascinating. The Joyce

method makes us realize that there are viscous depths beneath our sunlit universe. There is existence beyond language. A. N. Whitehead, in his *Adventures of Ideas,* keeps insisting that the final cosmologies are only partly expressed, can only be partly expressed, in language. There is more to this world than can be covered by lucid, coherent discourse. At the opposite poles, the Obscurantists and the Illuminati teach us the same lesson.

3. The third step is the barely conscious. It is the colloquial level, that of everyday careless speech. Monsieur Jourdain had been using prose all his life without being aware of it: I surmise that many illiterates speak without any sense of constraint. They call a cat a cat simply because it is the cat's name. They know that language is not inborn: children have to acquire it. But it is as natural as clothes are for the vast majority of mankind.

Many scholars consider this the normal level. Whatever lies below is only pre-language; whatever goes beyond is artificial, and therefore secondary. To correct popular speech according to formal canons is sheer pedantry: language must be accepted as a datum. Malherbe, who as a rule was a tyrannical purist, could occasionally brush aside his painful learning: the masters of French, he averred, are the common laborers at the Hay Wharf. The French Academy made "usage" the only norm. "Usage" in polite society, to be sure; but the distinction is a snobbish criterion which our democracy was bound to reject. A. G. Kennedy, in his excellent *Current English,* admits that whatever is said can be said. If America splits the infinitive, why, the infinitive is split, and no rule will mend it. I have fought—not very hard—against *middle-of-the-road, to center round, to contact,* and *to transpire* in the sense of *to happen.* What is the use? Superciliousness is the sin against the Holy Ghost.

It must be borne in mind, however, that this "natural" level of language does not exist naturally. If go-as-you-please were the only rule, our speech would change as fast as our slang—and O. Henry already needs a glossary. In my family, the set of baby terms, evolved through a compromise between the infant and its slaves, was totally

Literature

different with each child. It is said that missionaries, returning to primitive tribes after a lapse of years, have had to learn the language anew.

4. Popular speech is arrested in its evolution by standard speech. This is the fourth level: good plain vernacular, without pretension, but consciously resisting disruption and change. When a country has a settled government, especially courts of justice, when it has central markets, a tradition, a literature (even though it be oral), it no longer lives in a state of nature, and its language no longer is natural. It becomes standardized. Historical oddities remain imbedded in it, for the delight and despair of grammarians; but on the whole it submits to a code. Verbs are no longer "strong" enough to go it alone: they conform to established patterns or conjugations. It is as hard, in French or in English, to coin a new irregular verb as it is for an orderly citizen to be an absolute individualist. Affixes become reliable tools; derivatives form well-behaved families. A grammar is not a haphazard collection of precedents: it is a set of rules. Departures from the rules are tolerated, but severely branded as *exceptions*. A language like French or English is therefore composed of four elements: a substratum transmitted on the barely conscious plane; a limited number of nonlogical forms, accepted as precedents, fixed and definitely taught, but only as exceptions; a code of laws based, if not on logic, at any rate on analogy; and finally, a small leeway of free individual creation. It takes a good many years to teach a child correct "natural" English.

5. The plain vernacular may be an excellent literary medium. However, we do not merely acknowledge the ornate: we welcome it. Our speech is not all Yea, yea; nay, nay. Shakespeare could speak with the tongues of yokels; he could be satisfied with such simplicities as "To be or not to be," or "The rest is silence." But he is Shakespeare still when he says: "No, this my hand will rather the multitudinous sea incarnadine." As soon as style is present, however unobtrusive, a new level is reached, the fifth, as different from the literate standard as that standard is from the untutored popular.

Education of a Humanist

There is no writer worthy of the name who does not have style, even though, like Stendhal, Mérimée, and Gide at certain moments of their careers, he may attempt to strip himself of all vain ornaments. The most austere among them wears his nudity with a difference.

In this zone of the elaborate, the lofty, the poetic, there are many degrees. First of all, there is the style which possesses such definite characteristics that it can be learned and practiced like an idiom. Latin, a living language until the sixteenth century, was killed by its offspring the Ciceronian and the Vergilian; for a language that is set is dead. Milton forged an instrument of his own; it would be easier to translate Miltonic into Latin than into the "natural" speech of Ring Lardner. Johnson reveled in the sesquipedalian: his definition of *network* is a priceless example of polysyllabic humor.[4] Carlyle, who started with plain English, evolved Carlylese, which, thank the Lord, died with its creator. During the war, "Turn off the light" was translated into official Johnsonese: "Illumination is required to be extinguished." If eloquence, poetry, and bureaucracy have languages of their own, so has the law, and so has religion. "Whoso believeth on Him" has a more spiritual ring than "All who believe in Him." In *Roughing It*, Mark Twain has the Miner and the Minister addressing each other from two levels of speech; and it takes them a long time to transact a very simple business.

The literary idiom may become a different language, not through tricks of vocabulary and syntax, but through a subdued accompaniment of allusions. There we have a language within a language. To the plain reader, the words and the meaning are plain. To the initiated, it is the overtones that tell the story. I need hardly mention, as a form of language, the deliberate affectations which may be as complex and as rigid as a code: Marinism, Gongorism, Euphuism, Preciosity, diseases or refinements which did not disappear in the seventeenth century under the rough therapy of Boileau and Molière. I can hardly pick up a book of modern poetry without being made

---

[4] "Anything reticulated or decussated, at equal distances, with interstices between the intersections."

Literature

to realize that the author and I do not use the same tongue. At times I find the new idiom easy to learn, and at times well worth learning. But I can pick my way through a page of Portuguese or Rumanian, which I have never studied, better than through certain contemporary lyrics.

6. We have thus reached a high degree of awareness and artificiality, far removed from the instinctive cry of fear or joy. The next step is easy enough. For the conscious artist, who deliberately spurns the triteness of common speech, there is nothing strange about the adoption of a medium totally different from the vernacular. Dante and Milton, when they wrote in Latin, were only a little farther removed from the common man than when they wrote in Italian or English. More books have been written in Latin since its alleged death than in the centuries of its triumphant life. Some, like *The Imitation of Christ* and *The Praise of Folly*, are counted among world masterpieces. It may be a shock to find Jean Jaurès as the author of a book in Latin (his minor doctor's thesis). Many have chosen to write in French, from Brunetto Latini and Marco Polo to Gabriele D'Annunzio and Oscar Wilde; and many in English, like Rabindranath Tagore and Jawaharlal Nehru, like Joseph Conrad and Lin Yutang. Thus the author completely escapes from the barely conscious use of his mother tongue. He knows, by definite experience, that language is an instrument which can be adopted by an act of will. Theorists will tell us that it cannot be done; that any Cockney's English is better than Conrad's because it is "natural" and Conrad's is "synthetic." But theories are a rather dismal form of humor.

7. Now we are frankly in the domain of the "artificial," that is to say, of consciousness, order, planning. We have seen that all grammar is meant to bring out the inner logic of a language; to extend to its uttermost limits the area of normalization (*standard English*); to reduce the "pockets" of illogical survivals, which remain like erratic blocks, or quaint feudal customs, or folk superstitions (*exceptions*). If you carry this normative tendency a little farther, you will want not merely to minimize but to eliminate the "abuses"

or absurdities which are still imbedded in natural speech, and which serve no valid purpose: no verb is less expressive for being regular. Descartes, Leibniz, and, nearly three centuries later, Peano, wanted to streamline Latin, just as Ogden and Richards, in their Basic, want to streamline English. I am convinced, and shall attempt to demonstrate that, from every point of view, Peano is right against Ogden and Richards. But the principle is scrupulously the same in both cases.

A streamlined natural language like Basic, or Peano's Interlingua, remains natural; it is purified, not synthetic. It would probably provide an excellent solution for our present needs: Basic and especially Interlingua are much easier to learn than the historical languages upon which they are based. This, however, is not likely to remain the final stage. If we follow the line of thought of men like Russell, Whitehead, or Carnap, we can descry the possibility of improving our instrument and turning it into a veritable algebra of thought. There was a time when crude rubber came almost exclusively from the Amazonian jungle. The plantations of hevea in Indonesia proved that, by taking thought, man could do much better than wild nature. But we are on the threshold of a new development. Already certain forms of synthetic rubber possess properties which cannot be matched in the natural or cultivated forms. In the past, so-called "philosophical languages" have been clumsy attempts. It is not merely possible, it is highly probable, that logicians, psychologists, phoneticians, and semanticists, if their efforts were integrated, could create a medium of expression immeasurably superior to Latin or English. Then, as in the noble plan of Lakanal under the French Revolution, "General Grammar" would be the keystone of education.

8. Here we become aware of the fact that even such a perfected instrument would not fulfill the whole purpose of language. Language is social, and therefore logical, for communication implies a common background, a set of accepted rules which, on the whole, must be in harmony with "common sense." Caprice is antisocial. Yet

Literature

there is also in language, from the instinctive level up, an element of self-expression and, in its utmost refinement, of self-exploration, apart from the desire to reach our fellow beings. A cry is not invariably a call. Santayana believes that dialogue is not the primary and original factor in language; that the "speaking to one's self" comes before communication; that language is first of all spontaneous music which only later, and in a very rough and uncertain manner, adapts itself to its rational function.[5] This theory may seem extreme and paradoxical; yet the individual creation of language, as an extension of personality, is a more reasonable hypothesis than a sort of Social Contract, a constitutional convention of beings who were previously dumb.

But we need not accept Santayana's conception in all its rigor to recognize that man seeks to express more than he can communicate. He hopes to be understood; he knows he cannot be fully understood, for every word he uses has connotations that he cannot fully share. Not the Experimental poet alone, but every one of us, is thus attempting to "put into words" his inmost self. Attempting and failing. Even in the speech of the common man there is an element which is cryptic, hermetic, or, in the etymological sense, "idiotic." Neither the speaker nor his interlocutor can fully measure the loss. Yet there is a wistful cast even on commonplace features: "Why can't you see what I see, feel what I feel? But what's the use? Let us be satisfied with the rough-and-ready."

Poets—some poets—are constantly striving to use language beyond the range of mere communication, as an assertion of their unicity. I believe this conscious effort is a mistake. It implies that you know what is unique in you; and this you can never know. Negatively, the attempt has an excellent effect. It prevents the poet from limiting himself artificially to the accepted common ground; it liberates him from the tyranny of the trite. There should be more to

---

[5] My attention was called to this theory of Santayana's by Alfonso Reyes, *El deslinde* (México: El Colegio de México, 1944), p. 174.

Education of a Humanist

language than common sense. The result of experimentation may be either to extend the area of agreement or to trace the limit between "mankind" and individual man.

On this level, language cannot be reduced to a grammar or a vocabulary: language is the man. I do not believe in verbal tricks to emphasize the difference—a "little language" like that of the *Journal to Stella,* or the idiosyncrasies of Gertrude Stein. The unique, which we may call the lyric note in its purity, may be revealed in the tritest words. We are here in a totally different sphere from the ideal of Leibniz, Ogden, or Russell. They are seeking unity; the lyrical note is the assertion of unicity.

9. The next step is not, logically, on a higher level. It implies rather a difference in technique. In practically all the realms of language from the third (colloquial speech) to the seventh (algebra of thought), language is accepted as a collective achievement, a tacit or explicit convention. The individual must submit to its law. In the first, second, and eighth zones (unconscious, subconscious, and expression of unicity), the collective, the conventional factor is subordinated. There is no rule: grammar abdicates, and the vocabulary is set free.

Now this emancipation may appear, even in colloquial speech, in the form of free creation. This is particularly true of American slang in its most vital forms. French *argot* is a much more standardized and traditional affair. *Argot* is really a dialect, whose domain is social instead of regional: the peculiar speech of schoolboys, soldiers, workers, or thieves, instead of that of Burgundy or Auvergne. The beauty of American slang is that it is either poetry (metaphor) or joyous nonsense. "I can do what I please with my own. If I choose to say buck, mazuma, lettuce, cartwheel, instead of currency, it is my business. I know that you, as a man and a brother, will gladly play the game." It is freedom of speech beyond the dreams of President Roosevelt.

Slang, not free and irresponsible, but with malice prepense, becomes journalistic or radio patter, a learned tongue not always in-

Literature

telligible to the trained philologist. The supreme achievement in that line is *Finnegans Wake*. There is no difference, except in subtlety, between such current words as *smog, slanguage,* or *cinemactress* and the most recondite creations of James Joyce.[6]

10. The ultimate level is Silence. Ernest Hello had properly called it the natural language of the mystic. This is no absurdity: language can give us a sense of the unspeakable, the unutterable, the ineffable. The greatest heights of poetry are not reached through words, but through the vibrations which continue beyond the words. Many are deaf to this inaudible music. They do not realize, for instance, that in Hugo's tremendous symphony there is a flute of weird tenuous poetry, and that at times the flute itself is hushed, and the soul is overwhelmed with silence. Words hack their way through the explicit and lead us to the brink. He who can hear beyond, let him hear.

THE WORLD OF BOOKS AND THE WORLD OF MEN

My work in French Civilization assumed that literature was an integral part of a people's life, and that the whole history of France was a necessary background to the study of her great writers. Conversely, literary works were the mirrors of France's multitudinous activities. A lifetime of teaching, research, and questioning has not disproved that assumption; indeed, it has given it the steadiness of a reasoned conviction. But from the very first, I challenged my fundamental hypothesis. I have kept testing it ever since. As a result, I grew conscious of necessary qualifications and adjustments. The relations between civilization and literature cannot be stated in the form of a few simple dogmas: it is a large and extremely complex field of investigation. The economic interpretation of history is certainly no universal key. And even Taine's formula—race, environment, and time—although far more comprehensive and, literally, more intelli-

---

[6] It has often been said that one of the chief purposes of language is to conceal thought. Language may be intended as a veil for the uninitiated. This covers such jargons as the idioms of the cliques, thieves' cant, *Rotwelsch,* hog Latin, and *largoji des loucherbems.*

gent, does not tell the whole truth. Our problem is: does it even approach the essential truth?

One first step was easy to take, as my readers, by this time, must be well aware. Very early, I had become liberated from the thrall of nationalism. Chauvinism and jingoism, both seen at close range, canceled each other. By shrieking that the English and the French were radically different, and destined to eternal enmity, the nationalists on both sides of the Channel had proved to me that they were strikingly alike. The cause of the clashes between two idolatries is the fanaticism common to both. What was obvious of political thought was even more evident of literature. French literature has had a longer and more continuous life than any other in the modern world; but the most elementary knowledge of the subject revealed that its history was the reverse of "national." In the Middle Ages, apart from the Latin literature addressed to all Christendom, forms and themes in the vernacular were Pan-European. The Arthurian cycle, the Romance of Reynard the Fox, do not belong to a single nation. The Renaissance was the rejection of a stagnant tradition and a return to the living fountainhead, classical antiquity. No dictator of Parnassus could be less nationalistic than Ronsard, unless it be Boileau: both tossed contemptuously aside five centuries of French achievements to recover and make their own the masterpieces of the ancient world. When the late eighteenth century yawned at last, "Who will deliver us from the Greeks and the Romans?" the result was not a return to French origins, but the imitation of German and especially of English models. The makers of French Romanticism were above all the oddly assorted quartet—Shakespeare, Ossian, Walter Scott, Lord Byron. Our conventional thought manages to ignore facts that "jump to the eyes."

World literature,[7] it has often been said, begins not in the graduate school but in the nursery. No child is such a trueborn little

[7] *World* here denotes not an actual condition but an unattainable limit. Here I mean simply a consideration of literature that ignores political and linguistic boundaries: the humanistic point of view.

Literature

American that he will indignantly reject Grimm's Fairy Tales, or Andersen's, or *Pinocchio*. Folklore themes are world-wide: Aurelio Macedonio Espinosa has tracked down the Tar Baby in the most unexpected places. Adolescent readers are not governed by any *Sinn Fein* spirit: for generations they enjoyed *The Three Musketeers* and *The Mysterious Island*. Adults without any claim to scholarship or sophistication reveled in *Monte Cristo, The Wandering Jew, The Mysteries of Paris, Les Misérables*. Today, the *petite bourgeoisie* which gets its reading direct from the wholesalers at a substantial rebate does not object if the author happens to be Stefan Zweig, Franz Werfel, or Erich Remarque. When it comes to the more discriminating circles and the conscious artists, the case is more evident still. At one time Anatole France, at another Proust, or Pirandello, or Thomas Mann, occupied the center of the stage. As I write, a critic would lose his self-respect if he did not bring into the discussion Kierkegaard, Kafka, Gide, and Sartre. For the realist, that is, the man who refuses to be hoodwinked by conventions, there are only two kinds of literature: not the old and the new, not the homegrown and the foreign, not even the good and the bad, but the quick and the dead. In this respect, the movement for making "Great Books" the center of education is doing admirable service: it breaks down the paltry and wholly artificial barriers of parochialism.

Books informed with the purest "Americanism," "of Americans, by Americans, for Americans," are shoveled by the hundred into early, unwept, nameless graves. An Austrian Jew writes the novelized biography of a French peasant girl under the Second Empire, and the book, in translation, becomes a "national" bestseller.[8] Does not this rather play havoc with the theory that literature is determined by social conditions? Let us admit cautiously that it is affected by them. The action, which may be slight, seldom is direct. When it can be traced, it has, of course, no bearing upon the artistic merit of the work. Institutions, manners, ethos, explain to a large extent the superficial resemblances between the man of genius and the competent

[8] Franz Werfel, *The Song of Bernadette*.

businessman of letters. They do not account for the difference between them, which is the secret of literature.

With rare exceptions, the greatest writers in a language are also those who soar most easily above the limitations of time and space. Successful mediocrities seldom cross the Atlantic, the Channel, or even the Rhine: it is the men of whom a nation is most justly proud who cease to belong to that nation alone. Their obvious local features do not create an obstacle. Nothing could be more intensely local than the London of Dickens, the Paris of Proust, the Dublin of Joyce, yet they are claimed as universal. The West is in danger of forgetting Turgenev, who was so sanely, so lucidly Western; but it has adopted Dostoevsky. Because he is more intensely Russian, and therefore has a more exotic appeal? No: interest in the unfamiliar is no doubt a factor of success, but a minor one. It is the deep human quality, not the picturesque vestments of a different age and clime, that is the key to our response. Dostoevsky is no travelogue writer, no anthropologist describing a "culture." The vistas he opens are within our own hearts.

Because greatness in literature is independent of race, environment, and time, great works of art are far less and far more than the faithful mirrors of society. Mirrors if you like, but with the distortion of a powerful personality, and a light which is not that of the common day. Can we study in Dante and Milton the faith of the average man? They were anything but average. Both were rejected by the masses of their fellow citizens, and their genius burned more fiercely because of their defeat. Victor Hugo attained his full stature only when he stood alone on his rock, while France almost unanimously threw herself at the feet of Louis Napoleon. There is much in literature that is not the placid reflection of the current scene, but satire, protest, escape, yearning. There is nothing strange about the paradox that the greatest moment in French Romanticism should be the reign of Louis Philippe, a royal Calvin Coolidge, wielding an umbrella instead of a sword. What a delicious social history of the time could be written with the dramas of Victor Hugo and Alex-

Literature

andre Dumas as our documents! Even Balzac, so marvelously realistic in detail, is not the chronicler but the Dante of his age. Rodin was well inspired in representing him recoiling before the spectacle he had evoked, with haunted eyes and an avenging rictus. It was not a picture that he gave us but a vision.

Great books, like great pictures, provide magnificent illustrations for history, especially for the more popular kind. But as documents they must be used with the utmost caution. Imagine a biography of Marie de Médicis inspired by Rubens! Between that very commonplace woman and those vast gorgeous canvases, the connection is purely commercial. Those grand baroque allegories represent neither the convictions of the painter nor the spirit of the queen.

Literary history is a hybrid. Let me hasten to say that the word implies no condemnation, for there are hybrids that possess vigor, usefulness, and grace. It is inseparable from social history: for what it deals with is recognition, diffusion, success, that is to say, social phenomena. The work which is spurned as passé becomes a period piece, and as such takes its place in the total picture of the period: there are books which are the equivalents of the crinoline, of horsehair furniture, of steel engravings, of the antimacassar and the aspidistra. But literary history is also entangled with criticism. Inevitably so; let me revert unblushingly to my theme song: in order to appreciate a masterpiece, we must be acquainted with its language, and the language implies the mores—customs, manners, conventions—the style in the sense of prevailing fashion. There must be a mental transposition, amounting almost to a translation, from the English of Shakespeare to the English of our own days. This is the indispensable preliminary to criticism; it is not criticism itself. Many scholars are not fully conscious of the difference. We too often see a mountainous pedestal of information, bearing aloft a tiny and woefully conventional statue of aesthetic discrimination.

Literature as an art is independent: I believe in the unfashionable doctrine of Art for Art's Sake. Supreme values are not determined by race, environment, and time: else the great classics would not be alive today. This is the fundamental truth which should never be eclipsed in our minds. The history of literature is not coextensive with the understanding and enjoyment of literature. And that history itself is not autonomous: books do not grow in a vacuum, and books do not grow purely out of other books. At all times, the essential relation is not between book and book, but between book and life. A revolution in literature is part of a general revolution in thought, itself inseparable from a change in social conditions. The great spirit of confidence, energy, adventure, which is the true glory of the Renaissance, and which was so admirably expressed by Rabelais, did not originate in the flight of a few grammarians from Constantinople: it is the same spirit that stirred in discoverers, conquistadors, reformers. Classicism, the Enlightenment, Romanticism, Realism, were not mere literary fashions. Even esoteric movements, the Symbolist and Decadent schools of the Yellow Nineties, the Ecclesiastes mood of the sophisticates after the First World War, were odd manifestations of a universal *malaise*. Political history, social history, economic history, literary history, are constantly fed from the common reservoir which we must call vaguely "the spirit of the time."

These considerations should throw some light on the problem of the "Great Books." That we should read "great books" rather than poor ones is a venerable truism; that we should make them the core of a liberal education is not quite so obvious. My attitude toward the plan so successfully carried out at St. John's College and Chicago will be called by some of my friends ambiguous, or perhaps—since the word is now in fashion—"ambivalent." It is definitely friendly; and, because criticism is my rule of life, it is no less definitely critical.

In the first place, it is evident that the whole of life is not covered by a hundred books. Erasmus and Rabelais are splendid manifestations of the Renaissance: they are not the whole Renaissance. Luther is greater than anything he wrote, and the Reformation is im-

Literature

measurably greater than Luther. Certain immense changes, of the utmost importance to mankind, never were recorded in commensurate books. The Industrial Revolution had incalculable consequences; but even if James Watt had happened to write a book, it might very well not have deserved to be considered a world classic. And in the mounting tide of socialism for the last century and a half, no single book, however mighty, can be treated even as an adequate symbol.

One of the boasted advantages of the proposed method is to go back directly to the source, pure and uncontaminated: not books about books, but the original works themselves. Yet if we want fully to understand any one of these masterpieces, we have to study not its bare text alone but the antecedents and concomitants that explain it. Most of the books on the proposed list are termed "great" because they were moments in history: we cannot pick up *Das Kapital* as though it had appeared this morning. I defy any one to read Marx intelligently unless he also reads about Marx and his times.

To isolate a few books out of millions, and to assume that they and they alone are necessary and sufficient, is to transfer to the world of books the Carlylean delusion of hero-worship. It is not true that all we see in history is but the prolonged shadow of a few great men, be their instrument the pen or the sword. We shall discuss Carlyle's thesis at greater length in our chapter on History. Suffice it to say that of such "heroes," many seem so great only because their puny stature is projected upon a gigantic screen. I shall not adduce the example of Hitler, whose memory is somewhat under a cloud at present. Napoleon, whose primacy as a maker of history is undisputed, will serve our purpose. Had Napoleon been born fifty years earlier or later, it is not the face of the world that would have been changed but only the Napoleonic Legend. He knew, with his curious blend of mysticism and bourgeois common sense, that his "Destiny" was not framed by his own will; he was conscious of being swayed by *la force des choses,* the irresistible urge of things. From day to day, in dramatic episodes, individual men and individual books seem to have a sharp, intense, vivid existence —like an individual wave just as it breaks on the shore; but the tide, not the wave, is the substantial reality.

I am no scientist; but I have heard scientists question the wisdom of teaching science through the works of the past. The very nature of science is to disregard tradition and courteously to rule out individual authority. Nothing is true simply because Euclid, Ptolemy, Kepler, Newton, or Einstein said so. The ascertained, classified, organized facts accumulate; the method grows more exacting, more searching; the actual work of any particular scientist is incorporated in the general body of science. The gropings of a genius have a personal, not a scientific, interest. As the merest layman, I have no right to speak about, say, Lyell's *Elements of Geology* or Darwin's *Origin of Species,* both epochmaking books. But I happened, as I shall explain later, to grow professionally interested in Malthus. The problem of population is of the utmost importance to mankind; it might well become the all-absorbing one if the time comes when even standing room can no longer be found upon this earth. Malthus had the merit of focusing the problem so sharply that his name remains inseparable from it. Moreover, he started a rebellion against the fundamental optimism of the Christians ("God's in His heaven"), of Rousseau ("Man is good"), even of Adam Smith ("the guiding hand"). Long before Unamuno, and in the dreariest prose, he too had a tragic sentiment of life.[9] No history of thought would be adequate without at least a paragraph devoted to that formidable question mark in the garb of a country parson. Political scientists may well desire, periodically, to reëxamine the pregnant *Essay* itself. But is there any reason why our young people should have to wade through hundreds of pages of antiquated, inaccurate, ill-digested facts? For a man's general education, a good textbook on "Theories of Population" would be much more to the point.

[9] No, I am not going to make him the first of the Existentialists.

Literature

As the "Great Books" idea weakens the connection between the author and his times, it loosens also the chain between an author, his predecessors, and his successors. There are no Melchizedeks in science: every idea has a history and a pre-history. Malthus himself was rather surprised to find that his "discovery" had been anticipated, or at least adumbrated. Only the unwary will entertain the idea that artificial languages were "invented" by Dr. Zamenhof, or flying machines by the Wright Brothers. And ulterior development is an essential factor in the fame, that is to say, in the importance, of a man. A pioneer whose thought disappears altogether does not belong to history. Imagine Jesus without disciples! Marx is important because of Marxism; and Marxism is not a single formula but the whole Marxist movement. Scientific research could proceed without formal history, starting from our present knowledge and with our present equipment. But if we do study the history of science, it must be scientific, not sensational; it must trace the long and complex growth, not focus our attention exclusively upon isolated peaks. If we are told that, in Introductions, Notes, Aids to Study, Lectures, and the like, all these elements will receive proper treatment, then we shall have Histories of Science, of Philosophy, of Politics, and so forth, with selected texts as illustrations. Which is exactly what has been done, often indifferently, but at times very well, for several generations.

The chief weakness of the "Great Books" idea is that, in spite of the rare intellectual quality of its promoters, no clear criterion of "greatness" is revealed by their choice. Their list represents a vague consensus, a composite image of many compromises. There is of course no single authoritative collection of "Great Books" as—with a twilight zone of Apocrypha—there is a Canon of Holy Scripture. The best that can be said of any such list—Sir John Lubbock's, for instance—is that it is "as good as the rest." There will always be omissions to be deplored, admissions that will rouse mild astonishment. The bulk of the list is composed of "safe" names, about which there is polite if at times unenthusiastic agree-

Education of a Humanist

ment, a convention not outrageous enough to call for a challenge. It is simply not true that all these "Books that every Child Ought to Know" are indispensable to culture. Many intelligent men, past and present, have read most of them "by title only," and have derived greater sustenance from works not on the approved syllabus.

A great temptation in drawing up such a canon is the distributive, the encyclopedic method. There must be samples of everything: this introduces a standard very different from that of intrinsic value. Inferior works have to be brought in so as to preserve the balance between kinds, countries, periods. For the sake of completeness, the collection is stuffed with books which are admirably suitable to the composite statistical Man, but which do not appeal to this or that individual reader. Upon all such series lies heavily the curse of the ready-made: it is good, it is practical, it is cheap, it does not quite fit any one.

But the chief ambiguity in selecting the Hundred Best Books results from the effort to combine two criteria, the intrinsic (artistic or scientific) and the social: books that live because of their beauty and truth, books which once were events in the history of mankind. When the two criteria happen to be in agreement, it is little short of a miracle. The most miraculous case of all is that of Plato. St. Paul, in rare passages, reaches supreme heights of spiritual and literary power; Jean Jacques Rousseau was not merely a portent, but, once in a while, a poet. But as a rule, the scales are not the same. It cannot be denied that the poetry of Emily Dickinson, of Keats, of Blake, failed to deflect the course of human events, while Thomas Paine with his *Crisis*, or Harriet Beecher Stowe with *Uncle Tom's Cabin*, appreciably did. If *Hamlet* had never been written, mankind would have been deprived of a jewel; but, because Luther nailed his ninety-five theses on the church door at Wittenberg, the lives of millions were transformed. There is an abyss between a classic and a document.

Literature

Many years ago, a British publisher asked me whether I would write for him "The Fifteen Decisive Books of the World." The scheme was obviously inspired by *The Fifteen Decisive Battles,* by Sir Edward Shepherd Creasy, a hardy perennial in the book trade.[10] I do not remember why the deal fell through, unregretted. But I had given the subject some thought. I wanted to work out the problem on a definite instance. In connection with French civilization, I had had to look into the population problem, with Malthus looming vaguely in the background. I tackled the *Essay on the Principle of Population as it affects the Future Improvement of Society,* with all the biographical and critical data thereunto appertaining. I watched an epoch-making book in the act of making an epoch. It was a good experiment: the work was important enough to be worth observing, the influence narrow enough to be observable. It taught me a few things which could be applied to more obvious and mightier books. Above all, it left me puzzled: do we mean anything definite when we say that *The Prince,* or *The Origin of Species,* or *Das Kapital* are decisive books?

For some twenty years, I had a series of symposia on the subject with my advanced students.[11] We did not solve the riddle, but we had some good mental exercise in the attempt: it was a twentieth-century equivalent of "How many angels can stand on the point of a needle?" We derived some enlightenment from the "List of the Twenty Five Volumes three noted scholars, John Dewey, Edward Weeks, and Charles A. Beard, considered to have had the most influence on thought and action during the last half-century" (1936). We came to the safe conclusion that if one noted scholar could be muddled, the combined efforts of three noted scholars were confusion in the third power. Good pragmatists, they mentioned, haphazard, those works that had been most talked about, those titles which had crashed the front page. People discuss books

---

[10] First published 1851.
[11] The consolidated result of these polls will be found in my *Preface to World Literature,* pp. 476-77.

they neither enjoy nor believe in, not seldom books they have not read and do not intend to read, books that are an annoyance rather than a force. Notoriety and influence are not identical.

Although the Three Noted Scholars defined their problem a little more closely than other list-concocters, they made no clear distinction between *great, good, successful, influential, decisive.* The relation between *great* and *good* in particular raises innumerable problems. It is difficult to deny some kind of greatness to Napoleon and Hitler. Even though that greatness was due to circumstances, there must have been in those men evil elements—insane egotism, ruthlessness, willful blindness to distant consequences—which enabled them to take advantage of their opportunities. Hence a sinister "greatness" denied to Lafayette. In the literary sphere, it would be difficult to call good, in any sense of the term, *The Songs of Maldoror* and *Voyage to the End of the Night.* They are obviously not moral, they are full of technical flaws, and they do not even give the impression of sincerity. I am inclined to pass the same judgment on *The Flowers of Evil,* even though we are now taught to ejaculate: *Sanctus Baudelaire, ora pro nobis!* Yet they are acknowledged as *great* books. What is the secret of their power? It is painfully evident that the "good," in practical life as well as in poetry, may be poles asunder from the great. Indeed, we constantly have to fight the stupid prejudice that the good cannot possibly be great. To measure success needs an intricate sliding scale: of Kafka's *Castle,* only a few thousand copies were sold in this country; of Sheldon's *In His Steps,* ten million. Votes have to be not merely counted but weighed; and who is to weigh the weighers?

Influential also is a term which requires careful analysis. In the purely literary sphere, we call influential an author who has had many imitators, like Scott and Byron; imitators who may be greater than their models, for *I Promessi Sposi* and *Notre Dame de Paris* are held by many to be better than any of Scott's romances, and Alexandre Dumas is undoubtedly more popular than his master.

Literature

But, paradoxically, the very greatest, because they discourage imitation, are not influential in that sense. There were no pullulating Campistrons to follow Dante, Shakespeare, or Cervantes: their masterpieces are Land's Ends, abrupt promontories. If we reach beyond the limits of literary art, we find that the influence of great writers upon life is pitifully small. Hugo's dream of the poet as shepherd of the nations is but a romantic Utopia. The men who deliberately adopted a Byronic, a Balzacian, a Baudelairian attitude were *poseurs* to begin with. If it can be said of Hitler that he made himself, consciously, a Nietzschean Superman and a Wagnerian hero, so much the worse for Nietzsche and for Wagner.

We must revert, therefore, to our fundamental distinction between art and history. Art does not seek influence—which is another way of asserting that it exists on its own ground and for its own sake only. History, on the contrary, is a concatenation of influences: the soil and the dead, as Barrès put it,[12] mass psychology and its unaccountable chain-reactions, facts of the most material kind, and, mingling with the facts, legends all the more potent for being vast and vague. I do not deny that among these innumerable factors, certain books have their place. But that place has very little relation with their aesthetic worth, and it is small at best in the warp and woof of history. Napoleon was neither made nor destroyed by a book (although Chateaubriand may have entertained certain delusions on the subject). Even his Legend is independent of any book: it is made up of traditional scenes and familiar attitudes, stage properties such as the cocked hat and the gray riding coat, pictures, statues, a stiff but impressive style of interior decoration, the tomb under the great gilded dome, the massive arch closing the grand vista of the Champs Elysées.

A place apart must be reserved for the sacred books of any faith. To the believer, they should be "decisive" in every sense of the term.

---

[12] In more diffuse and less poetical language, the geographical environment and the tradition. Hitler substituted blood (race) for tradition: *Blut und Boden.*

Education of a Humanist

Accepting them as the ultimate authority gives a new meaning to a man's life. They guide the faithful on every issue; and beyond the range of his daily experience, they determine his view of first and last things. For the man who is not a convert, however, they are mere documents. If he is free from fanaticism, he will examine them with sympathetic curiosity. In most cases, he will feel justified in ignoring them altogether. For the vast majority of mankind, the Koran, the works of Swedenborg, *The Book of Mormon,* or *Science and Health* are not an essential part of culture.

But let us examine more closely the crucial instance, the "decisiveness" of the Bible for Christians. Incidentally, the Bible happens to be, in parts, great literature. I say incidentally, because, for earnest believers, such a consideration is irrelevant and almost sacrilegious, as objectionable as it would be to dwell on the "good looks" of the Holy Virgin. If we used the aesthetic criterion, we should be obliged to conclude that the bulk of Leviticus or Deuteronomy was decidedly not "inspired."

What has the Bible decided for mankind? After nineteen hundred years, it has not conquered the world. The Christians are still a minority. Fifty years ago, it looked as though the Christian nations were destined to inherit the earth: not, however, because they were meek, but because they could shoot. Today, Asia is resurgent; Russia is in the doubtful column; and it would be hard to appraise the gains and losses of orthodox religion among the nations of the West.

Even within established Christianity there has been no decision on the essential issue: the very standing of the Bible, the nature of its authority. Three totally different attitudes still prevail, and they are irreconcilable. For at least half of the Christian world, the Bible is subordinated to the Church, in whom abides the spirit of God. The Church was established by Christ Himself before a single page of the New Testament had been written. It was the Church that selected the books of the canon and endowed them with their sacred character. For the Protestant Fundamentalists, the Bible is the

Literature

sole and absolute authority; every jot and tittle in it is literally inspired, inerrant, an infallible rule of faith and life. For the unthinking—and I am afraid they are the majority in any denomination—the Bible alone among books is not merely great, but divinely inspired; it is not, however, inspired through and through. The sensible man knows how to pick and choose: "This is mere folklore; this is tribal chronicle; this is lyric or epic poetry on the human plane, but of the highest order; this is the very word of God."—"How do you know?"—"It must be the word of God, for it agrees with what I think."

There is but a shade between this "liberal" conception and that of the respectful and sympathetic outsider: "Yes, the Bible is inspired in parts, to a higher degree perhaps, but in the same way as the other sacred books of mankind. A Bible of Bibles has been repeatedly offered to us. Nay more: there is no difference between the grandest passages in the Bible and the secular masterpieces deeply concerned with spiritual issues. The Book of Job is inspired in the same sense as *Prometheus Bound* and *Prometheus Unbound*. Ecclesiastes offers the same disenchanted wisdom as the *Maxims* of La Rochefoucauld, Jonah the same tolerant irony as *The Vision of Babouc;* the Apocalypse ranks with the *Divine Comedy*." All this proves of unspeakable comfort to middle-roaders and Laodiceans.

If the Bible had been "decisive," the Christian life would be practiced, and that would involve espousing poverty and peace. But what are the glaring facts? Our science, our social organization, our business system, our home and foreign policies are definitely not Christian, and at times frankly anti-Christian. Christianity in its purity has been relegated to Sunday mornings at eleven o'clock; and even for that brief hour it is accompanied, as a rule, by a display of luxury for which there seems to be very little scriptural warrant. If a Christian ideal is urged out of due time and place—on Monday and in the halls of Congress—there is an outcry on the part of church members in excellent standing against the radicals, the perfectionists, the starry-eyed, the do-gooders.

Education of a Humanist

All this is not an attack on religion, but exactly the reverse. It is not even a satire of those churches which "give the Devil his due" a trifle too generously. It would be sacrilegious to make the Bible responsible for the confusion, the jealousy, the hatred, the terror which lash our souls at the present hour. Christianity has not failed because it has not been tried. The lesson, for the modest purpose of our inquiry, is that even the most decisive of all books has not proved decisive. It has brought not peace but a sword. In dubious battle, it is still fighting its way.

It is something of an anticlimax to pass from the Bible to such works as *The Prince, Leviathan,* or *The Social Contract.* Here a distinction, which may well be essential, offers itself to our minds. There are books which seem to have a creative power of their own, books which make their authors, and in the refulgence of which the actual writer might be completely absorbed. Such books are sources; decisive influences proceed from them, not from a man's life or the activities of a group. There are books, on the contrary, which are the summing up, and, as it were, the consequence of a whole career, of a movement, of an epoch. The first are a revelation, the second a confirmation.

To take contrasting examples from the same period: Jean Jacques Rousseau's first *Discourse,* denying the benefits of civilization, came from an unknown writer, with the freshness of a paradox and the force of a new gospel. The *Encyclopaedia,* into which went an enormously larger amount of thought and knowledge, simply organized into a mighty war machine the efforts of a preëxisting school. The latter type of books may be called summative, and in some cases, conclusive.

The works that close a debate are not seldom buried in their victory. We have to make an effort to realize how great a man John Locke was: his thought, absorbed for two hundred years into the general stream, has become commonplace. Much of Voltaire is antiquated, not because he was proved wrong, but because he was too obviously right: we lose interest in his battles because they do not have to be fought again. Works see their vitality ebb away when they were too perfectly adequate to a particular purpose. The books which we call decisive are not those which settle a problem, but those which define it, and make us conscious of its commanding importance. So they do not decide: they challenge us to decide. They open controversies; when the controversies are absolutely closed, the books are dead. If Darwinism were as universally accepted as the law of gravitation, *The Origin of Species* would be merely a historical document.

On closer examination, the dividing line between the books which initiate and those which sum up a movement appears in many cases extremely hard to trace. In the field of religion, as a rule, the written word follows the teacher. Joseph Smith did not begin his apostolic career until he had *The Book of Mormon;* but Jesus first lived the Gospel, and Mohammed first acted the Koran. In the same career, the two processes may be seen at work. The *Communist Manifesto* was in a sense a revelation. It made Marx, and thus enabled Marx to shape Marxism as an extension of his own personality, a unique compound of vision, will power, organizing capacity, appalling knowledge, formidable arrogance. And, because Marx impressed and imposed himself so imperiously upon the Socialist world, *Das Kapital* was accepted blindfolded as the Koran of the new Mohammed. Had the ponderous treatise been written by a quiet professor, it would have been seriously discussed in a few learned periodicals, but it would never have created a party or even forced itself upon the attention of an existing party. To isolate, to overemphasize the book is a distortion of historic reality. *Das Kapital* is the fruit, not the cause, of a great movement.

The revelation that Rousseau brought in 1751 was not a new truth, summoned for the first time from the empyrean. It had long existed in solution throughout society.[13] Rousseau's chance words—perhaps a deliberate paradox—acted as a catalyzer and precipitated

---

[13] Cf. La Fontaine, *The Danubian Peasant;* and La Fontaine borrowed the theme from Guevara, who wrote a century before.

or crystallized a new faith. Rousseau had the luck, miraculous but not wholly undeserved, to attach his name to the emergent thought, as Amerigo Vespucci had given his to a new continent. But if preëxisting Rousseauism made Rousseau in its own image, Rousseau did not fail to return the compliment. He had been made a prophet, and he acted the part. His greatest book, *The Confessions,* was of course a summation. If it had not been for his immense and disputed prestige, he would not have dared to write, and no one would have cared to read, this romanced account of his wanderings, his turpitudes, and his squabbles.

I may seem to have swayed back and forth in this discussion of decisive books. My criterion, however, is definite. The only books that deserve to form the center of an education are those which stimulate because they are alive, in their beauty or in their challenge. Let the dead bury their dead. The books that once settled an issue deserve honorable mention, nothing more. They might not even receive that, for gratitude, in science, is not an indispensable virtue. We do not need the very words of the discoverers to be taught that the earth moves and that the blood circulates.

To attach unique importance to a few privileged books in the development of mankind is a belated form of bibliolatry, or bookworship, the disease which paralyzed both the Renaissance and the Reformation, and which paralyzes socialist thought today. Book learning may go by the name of scholarship, no doubt; it may also be known as pedantry. For a general education, history is needed, but history must be distilled from innumerable books, great and small, and from documents other than books—the land, the monuments, the fine arts, the artifacts, the folklore of a people. History, which is experience at second or third hand, is not enough. We need direct contact with life through the books that live, not through those that are dust. Above all, we must establish that contact with life through the experimental method, which is vital to science, and which has been unduly neglected by the humanities.

Literature

TEACHING LITERATURE OR TEACHING MEN?

So far, I have attempted to state two conclusions which were forced upon me by long years of meditation and experience. The first is that, in so far as history is needed to understand a literary masterpiece, that history cannot be limited to literature itself. Writers do not beget writers, in exclusive and unbroken chain: they are immersed in the whole life of their time. Even when a poet seeks refuge in his Ivory Tower, he is affected by the society he spurns or dreads. This means that pure literary history is as thin and unreal as sheer political history. If this fact were properly grasped, much of our college work would have to be recast.

The second conclusion is that historical knowledge, in literature, is merely preparatory. Even if it be indispensable, it does not reach the essence of the subject. When we do understand the language of an author, with all its connotations, shades, and overtones, we are ready to appreciate him; but our aesthetic response is not the inevitable fruit of our information. I might know everything about the upbringing and the career of Kathleen Winsor, and the exact circumstances under which *Forever Amber* was composed, without being committed to admiration for the result. Keats knew literally nothing about Homer—except perhaps that he was born in seven different cities—when he was struck with awe by the majesty of the old poet. I believe it is possible for the teacher to foster the development of taste; it is indeed his highest duty. But, in order to do so, he will have to go beyond erudition.

I advise therefore that all elementary courses in literary history be dropped; or, more exactly, that they be integrated into a basic course in Western Civilization. By Western Civilization I mean the achievements of the group necessary and sufficient to explain our own lives. We cannot understand America today without Judea, Greece, Rome, the Renaissance, the Reformation, the Enlightenment; we can understand it without Mohammed or Lao-tse. It is a central

Education of a Humanist

article of my creed that mankind is one. But that oneness is revealed in philosophy and science, not in history. The converging and the clashing of all traditions is a phenomenon of the present day; their merging and their harmony are the task and the hope of tomorrow. But in the past, large groups have had an almost self-contained existence. Isolation, cultural autarchy, now antiquated, were real only yesterday; and it is with yesterday that history has to deal. For college freshmen, a study at third hand of ancient China would be inert knowledge; a study of Rome could be made alive.

Most colleges offer such a course. In my opinion, its proper place would be in the upper grades of the high school, for every literate citizen should have the benefit of such a training. It offers immense difficulties. Some colleges yield to the temptation of distributing the various lectures among specialists: the result, as a rule, is deadly. The best specialists are not invariably best qualified to give a popular account of their subject. Even if they should be, as some of them are, lucid and pleasant expositors, the main point of the course is likely to be lost: to wit, the integration of all aspects of civilization. Of course, no one, not even Arnold J. Toynbee, F. S. C. Northrop, or Will Durant, is an authority in every field. Neither is any one a thorough master of a single century in a single literature: much of every man's work, as the reader is well aware, has to be done with secondary sources.

Because the task appears so hopeless, it is at times entrusted to young instructors, and even to graduate assistants, with a senior faculty member as coördinator. As a rule, they are guided by textbooks, some of which are incredibly bad; even when they are honorable as well as profusely illustrated, they are wholly devoid of philosophical value. Such work should on the contrary be the crown of a man's career. In my School of Humanities, a scholar of ripe experience would be selected a few years ahead of time, so as to prepare himself for the great ordeal and the great opportunity. He would be picked out from any of the learned disciplines—philosophy, science, law, history, letters. He might be a Dewey, a Huxley, a

Literature

Roscoe Pound, a Toynbee, an Irving Babbitt. The one qualification would be a rich and orderly mind. He would teach "all things knowable" to freshmen for the last decade of his academic life.

The objection of superficiality would be valid [14] if this introductory course were also to be the last of its kind. This is too often the case. As a result, I had graduate students taking for instance my seminar on The Spirit of 1848 who were absolutely unprepared for the work. Several years back, they must have had a course, good or bad, but inevitably sketchy, in "Civilization." Immediately afterward, however, they had to devote themselves to "serious," that is, to splintered knowledge. The general survey should be followed by a course of the same kind, but on a totally different scale. Instead of taking a sweeping view of thirty centuries, the field should be limited to a single generation, three or four decades. If a whole year were devoted to such a subject, it would be possible for students to become directly acquainted with the documents. Masterpieces would naturally be included and receive preferential treatment; but only in so far as they were typical of the age.[15]

After this training, students could, if they chose, do some more thorough work in "integral history," concentrating, by the same method, on a single year, a single event, a single book. They could also, without danger, elect highly specialized subjects: some fine points in Anglo-Saxon, or in the grammar of the various periods; definite and minute problems in chronology, textual criticism, prosody, bibliography. All these are legitimate and desirable, provided they fall into their proper places within a general scheme. I am not

---

[14] Professor C. H. C. Wright defined General Literature as "a breathless attempt to keep up with God and H. G. Wells." Of course, the brilliant and facile generality-monger must be ruled out.

[15] The divisions adopted in the series, *The Rise of Modern Europe,* are good examples of what I have in mind: *A Decade of Revolution* (1789-1799), by Crane Brinton; *Europe and the French Imperium* (1799-1814), by Geoffrey Bruun; *Reaction and Revolution* (1815-1832), by Frederick B. Artz; *Liberalism, Nationalism and Socialism* (1832-1852), by William L. Langer; *Realism and Nationalism* (1852-1871), by Robert C. Binkley; *A Generation of Materialism* (1871-1900), by Carlton J. H. Hayes.

attempting to discourage exhaustive and recondite research: I am only seeking to define its proper foundation, which is general culture, and its ultimate aim, which is the advancement of knowledge and the deepening of wisdom. It was excellent that in the Middle Ages every stone should be cut, polished, and carved with the most scrupulous, the most loving care, as if the proper handling of the chisel were a service to God and man. But a multitude of devoted stonecutters could never build a cathedral. They would not even provide the proper material. There must be a design, corresponding to a purpose.

Now we take the "language" for granted. Can we teach "literature"? Yes, if by teaching we mean not the transmission of infallible tricks but the fine tuning of an instrument.

I shall not waste my breath in rejecting every kind of literary dogma. Those who crave absolute standards will never be convinced by my arguments: I cannot pierce their triple carapace. To fresh minds, the facts are plain: there have been many schools in literary history, each blessing and damning as though it were in sole possession of august Truth. Unless we espouse one of them—blindfolded and out of sheer despair—we must conclude that their contradictions destroy their claims. No lover of literature today would accept Boileau's condemnation of Ronsard, nor Hugo's rejection of Boileau. The Naturalists in their turn jeered at the Romanticists, and the Symbolists at the Naturalists, and the Surrealists at all those who groped and stumbled in the light, when darkness alone could reveal the truth. Every dogma is an arbitrary cross section of reality. On a given plane, it may offer an intelligible picture, which is nothing but a self-portrait of the theorist; but it ignores, blurs, or distorts everything that does not belong to that particular plane. The quest, the method, the stubborn facts are the essential data; doctrines are but partial and provisional hypotheses. I need not repeat that my attitude is exactly the same with regard to all other orthodoxies, political, economic, or religious.

Literature

As definitely as dogmatism, I reject the pragmatism which makes success the sole criterion. Under success, I include not merely popularity, but the acclaim of the elites, and even that of posterity. Fame is but a prolonged Gallup poll; in matters of the spirit, I do not believe in majorities, even when they decide to "make the vote unanimous." The pragmatic method is the inculcation of "good taste." Now "good taste" is sheer conformity. It means joining the proper club: the right people admire such a book, therefore I too must force myself to admire it—honestly if I can. If the elites had not been rudely challenged, we should be worshiping Jupiter still. The first text to ponder in literary criticism is Hans Christian Andersen's apologue, *The Emperor's New Clothes*.

The foundation of literature is taste. By taste I do not mean membership in an infallible book club, and not a set of formal rules: this is but taste at second hand, an ersatz for your own palate. I do not mean the fastidiousness of a Pococurante [16] who, in the most exquisite work of art, could see nothing but the flaw. Taste is first of all the capacity for tasting. Some are born color-blind, some are tone-deaf, some are taste-less. In them, a savor, however pungent, brings forth no spontaneous response.

Even though such people should master to perfection the jargon of the connoisseur, and be well versed in the chemistry of the work of art, their infirmity debars them from the aesthetic realm. The illiterate who sincerely enjoys melodrama, farce, or sentiment is at least a prospective catechumen. The man who thinks of art in terms of success, erudition, or technique is simply an intruder, a profiteer. The germ of the truth is not in him.

It is safer of course to admire nothing except by permission of the authorities. But it argues a timidity, a servility, which is demeaning. A man must have the courage of his own taste; or, in Blake's words, he must not allow himself to be "connoisseur'd out of his senses." In *Preface to World Literature,* I drew up in parallel lists the qualities found in true art and the corresponding imitations

[16] In Voltaire's *Candide.*

Education of a Humanist

in *Kitsch,* or spurious art: the grandiose as a "showing off" of the grand, the gaudy or gorgeous as vulgar ostentation of riches, the smart or sophisticated as a display of cleverness or subtlety—all this to impress the more primitive minds. Note that the material may be genuine; it is the intention that turns it into *Kitsch:* the gorgeous is pretentious, even though the gold be real gold and not tinsel. Let us pity the yokels who are taken in by such tricks. Aye, but let us envy them too.

For if their own response is strong and sincere, there is something authentic at the core of their delusion. Under the meretricious garments, they divine, shrinking, ashamed, but not destroyed, the spirit of beauty. All art is play-acting, pretending, and we must for a while suspend our rigorous disbelief. If, in the austere name of Truth, Plato succeeded in banishing poets from the Republic, if the Puritans were allowed to frown away the stage and the novel, the world would be the poorer. It is better to admire something crude, excessive, not wholly sincere, than to be incapable of admiration. Let us guard against the purists: the great classical architect Tolsa who abominated the Churrigueresco style because it was tormented and gaudy; the well-bred readers who spurned Ring Lardner or Damon Runyon; Irving Babbitt who singled out Charlie Chaplin's success as an example of modern vulgarity; the academicians who are blind to the folklore quality of certain comic strips. All are examples of "taste" as self-mutilation. As a Berkeley colleague of mine quaintly expressed it, "The man who does not get a kick out of a Varga girl is missing something."

Taste, in the positive sense of spontaneous response, is then our raw material. We must not destroy it, we must not ignore it, we must not stifle it with rules and conventions. But we have to admit that it is very raw. If we are to progress, we need an instrument, and this instrument is *taste* as the faculty of discrimination. I do not mean discrimination according to a prescribed pattern, the work of an inspector checking up on specifications. I mean the genuine capacity to say: "I like this; I do not like that." You can leave the

Literature

glutton to his voracity, and the Pococurante to his self-destroying fastidiousness: the man who enjoys everything and the man who enjoys nothing are equally hopeless. However crude the criticism may be at first, if it exists at all we have the possibility of a literary education.

The first step, therefore, is to enjoy; the second is to be conscious of differences; the third, no less essential, is to ask one's self: Why? With this magic word, infinite vistas open. Literary criticism is then seen in its true light as self-criticism, as exploration of one's own personality. Taste, as a physical sense, is the guardian of the gate (alas! the guardian has long ceased to be infallible); it approves of what is "good for us"; it warns us against what might do us harm. Literary taste also is the defender of our individuality. It bars the way to thoughts that would weaken or destroy us; it welcomes those which strengthen the self that is struggling and growing within us. (Taste may therefore be perverse: for there is in us, infinitesimal or irresistible, a desire for self-destruction.) The timid think exclusively of protection: keep away from *Ulysses*, it might upset your stomach. The self-confident are ready for adventure and conquest: let us tackle *Finnegans Wake*, the risk is worth taking. But in all cases, "the care and feeding of the infant self" is the key.

This is not sheer egotism. Indeed, it is compatible with the most starry-eyed desire for service. It is possible to build up our selves as instruments for a great cause. But the immediate purpose is to benefit the individual, not to make him a better cog in the monstrous totalitarian machine, communist, nazi, or plutocratic.

That is why no attempt should be made to impose a taste. We must foster at every turn the three essential powers: the power to enjoy, the power to discriminate, the power to question. For this kind of an education I know of but two methods, which should be intimately combined: directed reading and creative writing.

Directed reading. Find out, in conversation, what are the student's interests, and then tell him: "If this is the kind of things you

Education of a Humanist

like, then I believe that such or such a book would appeal to you." It need not be one of the world's masterpieces. I am convinced that a novice in mountain climbing had better not start with Mount Everest, and a child will be well advised to attempt *Voyage to the Center of the Earth* before Dante's *Inferno*. Recommend the book that with the greatest honesty will give the student what he legitimately wants. In the course of the reading, questions should be welcome. When the task is over, checking up on plot, characters, and style may not come amiss; but the essential question will be: "What did the book mean to *you?*"

The teacher as guide will thus deepen and purify the student's own taste, without attempting to alter it radically. He may also enrich it, by rousing interests hitherto dormant. He should strive to break down walls of prejudices: "Are you sure you would not like this kind of literature? Have you given it an honest trial, under favorable circumstances?" All too frequently, the teacher, in college, has to repair the harm done by clumsy pedants. I have had students whose sole memory of a high school course in Shakespeare was "Never again!" I do not believe in acquired tastes. But it is possible to give an unconscious, a neglected taste a chance to grow, a wounded taste a chance to heal.

The task of "director" is infinitely more delicate than that of a "doctor" expounding the approved doctrine, supported by Holy Writ, that is, an approved list of classics. He has to deal with individuals: he cannot treat them as so many standardized tin cans, to be packed with wholesome standardized products. There is a fine casuistry for the "director," as there is for the confessor. Should he deliberately permit the student to read a bad book, so as to have a chance to point out its ill effects? Should he allow him to follow one particular aspect of his taste until he grows weary? The youngster might never tire; some drugs are habit-forming.[17] Should he

[17] The Standford psychologist Frank Angell caught his very young son smoking a cigarette. Thereupon he offered him the biggest, blackest cigar he could procure. The boy smoked it to the end, with manifest relish, and gratefully remarked: "Say,

Literature

avoid recommending difficult books? When their interest is excited, young people welcome difficulty. They all read *Ulysses* when it had to be smuggled, at fifteen dollars a copy; and I'd rank *Ulysses* as a tougher assignment than *Piers Plowman*.

Students form spontaneous "coöperatives" for the education of their taste. The result is not seldom stimulating. No course was ever so fruitful for me as my exchange of suggestions and impressions with Albert Thierry. We were not in miraculous agreement: I still maintain that his admiration for J. H. Rosny was excessive. But even when he made me read a book which I found unpalatable, we profited by the discussion. Such comradeship is rarely possible between teacher and pupil, even between parent and child. But there are compensations. The young are not systematically hostile to their elders. I found them willing to give the professor a hearing, provided he did not "pull his rank." As a matter of fact, many were far too receptive. They were eager to swallow prescriptions. It did them little harm: some of the books assigned genuinely appealed to them, and the rest were forgotten on the morrow of the final examination. Still, their docility involved a waste.

Unfortunately, perhaps, we cannot have an individual preceptor for every child, as in Rousseau's pedagogical fairy tale. Much of our education has to work on the assembly-line system: it might pay us to teach less and to devote more care to what little we teach. A compromise, however, can be reached: individual needs cannot be wholly ignored. For the care of the body, we are beginning fully to recognize idiosyncrasies. Pupils are checked up one by one, sent to corrective clinics. We do not transfuse blood without ascertaining what type is needed. We have discovered the marvelous word *allergy:* our simple-minded fathers said: "What is one man's meat is another man's poison." All these conceptions may yet be trans-

---

Dad! That's some cigar! Where do you get them?" I have never recommended the "Divine Marquis" de Sade to my students in the hope that it would turn them against pornography.

Education of a Humanist

ferred from the medical to the literary field. Since ours is a "business culture," let us use a simile in harmony with our folkways. We cannot afford to clothe all minds to measure. We do not want to impose upon all a uniform garment, rigorously of the same material, design, and size. Our best hope is to have a large assortment of the ready-made, with skillful men in charge of the necessary alterations.[18]

Creative writing. This seems to me the best approach to the understanding and enjoyment of literature. I am leaving out of consideration the obvious: that every man, whatever his job, should be able to express himself intelligibly. This is the justification of our courses in Composition, which can never be thorough enough. "Writing" does deserve its place among the three R's.

It is a plain fact that an active practical knowledge of any craft enhances our interest in it, rudimentary as that knowledge may be. I appreciate football because, in the crudest fashion in France, in a very spotty manner in England, I had played some sort of football. I cannot rave about baseball, as all sane Americans do, because it was not part of my experience. To play (not under stern parental compulsion) any kind of instrument is indispensable to a well-developed musical taste. Appreciation is embryonic re-creation. There is a double empathy, or sympathetic response: we enjoy a book not merely because we live it with the characters, but because we write it anew, in shadowy fashion, with the author. We rejoice in his skill; we smile indulgently at his too labored "felicities"; we are impatient when he "muffs" a chance. Reading Shakespeare is collaborating with Shakespeare; the more active the collaboration, the more intelligent the reading.

[18] Such Directed Reading courses used to be offered at Stanford, but not under the best circumstances. The "directors" were volunteers, and in many cases amateurs. Their unrewarded enthusiasm soon flagged, especially since the professionals looked down upon the experiment as a fad or a luxury. In my courses, the directed reading was more important than the lectures. I gave a long list to choose from and welcomed additions suggested by the students. Guidance is needed. A student, interested in Joan of Arc, and having heard me refer to Voltaire as the founder of modern history, read *La Pucelle*—with consternation.

Literature

This is the well-known theoretical basis for the "creative" method. It is inseparable from the "receptive." Books inspire our desire to compose; composition sends us back to books with a keener zest. The combination of the two is the equivalent of experimentation in the sciences: teaching and testing go hand in hand. There is no better way of discovering the fine points of a craft than to practice it yourself: this is merely a practical advantage, incidental, but not negligible. I learned very early the stiff and absurd rules of French versification because I was moved to write verse; and, naturally, I was moved to write because I had read. Perhaps it would pay to master the technical tricks of a great poet, if only in order to realize how much of his power lies beyond the mere tricks. Pastiche is an admirable instrument of criticism. When pastiche turns into parody, it involves a severe judgment, either of model or of imitator.

"Creative" writing almost inevitably begins in imitation, which is not unhealthy. It normally grows beyond that stage. I am not thinking of revealing geniuses to themselves; I am thinking simply of preparing plain citizens, qualified to follow their own thoughts lucidly, courageously, critically. I am thinking also of John Doe's place in the literary world. What authors crave for, if they publish at all, is a receptive audience, and only he who *does,* in however humble a fashion, has the right to criticize. Poets want not a passive herd but a jury of free men; and no man is free unless he has thoughts of his own and words at his command. It would be well to break down the artificial distinction between the initiated and the *profanum vulgus.* There are innumerable degrees in the literary hierarchy, shifting according to the point of view. Far above the competent man of letters is the true poet; but the modest reader, if his response be sincere, also belongs to the brotherhood. "I, too, can write!" is the cry of emancipation from the cliques. The man who knows what it means to struggle with thoughts and words cannot be bluffed into abject submission.

From the first to the last day of a man's schooling (that is, to the last day of his life), constant training in self-expression is required.

Education of a Humanist

I have known men whose responsibilities grew faster than their power of articulate thought. To be deliberately heretical, I believe that such was the case with Henry James. His later novels were manifestly richer and deeper than his earlier ones; his art had improved also; but it had not kept pace with the progress of his mind. It is better no doubt that he should have attempted the more difficult field, even with inadequate equipment; it would have been best if he had grown harmoniously, mind and style. The riper James needed a stiff course in English composition. But who could have guided him? Perhaps his psychological brother?[19]

Our education too often sags in the middle. As I noted before, we have an elementary course in Civilization, and the same difficult technique is taken up again in graduate seminars; but there is no adequate link between them. In the same way, we have Composition classes, often considered as clinics for obvious defects ("Bonehead English"); at the other end of the academic scale, we find professional training, often of the highest quality, for would-be novelists, dramatists, and poets. Creative writing is the very core of the Humanities: no college term should go without it. Except at first perhaps, it need not be of a general nature. A course in philosophy or history should be also, to a very large extent, a course in creative philosophical and historical writing. This was my experience with such masters as Georges Dumas and Paul Wiriath: I owe more to them than to any of my literature teachers. The power to organize thought is one with the capacity for absorbing ideas. We have an oversupply of windbags and sponges: we need living minds.

A personal testimony: in my high school training (which included the equivalent of the lower division in an American college curriculum), the one element which stands out to this day in my grateful memory is the work in French Composition, which, I repeat, was not limited to classes in literature. It was our favorite sport.

---

[19] Of course, the opposite danger is of more frequent occurrence: the man who arrests the growth of his thought so as not to disturb the purity of his style. That accusation was leveled at James Branch Cabell.

Literature

We rejoiced when a subject was offered which we found congenial; we accepted the challenge when the topic was difficult. We waited eagerly for the public discussion of our themes. And if our essays were read in class, we saw the first delightful dawn of fame . . . *Et in Arcadia ego* . . .

IV. History

GROWTH OF THE HISTORICAL SPIRIT

At no time did I figure as a formal member of a history department. But the Sons of Herodotus never treated me as a stranger. My courses and books on French Civilization proved my family claim: a mottled sheep perhaps, but one of the fold. When I returned to Stanford, from 1925 to 1946, I offered a number of seminars which, although not of the conventional type, were well within the vast limits of the subject: The Growth of the Historical Spirit, The Napoleonic Legend, The Spirit of 1848. I was asked to address the American Historical Association without being a member,[1] and to contribute the historical introduction to a symposium on Nationalism.[2] I was given more historical books to review, especially about Napoleon I, than was altogether to my taste; I should have preferred to keep a more even balance between history and pure literature.

Persuaded that no university teaching should be the mere transmission of accepted ideas, I was compelled to ask myself: "I am teaching history: but what is history?" A very plain answer first came to my mind: the study of the human past. On second thought, it appeared ambiguous. The first cause of confusion is that the term denotes at the same time the *science* and the *material:* botany is the study of plants, but history is the study of history.

[1] St. Louis, December 28, 1921.
[2] The Annals of the American Academy of Political and Social Science: "The World Trend Toward Nationalism" (Philadelphia, July 1934).

Education of a Humanist

In the widest sense, history is the sum total of everything that has happened in the world, in so far as it affects man: the Bible properly begins with Creation; Voltaire and H. G. Wells with astronomy and geology. In a narrower sense, history is the record of human events: but both terms require further definition. *Record* would seem to imply the intention of preserving the memory of a fact; and for a long time, history limited itself to what may be called deliberate documents—annals, archives, memoirs, commemorative monuments, inscriptions, medals. But every vestige of the past is a document. Paleontology, anthropology, and pre-history are historical sciences. The remains of *Homo sinensis* are part of the record, and far more significant than most scraps of paper. The artifacts even of a recent period, never intended to enlighten posterity, take their due place in the chronicle.

The words *human events* also might be misguiding. Catastrophes which obviously affect man's life cannot be denied the character of historical events, although they cannot be controlled by man: the eruption of Mount Pelée, for instance, or the disastrous vagaries of the Hwang Ho. But history is not a series of sensational headlines; suddenness is not a necessary quality of significant change. If an earthquake or a flood are factors, so is the gradual desiccation of a vast area. We must strive to free outselves from the melodramatic bias: racial improvement or decay continued by imperceptible steps over a number of centuries counts for more than the virulent outbreaks of plague, typhus, cholera, revolution, or war. In this amorphous mass, I could find definiteness only in relativity: the field of history is determined by the standpoint, the angle of vision, the penetration, of the observer. Everything is history which, in the historian's estimation, may have affected man's existence.

These elementary considerations convinced me that objectivity is not the impossible absence of a definite observer, but a judicial quality in the observer's mind. They made me realize how shallow, how naïve was Leopold von Ranke's formula when detached from its context: "The present enquiry will simply show how it actually

History

happened."[3] But what is the *it* that happened? History is not the haphazard accumulation of disconnected facts. Let us not forget that everything that exists in the world is a survival, a vestige, therefore a potential document: the historian must select out of that mass that which seems to him relevant.

This selection takes many forms. Bossuet, with magnificent assurance, limits himself to those events which demonstrate the action of Divine Providence. Victor Hugo, in delightful chapters of *Les Misérables* and *Ninety-Three,* the Goncourts, Philip Guedalla, Frederick L. Allen in *Only Yesterday,* pile up picturesque, amusing, minute details, without any apparent sequence; but, with that *pointilliste* technique, they expect to produce an intelligible picture. Many historians, dealing with the latter part of the eighteenth century, carefully noted changes in the British ministry, but overlooked enclosure acts, "deserted villages," and the spread of "dark satanic mills," as beneath the dignity of history. In 1859, "what actually happened" in France were repressive measures, administered by General Espinasse after Orsini had attempted to murder Napoleon III; but it was also the introduction of American vines which carried the phylloxera blight, a worse "villain" than Espinasse, and much better remembered by the population. And which was the more "significant": the confused fighting in Germany, in which René Descartes was engaged in his philosophical, semidetached way, or his winter meditations by the stove, which were to lead to the *Discourse on Method?* Granting that history should not be the propounding of a doctrine, it is at any rate the testing of a hypothesis.

We have already seen that every organized branch of knowledge was a consistent language: there can be no science of facts without thought and without words. In arriving at such a system of conception and expression, we have to make use of several approaches, adopting each in turn as it suits our purpose, abandoning each when

---

[3] Ranke was obviously deprecating any willful distortion of the facts, and repudiating any thought of judging and teaching, that is, of being the servant of a cause: history for history's sake.

it diverges from the goal. The first of these approaches is the pragmatic: we must start from the facts of the case. Factgathering, however, will not suffice. Irrelevant facts, Ranke would admit, are worthless; and relevancy depends upon a conception of values which transcends empiricism. But how can we arrive at a criterion of value? If we give freest play to the critical spirit, shall we not drift on the aimless flood of Pyrrhonism? Pyrrhonism unchecked is self-devouring; doubt dissolves everything, including systematic doubt. If on the contrary we affirm principles which must not be challenged, are we not committing ourselves to an absolutism or a dogmatism of the strictest kind? Learned and subtle as the expression of a theology may be, it is a denial of free thought, and thought sickens in a cage.

If we want to preserve the dignity of thought, which, as Pascal said, is the whole dignity of man, we must guard against looseness. But looseness has two aspects. The most familiar is inconsistency within, all the way from mere vagueness to chaos absolute. The second is inconstistency with the rest of the world. A taut homogeneous thought may be called "loose" if it is not properly connected with other thoughts. It has inner coherence, yet it is an anarchical element, like a bit of pure iron in an article of food. The crude, the one-sided, the fanatical must be called "loose" no less than the flabby or the capricious. The Empiricists and the Pyrrhonians offer examples of looseness in the primary sense: their mind is but a chance heap. The Absolutists are loose in the second sense. They have neat little spheres of dogma, definite and organized. But these compact little spheres float and at times collide in an enormous sea of thoughts and facts which they proudly ignore.

Solvitur ambulando: to blend methods at the same moment and on the same plane is a sure recipe for confusion; to use them in succession, each correcting and enriching the other, might well be our salvation. An ill-defined interest attracts our attention to certain facts, or a chance juxtaposition of facts rouses in us an interest, still inchoate. We attempt to focus, to sharpen, to define that interest;

History

but we know that our definition is only provisional. Yet, within its range, the definition will bring more facts into clearer light. Upon this working hypothesis, we now train our critical batteries, mustering all the facts at our command. The hypothesis may collapse utterly; it may break down, but, in its very failure, suggest the possibility of a stronger one; it may resist every assault. But even in that case, it will not stand unaltered; some of its original elements are bound to crumble, and new supports will be discovered that were not surmised at the beginning. At every moment, there is some confusion and some conflict; but at every moment, also, there is a guiding principle. At no time are doubts brutally silenced; at no time are facts willfully denied. This is living order; the whole thing is not a status but a process. The pattern of thought, undecipherable or absurd in a single still picture, exists in motion, in time, and is revealed by the study of time, which is history.

The "sense of history"[4] was revealed to me, when I was still in high school, through Zeno of Elea and his paradox of the arrow. His other logical tricks, particularly that of Achilles and the Tortoise, are pretty obvious fallacies. But if we mentally divide time into its atomic particles, at any one of these infinitesimal moments the arrow can occupy only one position; for it is absurd that a body should be, at the same instant, in two different places. Pile up these innumerable immobilities and you cannot get motion: the arrow refuses to fly. Since motion is a fact, our logic must be at fault. This is deeper than a verbal legerdemain: logic cannot account for motion, therefore motion must be taken for granted. If we accept motion as

---

[4] Another fine example of ambiguity. The "sense of history" here is a "feeling for history," the sense that history exists. It could also be "the meaning of history": this certainly was not revealed to me, then or later. Humanly speaking, much of history seems to me to have no sense. Finally, it might denote "the direction of history," a teleological conception. Bossuet had a great mind and Maurras a subtle one; but history and they went in different directions. From my point of view, they missed "the sense of history."

a primary datum, immobility is easily explained: it is the delusion, or rather the condition, which arises when two or more bodies move exactly in the same direction and at the same rate. I call my desk motionless, although I am (theoretically) aware that it follows the earth's spinning and circling, because I am carried by exactly the same gyrations.

In the same way, we cannot explain time in terms of timelessness or eternity. There is no atom of time at which time is arrested: in its most infinitesimal particle, time retains its essential quality, which is *flow*. What we call permanency ("time-defying") is the result of courses pursued at the same speed and on parallel tracks. The Eternal Verities will remain eternal in our eyes so long as they and we grow together. If they should stop in the year 1776, while we proceed, they would soon be lost to view. On the other hand, if their inner force, their dynamism, should carry them forward—from a vague human equality, for instance, to full racial equality; from political democracy to social democracy; from local federation to world federation—while our minds still clung to the year 1776, there would again be a disruption. The "Verities" would have become Utopias, which all safe and sound men would properly deprecate.

Just as there is no "eternal" in human affairs—no, not even the rules of Aristotle or the principles of Adam Smith—so there is no "instantaneous" either. Existence implies duration: a cube without the capacity of enduring besides us, were it only for a fraction of a second, would make no impression upon our consciousness. No gesture, no word, can be said to exist per se: they have no meaning except in the endless chain of their antecedents and consequents. There can be no pure journalism (I am using "pure" in its philosophical, not in its moral, sense): even the journalist who forgets at once everything that he has wired to his news agency, and who is concerned only with the fugitive moment, must be, willy-nilly, something of a historian. If he wants to give us the very latest words of Winston Churchill, it is because he knows that Winston Churchill existed yesterday and will be remembered tomorrow. The inconceivable being without any past and without any future would not be news.[5]

This is—in vague adumbration as yet—that historical spirit which seems to be the condition of modern thought: the category of *becoming*. And, naturally, we are led to consider it historically, not as an unchangeable verity, but as itself a growth. Our ancestors never were entirely without a sense of the past. Few men have sincerely believed that, in terms of human experience, time is a delusion; and the disenchanted *Plus ça change, plus c'est la même chose* of Ecclesiastes was a willful paradox. On the other hand, the anti-historical mind is with us still. Even now it would clutch the "Eternal Verities" in politics, religion, literature—eternal! the direct negation of time and history. To reconcile manifest change with the changeless pattern that they posit, some anti-historical minds still harbor the concept of "eternal cycles": growth and decay within one revolution of the time-wheel, but with an inexorable recurrence of the same delusive change.

So the historical spirit does not follow a single, well-defined line. It assumes many forms and suffers many defeats. If we question our own minds, we shall find that our historical spirit is extremely uneven. Our various thoughts move each in its own tempo. We may be static in religion, dynamic in politics, as Gladstone and Bryan were; we may welcome change in one art and resist it in another; we may be revolutionary in matters of prosody and conservative on points of syntax. And, especially, we are apt to scorn our neighbor because his rate of motion is faster or more sluggish than our own. He is antiquated if he clings to the values of yesterday; he is uncultured if he ignores the values of the day before.

The study of the historical spirit is therefore exceedingly complex; hardly more complex, however, than that of other movements in

---

[5] It follows that Walter Pater's doctrine, at the end of *The Renaissance*, "only for the moment's sake," is a fallacy. The moment does not exist, only the sequence of moments.

Education of a Humanist

thought, Romanticism for example. Like Romanticism, the historical spirit may be all things to all men; like Romanticism, it pervades the ages (Satan is said to be the first Romantic; he might also be said to have inaugurated history); but, like Romanticism, it reaches full consciousness in certain periods only. That is why, in our discussions at Stanford, we limited ourselves to the last three centuries of its growth. We began with what Paul Hazard has called *la crise de la conscience européenne,* a revolution in thought which required some forty years, with 1688 as the central point.

Before that time, there were human events, and their chronicling, and a sense of the past; yet the whole attitude was predominantly anti-historical. For the medieval mind, the world was much as it had ever been, even in details of costumes and manners; only it was growing steadily worse. On the practical plane, evil was conceived as departure from custom. Charters did not register the conquest of new liberties; they made ancient rights more explicit, so that they might be better preserved. On the spiritual plane, the essential truths were thought of as eternal, and committed to the keeping of the eternal Church; our earthly life was but a brief prologue to eternity.

The Renaissance and the Reformation, rebellions against medievalism, were themselves anti-historical. The only change of which they were aware they called decadence: mankind had erred and strayed from the eternal paths of classic wisdom and the Christian revelation. The ideal of the sixteenth century was to blot out Time and revert to the Augustan age and the era of the Apostles. There was a secret dynamism in that hankering for fixity; and other forces were at work, manifest in Rabelais and much later in Bacon; but the prevailing cast of thought was averse to change;[6] the only

---

[6] Then gin I thinke on that which Nature sayd
Of that same time when no more Change shall be,
But stedfast rest on all things firmely stayd
Upon the pillours of Eternity
That is the contrayr to Mutabilitie.
—*Edmund Spenser*

History

change admitted as legitimate was the return to unchangeable law.

The modern historical spirit was born of religious controversy. The Protestants sought to prove that Catholicism had departed from primitive Christianity; the Catholics, that Protestantism was at variance with what had been believed at all times, everywhere, by all men. The masterpiece in that line of argument is Bossuet's *Variations:* the Protestant churches have fluctuated with time; therefore they cannot be in possession of the truth, which is timeless.[7] Each party sought to fasten upon the other the stigma of historical development, and to a large extent both were successful; but in the process both had to appeal to history.

The historico-theological issue was already clear in Spinoza's *Tractate.* The forcible suppression of Protestantism in France did not stifle the dispute; it had the effect of substituting free thought for Calvinism as the chief opponent of orthodoxy. The *Historical Dictionary* of the emancipated Huguenot Bayle was to be the chief arsenal of the Voltairians. For the great historians of the Enlightenment, Voltaire himself, Hume, Gibbon, history was a war machine against abuses, prejudices, and superstitions. The past, far from being holy in their eyes, appeared as a mass of ignorance and cruelty. The blind and often ferocious defense of tradition was in Voltaire's mind *l'infâme,* which must be crushed if the humane spirit is to live.

The Romantic reaction has dealt harshly with the Enlightenment. To be aware of past evils is not necessarily "unhistorical." A motorist finds dark glasses more effective than rosy ones. Logically enough, the apparent pessimism of Voltaire and Gibbon was but the obverse of a deeper optimism. They believed with Rabelais that mankind was at last "out of Gothic night." They were progressivists, and Condorcet was their disciple.[8] So were also, alas!

---

[7] It is curious to note how completely Newman, two centuries and a half later, reversed Bossuet's position. Protestantism he condemned as unhistorical, because it had remained arrested in the Apostolic revelation; the Catholic Church on the contrary is the living and growing instrument of a progressive revelation.

[8] The same issue—progressivism versus tradition—was fought indecisively on the

Education of a Humanist

the innumerable Philistines who, in the nineteenth century, sang hymns to progress. But the progressivism of the masters was sober; they knew how slow, painful, and precarious human advance had been in the past; they did not anticipate the sudden coming of a new heaven and a new earth.

Parallel with the Enlightenment, and in certain cases within the Enlightenment, there grew an antagonistic force: Primitivism, the cult of the unconscious, a rebellion against the intellectual discipline which is the essence of civilization. This force, of its very nature, was obscure and Protean. We find it already in Vico, that Melchizedek among historical thinkers, without ancestry and without progeny. For Vico, those myths which Voltaire would have denounced as delusions or lies were the spontaneous expression of a people's soul, the vital element in all poetry, deeper than formal truth. We easily recognize the trend which, half a century later and quite independently, was expressed by Herder, and which informs Wolf's *Prolegomena*. Homer was no longer considered an "artful" poet, applying or creating the "rules" of the epic; the *Iliad* and the *Odyssey* were but the crystallization of folklore. A deliberately manufactured epic, like *La Henriade*, or even the *Aeneid*, is bound to be lifeless in comparison; conscious tricks are no substitute for the unspoilt glow of enthusiasm and faith. A modern man can be a true poet only by rejecting the slow conquests of civilization and by being a primitive at heart, in direct touch with the timeless.[9]

Both schools, Rationalistic Progressivism and Anti-Rational Primitivism, sinned against the historical spirit when they failed to

---

cultural field, with the Quarrel of the Ancients and the Moderns. The champions were halfhearted on both sides, and the Modernists were second-raters; so the controversy proved abortive. It was to reappear, a century later, with the attacks against Greco-Roman tyranny: *Qui nous délivrera des Grecs et des Romains?*

[9] The Primitivism of Rousseau was far less historical than that of Herder, although there is a definite connection between the two. Rousseau is still a *philosophe* in his belief that man would be happy if he were free from superstitions; only he considered civilization and progress (as Pius IX did a century later) as the most noxious of all superstitions.

History

recognize that reason, that is to say, awareness, is itself a growth. Voltaire took it for granted that men living in remote ages were as cunning as himself, and that the origin of myths and superstitions was to be found in deliberate fraud: Mohammed was but an unscrupulous Voltairian. The Primitivists, on the other hand, spoke as though eighteenth-century minds were no sharper tools than the brains of the Old Stone Age.

For the Primitivists, thought was not a conquest but a blight; as soon as men knew what they were doing, they were bound to go wrong. Against awareness and planning, the Primitivists extolled with Burke "the wisdom of prejudice." This was of course less a philosophy than a convenient rationalization of the conservative bias. The *status quo* which could no longer be upheld as an Eternal Verity was defended as the inevitable result of organic growth. A written constitution is valid, although unnecessary, in so far as it embodies precedent; it is futile and dangerous when it appeals to reason. To such minds, Jefferson is hardly less of a scandal than Tom Paine. We must quote again Joseph de Maistre's lofty denial that the proposed city of Washington would ever come into being; for a city must grow from obscure beginnings and cannot be founded by a definite act of the human will.

A third element developed in the eighteenth century. The period was restless and adventurous, not satisfied with the smooth perfection of its setting and the luminous clarity of its thought. Reason, common sense, commonplace, are all too often interchangeable. So the Age of Reason deliberately sought the strange in many domains: in a curious revival of mysteries as well as in scientific discoveries, in the exploration of space and time, in the far away and the long ago. The quest for the picturesque was one of the manifestations of this craving. The sophisticates gave up the conscious architecture of formal gardens; they returned to wild nature by building fake waterfalls and artificial crags; in the same spirit, they erected pagodas and Gothic ruins; in the same spirit again, they wrote "Gothick" novels and forged medieval or primitive

Education of a Humanist

poems; the rebellion against the humdrum led to a carnival of make-believe.

This love of the "Romantic" in the early sense of the term gradually lost its most glaring absurdities. It was purified into the art of Scott, in which "romance" was tempered and heightened by a large admixture of shrewd realism. The romancers, in their turn, begat the Romantic historians, who honestly sought accuracy, but for whom drama and color were the supreme object of research and the warrant of truth. Voltaire was then voted no historian at all, for in the Middle Ages he saw the dull suffering of the people rather than the gay pennons and resplendent armors of the knights. It can easily be seen how this flamboyant aspect of the historical spirit would blend with primitivism, anti-intellectualism, and the conservatism of Burke. Together, they formed an admirable defense against the Revolution.

Picturesqueness is an aspect of the problem which historians of literature, for generations, have rather overemphasized. It never was the chief element, either in Romantic poetry or in Romantic history. But, however superficial, it is not to be neglected. It affected art, politics, and most of all religion. If we had Ritualism, Coronation pageants, a Hohenzollern Empire; if we have Gothic railway stations for London commuters, gloomy medieval cells for twentieth-century students, medieval shrines for modernist preachers, it is because Dr. Syntax, after many others, started for his momentous tour in search of the Picturesque.

The nineteenth century had become, in several different ways, historically minded; but there were two domains which had not yet been fully conquered: philosophy and science. Philosophy deals with the permanent; the Progressivists were philosophers in so far as they sought to free "eternal" reason from the shackles of tradition; the conservatives appealed to the eternal truths of revelation, or to the unchangeable facts of human nature. Even among the Romanticists, many still refused to recognize the validity of

History

change and the ineluctable power of time. It was Hegel who operated what may be termed the historical revolution in philosophy, by substituting a dynamic logic for the static logic of the Aristotelians. Instead of rejecting contradiction as the sign of the absurd, Hegel made it the fundamental element in his method. With stiff mechanical steps, but irresistibly, his dialectics proceeded through thesis and antithesis to synthesis, itself a new link in the endless chain. Such a philosophy of conflict and motion was profoundly romantic; born of the Romantic age, it was darkly heralded by Blake, the purest of the Romanticists; and ultimately it would lead to Bergsonism which, quite consciously, is Romanticism undefiled.

The last victory, and perhaps the most fruitful, was in the field of science. In the seventeenth and eighteenth centuries, the archetypal discipline was mathematics, which dwells in the eternal. The scientist par excellence was Newton. Even metaphysics and theology would ultimately yield primacy to Celestial Mechanics, a development which would have filled Copernicus and Newton with dismay. Asked, "Where is God in your system?" Laplace replied, "Sire, I need no such hypothesis." But already with Buffon in his *Epochs,* with Lamarck, with Cuvier and his paleontology, the natural sciences were assuming leadership; and they did so in the form of historical sciences. This tendency came to a head with Lyell's geology; and again with Lyell as with Bossuet, Bayle, and Voltaire, we find religious controversy at the bottom of the historical problem, "the age of rocks versus the Rock of Ages," the slow unfolding of time as a challenge to an unchanging revelation. This dramatic new force is connected in our minds with Darwin, Wallace, Spencer. But the doctrine of evolution is simply the historical spirit; natural science was the last, not the first, of human disciplines to follow its guidance. Ernest Renan definitely said that he, a mere layman in these matters, was inclined to accept the Darwinian hypothesis simply because it was in line with the ruling principles of European thought for the last fifty years.

Education of a Humanist

We need hardly point out that the natural sciences, grown historical, reacted in their turn upon philosophy, politics, history, and literature. They colored the conservatism of Taine as well as the "naturalism" of Zola; they provided Brunetière with a metaphor *(L'évolution des genres)* which he mistook for a scientific law. The heirs of Burke saw their belief in unconscious, infinitesimal growth confirmed; the rejection of "catastrophism" by the geologists was a telling argument against the radicals, and an apology for the slow broadening from precedent to precedent, for Fabian tactics, for the inevitability of gradualness. The Communists themselves, combining Hegel and Darwin, offered their social philosophy not as an absolute, not as a static ideal, but as an interpretation of history.

These indications, so rough as to be positively rude, are not meant to be even a hasty survey of the problem. Their purpose is to formulate two propositions, two working hypotheses, which it would take a long treatise to establish or disprove.

The first is that the growth of the historical spirit may be likened not to a melody but to a fugue. The same theme—the reality of change—is picked up by various instruments and in various keys. At times, theological controversy is the leader; then philosophy, then art, then history proper, philosophy again, art once more, the natural sciences. The development of that essential thought ignores all departmental fences: its study necessitates a School of Humanities. A Romantic historian like Carlyle is the heir of the romancers like Scott and of German philosophy, not the successor of rationalistic historians like Gibbon. The "naturalism" of Zola was shaped by Claude Bernard and indirectly by Darwin, far more than by the novelistic tradition of Lesage, Marivaux, Prévost. A history of scientific thought that should ignore philosophy and literature would be as full of gaps as a history of literature in purely literary terms.

History

The second proposition is that, of all the manifestations of the historical spirit, the most obvious are also the most superficial. The mere picturesqueness of certain Romanticists—historians as well as romancers, dramatists, or painters—belongs to the masked ball or the carnival rather than to sober science. The invincible attachment to the past, which the Tory mind identifies with the historical spirit, is in effect anti-historical, for the defense of "the good old days" denies the irresistible action of time. Unless men, like blinded horses, are doomed to tread forever in the same circle, it is literally impossible for them to "walk in their fathers' footsteps." We cannot even admit as a certainty that the historical spirit implies the notion of gradualness. The theories of Lyell and Darwin are not permanent; they take their place in the historical process; they evolve. They were but the geological and biological transcription of Victorian anti-Radicalism: they are period pieces, not eternal verities. De Vries, among others, has restored the notion of new departures under the name of mutations; catastrophes must have occurred in geological history, and we know too well that they do occur in human history. Perhaps the most profitable lesson of such a study is not to emphasize the flow of time, which few would dare to deny, but the extreme unevenness of that flow. The heavens are an immense chronometer; but the story of mankind is not predictable in terms of the clock.

THE FITFUL STREAM: "PERIODS" AND "GENERATIONS"

To talk of viewing mundane affairs *sub specie aeternitatis,* or even, more modestly, "from Sirius," is grandiloquent nonsense. It simply cannot be done. Within the limits of man's puny endeavor and ephemeral memory, inches and minutes count, a decade assumes significance, a century achieves dignity, a millennium is clothed with majesty. In the eyes of the Eternal, world-shaking events are but meaningless ripples on the changeless face of the everlasting present. Dmitri Merezhkovsky, in his two incredible books on Napoleon, would have us admit that his hero is exempt from the time-flow: he *knows-remembers,* future and past are one to him. He passed through history like a meteor; he does not belong to history. On the mystic plane this doctrine is unimpeachable: Jesus' prophecy of His own death was a fulfillment, that is to say, a memory. He had to manifest Himself to man in human time and space, but transcended them both. Léon Bloy, "pilgrim of the absolute," averred that the miracle of the Marne might have been due to the prayers of a humble little girl who would not be born for another two hundred years: *o altitudo!* To mix the two realms of thought, the mystic and the historical, is disconcerting. If we are to write history "as it actually happened," we must take for granted the irreversible flow of time. A delusion, I am sure. But that delusion is the inevitable condition of the game.

If metaphysics and history refuse to mix, natural science and history do not mix very well. Astronomy, geology, biology, those vast concentric circles, think in terms of the time-flow, but their units are aeons which dwarf human chronology. Man is only a creature of yesterday in the universe; recorded history, from its very dawn, embraces but a few paltry millennia. We know not what immense cycles within cycles are carrying us through the boundless cosmos. We are as completely lost in the physical infinite as we are in the metaphysical absolute. Humbly, we must adjust ourselves to our human scale. On a globe five inches in circumference, Mount Everest would be one thousandth of an inch, imperceptible to sight or touch: to us, Everest is an unscalable height. And Pascal may have been right about Cleopatra's nose: had it been a trifle shorter, the face of the world would have been changed. What if we are less than Lilliput? Let us make the best of our anthill. No Gulliver has appeared so far to make a mockery of our measurements.[10]

[10] Some people are not so impervious as I am to a sense of cosmic time. After a lecture by some astronometaphysician, of the Jeans-Eddington type, a member of the

History

Let us not flutter ineffectually through the impalpable inane: we are on earth, and our positive knowledge is confined within the the narrow bounds of our conscious collective memory. Inside that small circle of dubious light, the time-flow is a reality, and it is perceptible. We can trace the upbuilding of empires and their destruction. But the picture is bewildering. It does not fade gradually into penumbra and darkness: things of yesterday, almost within the reach of our hands, vanish utterly in an opaque void; while figures and voices reach us, miraculously alive, across ten or twenty centuries. There is no single, clear-cut, steady process of growth or decay: out of decrepitude strange new shoots arise.

There is no absolute law, not even the law of change. We have adopted the ancient dictum of Heraclitus: All things flow. But it ruthlessly simplifies the picture. All things flow, but at a different rate: else we would not be conscious of the flow. And does not flow imply direction? At times, we wonder if the good old metaphor of the stream is valid. At any rate, our experience is so brief that we might easily mistake an eddy for the main current. The Thames in London (beating the record of the most astute politicians) reverses its course twice a day.

All this is not radical Pyrrhonism, but relativism. From man's point of view, there can be no absolute history; and, from the point of view of the absolute, there can be no history at all. History in every sense of the term is man-made. It is the projection of man's terrors and longings upon the undefinable screen of the non-human world. If man ceased to suffer, to think, to strive, to hope, history would come to a stop.

During the First World War, I took exception to a phrase of Hugo Münsterberg: "Truth is a free creation of the intellect." It seemed to me an admirable definition of German truth in war time, that is, propaganda. I apologize to Münsterberg: philosophically, he

---

audience asked: "Professor, did you say that life on this planet would cease in five hundred *million* years, or five hundred *billion?*"—"I said *billion*." The man heaved a sigh of profound relief.

Education of a Humanist

was right. His formula did apply to propaganda; but I have never come across history that was not propaganda, that is, things deemed worthy of being propagated. Leopold von Ranke would have been shocked if he had been told that his immense labor was altogether futile: his aim was to disseminate those truths which he thought were of importance to mankind. Even the nonphilosophical historian holds an unconscious or unconfessed philosophy.

The crux is the freedom of the creative intellect. That freedom is not caprice: it is not so even in romance. Absolute caprice is the negation of the intellect itself. Our mind is a set of consistencies, imperfect no doubt, but indispensable. The intellect is free when it works according to its own law; freest when it is most conscious of the law and most perfectly in accord with it. And the first and greatest commandment is the first rule of Descartes: honesty. Do not cheat yourself by pretending that you know or believe that which you are not quite sure you know or believe. Self-purification through self-criticism. This is not "the law of History"; it is the law for historians.

History is a scheme superimposed by man upon the facts of his collective experience. So there is a double selection. One is wholly unconscious: our experience does not register the whole of Nature, nor even all in Nature that actually affects us. The second may be subconscious, or it may be deliberate: we retain only the facts which seem to us relevant. History, like literature (but is it not a branch of literature?), is a self-portrait of the human mind.

The sense of difference, which is the foundation of history, is a psychological phenomenon. It translates itself most naturally into the conception of periods. If it were continuous and even, Change would not be perceptible. A period forms a consistent picture, different from pictures of the same kind, and different from the scene under our own eyes. Because of that difference, periods are landmarks which enable us to appreciate the flow.

Now periods are man-made. This is quite evident if we follow a scheme according to which periods are determined by the activities of a definite group of men. The French Revolution created a new

History

calendar, because it was opening a new era; and we still have a tendency to call epochs by the name of some ruler or hero: Pericles, Augustus, Elizabeth, Louis XIV. We all know, however, that most periods are not cut according to such a dramatic pattern. A period is the result of a vast trend assuming consciousness. So a number of periods are clearly self-determined, as nations should be according to Napoleon III and Woodrow Wilson. A period begins with a Declaration of Independence: in terms of poker and politics, it is a "New Deal." There are a few such proclamations that ring clear in history. I am fond of quoting the stirring words of the Burgundian monk, Raoul Glaber: "The earth was shaking off the rags of its antiquity, and clothing itself anew with a white mantle of churches"; and those of Rabelais: "At last we are out of Gothic night!" Goethe claims that he said at Valmy: "In this place and at this hour a new era opens in the history of the world." The Third Estate, with Siéyès as its spokesman, and the proletarians, in their anthem *The International,* uttered the "epoch-making" words: "We were nothing; we must be everything." Hitler announced the advent of a New Order, which was to prevail for a thousand years. When such an assertion meets sufficient credence, a period is born.

Naturally, there are false dawns, abortive periods. Etienne Marcel might have heralded a new age in France, Wyclif and the Lollards in England, Lamartine, the Chartists, and the Frankfort Parliament in the Europe of 1848. The Empire of Charlemagne was short-lived; that of Napoleon proved a house of cards. Herbert Hoover, in 1929, closed the days of confusion and opened for America a new age of unchecked, ever-expanding Republican prosperity. Infant mortality is appalling among periods.

What about those periods which were not conscious of their own existence and had to be discovered retrospectively? Would that be a warrant of objective reality? The clearest case is that of the Machine Age or Industrial Revolution. Some of the most famous British statesmen, Palmerston, Balfour, Winston Churchill, never were clearly aware of it. They kept dealing the cards exactly as if the

Education of a Humanist

clock of history had stopped in 1688. Most churchmen, squires, scholars, tradespeople, did not realize the advent of the new dispensation. For them, the new gadgets were merely conveniences or nuisances; if they wanted to spend a season at Bath, it was a matter of secondary importance whether they journeyed thither by coach, train, or plane; and to the present day, they prefer candles to electric bulbs. But the long delay in discerning and defining the period does not alter its man-made character. It too was "a free creation of the human intellect." We are now machine-conscious, and we are rewriting history in terms of the machine, brushing aside religious movements as immaterial and antiquated. It may be that our successors will rewrite history in terms of psychology or dietetics, pre-Freudian and pre-vitamin ages being the dim epochs before the Flood.

The period problem is strikingly illustrated by the events of today. We unanimously voted that the atomic bomb had opened a new era. Then we realized that the world remained curiously unchanged. For a few keen-minded observers like Robert Hutchins and Mortimer Adler, it was indeed a revelation. But the statesmen keep playing the same orthodox game of power politics as Elizabeth, Richelieu, Frederick II, Napoleon, Bismarck, and the same smart diplomatic tricks as Talleyrand. The cream of the jest is that they call their ignoring of the new factor "realistic." Generals are still demanding universal military service, as in the days of the French Revolution. On the other hand, the lessons that impressed themselves upon Hutchins and Adler as a consequence of the new power—the necessity of peace and therefore of a world state, the pooling of knowledge, the exploitation in common of natural resources, an economy of abundance—all these things had been clearly advocated long before atomic energy was even a dream. The new discovery is not a revolution but a sensational manifestation of a general advance in human technique. No more than other and hardly less brilliant manifestations is it capable by itself to impose a change in human relations, or to enlighten the human conscience. It did not and could

History

not bring wisdom: it has only multiplied the perils of unwisdom. Socrates and Jesus are more imperiously needed today than in any previous age.[11]

The merest conventions are soon accepted as objective realities. It is hard to make students realize that "Antiquity" did not come to a sudden end, like a presidential term, in 476, and the "Middle Ages" in 1453. A friend of mine took me to see the great monument on the battlefield of San Jacinto. Over the door there was a six-pointed star, which is not the pattern used on the Texas flag. I called his attention to this oddity. He remarked ingenuously: "Of course! How absurd! The stars in the heavens have only five points." And he believed it.

Periods exist in the consciousness either of contemporaries or of later ages. They are therefore psychological phenomena: the most essential thing about them is their "spirit." When German was the sole language that conferred dignity upon confused thought, we proudly used the term *Zeitgeist*.

The "spirit" of a period, when analyzed, resolves itself into the same elements as other manifestations of collective psychology, such as religious faith, party allegiance, or simply style or vogue. There is in every case a determined minority for whom the spirit is very real and all important; a large fringe of passive but sympathetic followers; a still larger fringe of people who repeat the current shibboleth with polite or cautious indifference, simply because they do not believe that it is worth fighting about; and a minority of conscious opponents, whom the majority strives to suppress, or at least to

---

[11] A curious case of a period that should have been: we are tempted to believe that the change from the Ptolemaic to the Copernican cosmogony should have determined a general revolution in thought. There is no trace of such a change. Priests, philosophers, poets, statesmen, soldiers, merchants, laborers, behave strictly today as though the earth were motionless, and indeed as though it were flat. The tremendous discovery has not changed the testimony of our senses and our figures of speech: for Hemingway as for Ecclesiastes, "the sun also rises." The Copernican system has not weakened faith; it has not made man more humble. Why should it?

repress and discourage. I could find no trace in history of any time when opinion was spontaneously unanimous. In the age of faith, so cherished by Henry Adams for its unity, there were free-thinkers, heretics, witches, and devil-worshipers: we know of their existence through the persecutions they suffered. We do not know how many people managed to stay on the safe side of the Inquisition, but kept their own counsel. At the time of Joan of Arc, purest incarnation of the national soul, many excellent Frenchmen were on the side of the Paris king, Henry VI of England, or of the Burgundians. Clemenceau imposed upon France an indomitable will-to-victory by methods which the totalitarians had only to copy and amplify. I need not comment again upon the activities of the Un-American Committee. It always takes an inquisition to maintain an orthodoxy; and Mrs. Grundy, being ubiquitous, is more effective than Torquemada.

If we examine the situation a little more closely, we shall find that even the minority in control, which imposes its own state of mind as the official *Zeitgeist,* never is, as it claims, "monolithic." In many cases, the agreement is nominal. The leaders are fanatical defenders of the faith—whether it be Christianity, the monarchy, the Fatherland, the Revolution, the race, Democracy, economic freedom, or the aesthetic attitude; but agreement prevails only so long as you do not attempt to define those sacred terms too precisely. People are never so "grimly resolved" as when they have stopped thinking; for reflection inevitably reveals contradictions and ambiguities. "What exactly do you mean?" is the Devil's most subtle snare.

I had the opportunity to study, over many years, two such "Spirits of the Time." The first was that of the classical age in France; the second, the strange synthesis that culminated in the European Revolutions of 1848. Their destinies were radically different. Classicism—dawn, noonday, and interminable twilight—lasted for three hundred years, and, at least for one majestic moment, silenced every opposition. The ardent faith of 1848 was but a flash, so fulgurating that for a few weeks it alone seemed real. But it was held with intense con-

History

sciousness by a mere handful of men; the masses, although they responded to its appeal, never fully understood it; and its downfall was sudden and irremediable.

Two things impressed me very forcibly about the Classical Age. The first is that its full maturity was extremely brief—a decade perhaps (1661–1672), at most a quarter of a century (1661–1687). Bayle, a product of that time, already belongs to the Enlightenment; Saint-Simon, who depicted the court with such savage vigor, is a feudal throwback with the freedom and intensity of a Romanticist; Pascal transcends all periods and schools.

The second thought is that the period, even during its short season of glorious plenitude, did not achieve inner peace. No doubt the protagonists of the classical ideal had superb assurance. Louis XIV, the Grand Monarch; Bossuet, theologian, historian, and statesman; Boileau, dictator of Parnassus; Lebrun, Mansard, Perrault, Lulli in the various arts; even Colbert in his economic policy and in his public works, all present the same style: disciplined magnificence. But that splendid outward order is not the fruit of a single doctrine; it results from a reconciliation, or rather from a truce, between two antagonistic principles: tradition and reason. The keynote is not an ideal, toward which all would strive with one accord: it is "reasonableness," moderation, that is to say, a form of resignation. So, under the smooth surface, we can trace tensions that will soon crack the majestic edifice. The king, first of the nobles, is most scrupulously respectful of their titles and privileges; but he governs through the *bourgeoisie,* whom the monarchy is thus training for the Revolution of 1789. A devout Christian with none of the Christian virtues, he obeys and defies the Pope. Bossuet, who preaches on "the eminent dignity of the poor," is an honored personage in that court of unprecedented and soul-destroying splendor. Boileau, who seems of reason all compact, is a bundle of contradictions. A pious son of the Church, he cannot repudiate, in literature, his pagan heritage; he maintains at the same time that art must love reason above all things and seek its inspiration from the ancient lies of mythology. He is indignant that any one should dispute the authority of Aristotle's *Poetics;* but he writes a spirited lampoon against the medical schools when they seek to uphold the infallibility of Aristotle in physiology. The apparent harmony of the age is not truly a synthesis but a compromise.

That compromise was bound to be short-lived, for the two forces which appeared united were moving in opposite directions. "Reason," in the form of philosophy, history, political thought, science, was gathering strength; "Tradition" was on the wane. As soon as the point of exact equilibrium was passed, unreasoning tradition appeared "unreasonable," a mass of privileges, abuses, superstitions; and the stage was set for Voltaire. Voltaire might still wear a pseudoclassical garb: his spirit no longer was that of Boileau and Bossuet. Louis XIV outlived the true classical age. Before he died, the authority of the Ancients had been challenged; La Bruyère had already said, "I am on the side of the people"; and the Grand Monarch had courted the favor of Samuel Bernard, a financier. The words "period of organic unity," in this crucial case, appear far too ambitious; we should speak of "the generation when a style reached its evanescent perfection."

Shall we imagine history as a serrated line, in which the peaks stand for the well-integrated periods, the notches between them for "times out of joint"? It would be more accurate to speak of dissolving pictures. The disruption of an ancient order is seldom abrupt. In the France of the eighteenth century, the traditional elements, Church, monarchy, aristocracy, Greco-Roman models, faded but slowly away: the magnificence which had clothed the great compromise was still a proud memory. Reason did not win a sharp battle against tradition: it rose invincibly through all the interstices of the past. And before it had triumphed, it was challenged in its turn by the Primitivism of Rousseau.

I am afraid that this scheme is not orthodox Hegelian dialectics. The classical thesis was far too complex to call forth a clear-cut antithesis. All its elements survived, but in changing proportions.

History

The Revolution itself was not the negation but the fulfillment of the Ancient Regime. It was severely classical in style and more authoritarian than Louis XIV.

With all due precautions, we may affirm that there was, in the minds of contemporaries, and that there still is in our own mind, a classical spirit; and that the moment, brief as it may be, when it was most sharply focused was the center of the classical age. Such definite coincidences are rare. There are periods which never found their spirit. It is impossible to define the two centuries and more that rolled uneasily by between the death of Saint Louis, the perfect medieval king, and the advent of Francis I, the typical Renaissance ruler. There was no rejection of the previous epoch, but, on the contrary—in scholasticism, in flamboyant Gothic art, in the elaborate trappings of chivalry—an exaggeration, almost a caricature, of its most salient features. It was not a time of sheer chaos and irremediable decadence; but there was—in France at any rate—no definite preparation for a new synthesis. We are compelled to use the stale and feeble word *transition*.

The faith of 1848 is, on the contrary, a spirit that failed to create its epoch; in Arnold Toynbee's quaint and pregnant phrase, "a turning point in history when history failed to turn." The mad and holy year, as the Germans called it, remains a puzzle, a menace, a remorse. That spirit was defeated, not destroyed. The bitterness of that defeat, the fear that never ceased to darken the precarious victory, the millennial hopes revealed for an instant and still unfulfilled, are tormenting us to this day. Metternich, the *Biedermeierzeit,* the early years of Victoria, the hesitant, timorous course of Louis Philippe the Citizen-King, all now belong hopelessly to the past: the problems of 1848 are our problems. The ghost of 1848 is haunting us.

How can we define a spirit? It cannot be caught in a mesh of theories, and it eludes statistics. Yet it has substance, for it shapes the activities of practical men. It is made up of innumerable facts fused by emotion. In a word, it is not a doctrine but a faith. It belongs to the history of religion, perhaps the only history worth our care. Without the emotion, the facts would remain a dead conglomerate. Without the facts, the emotion would evaporate in the void. In the spirit of 1848, the facts were provided by the six or seven revolutions which, uncoördinated in appearance, some of them barely conscious, had been underway for two hundred years. The emotional glow which finally welded them is loosely known as romanticism. The term is past apologizing for; but since no better one has been offered, this Protean monster will have to serve.

 The seven revolutions had shaken one pillar after another of the ancient edifice, traditional authority. The *rationalistic revolution,* with Descartes, was the most radical of all. Indeed, it would be radical even today: "Never receive a thing as true, unless it appears *to you* clearly and evidently to be such." But the *scientific revolution,* with Bacon, was earlier still: the triumph of the comparative, inductive, experimental method. The *theological revolution:* a hundred years of fierce controversy between Catholics and Protestants had finally released religious free thought, "natural religion." The three, Rationalism, Science, Theism, were to coalesce into the Enlightenment. The *financial revolution:* the modern techniques of insurance and banking, which had their origin in medieval Italy, were brought to perfection in Holland and England in the seventeenth century; and early in the eighteenth came the discovery of that magic force, credit. As a result, plutocracy or mercantile wealth could challenge the privileges of the feudal aristocracy and even of the king. Samuel Bernard imposed his terms on Louis XIV, and a foreign banker, Necker, was to be the receiver of the French Ancient Regime. The *industrial revolution,* which began obscurely with the steam pumps of Newcomen, and was not to be properly labeled and fully described for over a century. The *democratic revolution,* whose prophet was Rousseau, and which colored, even though it did not inspire, the rise of the American and French Republics. The *national revolution* at last, corollary of the democratic: it is not the king alone who is "France" or "England," but the Common Man; cities, provinces, countries, cannot be inherited, bought, stolen, conquered; it is the sovereign will of the people that determines their right to unite or secede.

Only an unphilosophical specialist or a too philosophical doctrinaire would claim that any one of these revolutions was the sole cause of all the rest. Each was apparently autonomous and followed its own timetable. Molière recorded the rise of the *bourgeoisie* (titled sharks see fit to flatter Monsieur Jourdain, the rich merchant), unaffected by Bacon, Descartes, Locke, or Bayle, and even less by the first steam engines of Denis Papin or Newcomen. The cross references are almost fortuitous. Werner Sombart's attempt to link and almost to equate Protestantism and Capitalism is a brilliant fallacy. There was capitalism in Florence under the Medici, and there could be no sharper description of the capitalistic ethos than Lesage's *Turcaret* in Catholic France.

The connection between any or all of these movements is not mechanical, and it is not logical and conscious. It simply means that the world was moving, in many directions, at different rates, beyond the power of the Classical Norm to control its development. Louis XIV, the aptest symbol of the classical synthesis, ended in complete bankruptcy. Mankind could no longer be guided by the eternal wisdom so dear to Bishop Bossuet, Ferdinand Brunetière, Irving Babbitt, and Mr. Thomas Stearns Eliot. Already by the middle of the eighteenth century, although the magnificent machine of tradition—monarchy, Church, academies, social hierarchy—was more ornate and more expensive than ever, it was no longer geared to reality.

In those epochs when a synthesis unquestionably prevails—the thirteenth, "Greatest of Centuries"; the Age of Louis XIV—sentiment has its place, but that place is subordinate. In art as well as in religion, and even in the personal relations between human beings, there are norms to which individual inclinations must yield. The Ego is condemned as hateful; what is purely individual is, etymologically, idiotic. Discipline, intellectual, moral, social, spiritual, is the

Education of a Humanist

first condition of sanity. When the synthesis shows signs of breaking down, on the contrary, discipline loses its vitality. It appears formal, irksome, deadening, and the great unruly forces are unleashed: imagination and passion. Note that these forces existed under Classicism: Pascal, or even Racine, cannot be described in terms of sheer conformity. But if these primeval energies were not destroyed, they were curbed. Now, by the middle of the eighteenth century, they were given a free rein. It is this shift from conformity to freedom, and even to anarchy, that we call Romanticism.

Any narrower or more positive definition will prove inadequate. Romanticism is not merely the Gothic, or the picturesque, or the primitive. Least of all is it, as Babbitt would have us believe, Rousseauistic optimism. It assumed innumerable forms. It was found in the Oriental tale and in the horror story; in the revival of Freemasonry and of the Rosicrucians; in fakers like Cagliostro and like that Saint-Germain whom Los Angeles has recently rediscovered; in the German Pietistic movement and in British Methodism. It was clearest of all in eleuteromania or liberty-worship, which logically means anarchism. We might find it difficult to persuade Mr. Herbert Hoover that his rugged individualism is the pure essence of Romanticism, as compared with the classic ideal of restraint professed by the Communists.

That release of untamed power was magnificent—a rebirth of forces that classic rule, in its later and more oppressive stage, had repressed almost out of existence. A greying world was aflame again. But, by its very nature, it was chaotic. Romanticism assumed all conceivable shapes and hues. The first clear note was that of rebellion: Rousseau's challenge to civilization, the *Sturm und Drang* of Schiller and Goethe in their early plays. This was found later in the anarchism of Shelley, in the defiant attitude of Byron, and even in Balzac: for the favorite hero of the great realist is Vautrin, the escaped convict, at war with society. Romanticism took the form of millennial hopes, but also of melancholy and despair; for a well-ordered, classical world, dull as it may be, is at any rate safe, comfortable, sociable. The individual, released from all bonds, sighs or shudders at the isolation he has sought. Romanticism is revolution, and Romanticism is reaction as well, a passionate love, not for the lackluster present, but for the storied past. This, and not political experience, dictated the attitude of Edmund Burke; it inspired Chateaubriand, and, at some stage in their careers, most of the German and French romanticists; it is the key to Carlyle's erratic thought. At certain moments, ever fleeting but inevitably recurring, Romanticism is Art for Art's Sake; in the collapse of all systematic values, Beauty alone survived. Keats was to give the pithiest form to that worship of pure Beauty; he died just as he was ready to leave it behind and seek his inspiration in "the giant agony of a world."

Romanticism therefore was confusion, and that confusion lasted for a hundred years, from the mid-eighteenth century to the mid-nineteenth. But out of that teeming chaos, a new synthesis was emerging. All the forces which had disrupted the classical world were being fused in the white heat of romantic imagination and passion. The result was a living faith, uniting free Christianity, democracy, and social justice. It was best represented, perhaps, by two French prophets never fully appreciated in the English-speaking world: Saint-Simon and Lamennais. It inspired George Sand, Lamartine, Michelet; it was to fill Hugo's epic, *Les Misérables*. But it was by no means special to France. It was, for instance, the core of Mazzini's thought. It was expressed in simple, almost naïve, but impassioned terms by Ebenezer Elliot, the Corn-Law Rhymer:

> When wilt Thou save the people,
> O God of Mercy, when?

It was to assume in Russia strange and troublous, but still recognizable, forms, with the Slavophiles, Dostoevsky and the later Tolstoy.

In the few years that preceded the Revolution of 1848, the issue became sharply drawn. Romanticism as a literary school had lost its glow. No longer poetry, but social democracy, the service of the people, became the chief vehicle of the Romantic spirit. Soon after

1840, both Lamartine and Hugo, the leaders of their generation, turned to politics. They had not lost their prophetic fire; but they felt that the hour of decision was at hand.

At the same time, the middle-class regime of Louis Philippe was hardening itself into its unlovely perfection. The national policy was isolationism, neutrality, peace at any price: "Let everyone stay at home and mind his own business." In home affairs, the profit motive was exalted. A Christian commonwealth, honor, chivalry, were shrugged away as romantic make-believe. The rights of the common man, social justice, social pity, were dismissed as the dreams of starry-eyed do-gooders. The one undeniable reality was wealth. Wealth was not merely the reward of virtue: it was virtue itself, since it was power. The Charter formally recognized the divine right of the moneybags. France's business was Business: only the men who had proved their mettle by acquiring or preserving wealth had a vote. The rabble, naturally, were kept out; so were the intellectuals, if they had no fortune but their intelligence. To every demand for an extension of the franchise, Guizot replied with faultless logic: "If you want a vote, qualify yourselves: get rich! *Enrichissez-vous!*"

This bourgeois millennium was the apotheosis of mediocrity and selfishness. "The Golden Mean," meanness with well-lined pockets, was the national idol. Between this smug mesocracy and the Romantic spirit in its final form, the fusion of Christianity, socialism, and democracy, there was an absolute antinomy. The leadership of the opposition went quite naturally to the most prominent, the most idealistic, the most religious poet of the Romantic school, Lamartine. And the verdict that he passed on the eminently practical and sensible rule of Louis Philippe was deadly: *La France s'ennuie,* France is bored.

In February 1848, France yawned Louis Philippe away. The very able king found his way to England, as plain Mr. Smith; the haughty philosopher Guizot followed the same road, disguised as an old woman. And France declared herself a democratic and social Republic.

History

There was, throughout the country and throughout Europe, a moment of boundless hope. People felt themselves liberated at last from the hateful obligation of being mean. The hucksters were no longer the rulers of the land. The spirit of '48 was so evidently religious, and even so specifically Christian, that the clergy at first acclaimed its triumph. They blessed the "trees of Liberty" that were solemnly planted everywhere. It was a moment like the night of August 4, 1789, when feudal privileges were given up by their beneficiaries. The Spirit, passionate and generous, stirred the whole of Europe—Madrid, Milan, Budapest, Vienna, Berlin, and even stodgy, insular London. But the new era failed to establish itself. A sudden vision of the fraternal Promised Land; four months of despairing hope and mounting anguish; then, in June, the catastrophe, and fulfillment deferred by over a hundred years.

HEROES, LEGENDS, AND MYTHS

Periods may be determined by events; they are not events in themselves. They are not the drama but only the backdrop of history. What are the characters that throng upon the stage? Obviously, they are men. The machine has not yet crowded flesh and blood out of the picture; and all abstractions—institutions, creeds, causes—have to manifest themselves through human voices and human deeds.

The raw material of history therefore is biographical. This plain fact accounts for the favor enjoyed by biography throughout the ages, for its vogue did not suddenly arise with Lytton Strachey, Emil Ludwig, and André Maurois. It accounts also for the "heroic" or personal interpretation of history, which likewise is of ancient origin and was not invented by Carlyle. Men are realities; trends or ideals are shadows.

I have as good a right to call myself a "realist" as anybody; and, purely in the name of realism, I challenge the idea that individuals as such are the subject matter of history. John Smith ate cabbage soup last Friday: it may be a fact, it is a bit of his biography, it is not history. It might become history if John Smith had other claims upon our interest besides his mere existence, either as an outstanding man or as a sample of the mass. Napoleon had the itch: we retain the fact, although its historical importance has yet to be determined; almost any fact connected with Napoleon might have a bearing upon the course of Empire. History is not idle gossip: it is an attempt to present human events of a certain magnitude in credible sequence. A small man in private life has no standing in history: he is "insignificant." But the man intrinsically or potentially great—Ibsen's ideal, greatest when most alone—is not historical either unless his strength and purity are known and understood. He has to become a hero in the eyes of witnesses, admirers, or adversaries, before he assumes his rightful place in history. Recognition, immediate or delayed, is the inevitable gate. "The mute inglorious Milton" we need not discuss: he is a mere hypothesis, incapable of proof. But the humble unsung hero is a fact of common experience. Every year the French Academy casts its net over the French people and draws out a few specimens of "virtue" to whom it awards the Montyon prizes: examples of obscure devotion and fortitude, only too rare among the mighty. There may be greater saints among those who retired from the world, and whom the world forgot, than among those who swayed multitudes. In history as in literature, there is no necessary connection, and no proportion whatever, between merit and importance.

Individuals count historically only as leaders, that is to say, as factors in collective action. History does not distribute Montyon prizes: wicked men, madmen, and even weak men cannot be expunged from the record if, at one moment, they seemed to have a following. Their significance may be purely fortuitous: the "dreary plain" of Waterloo was not worth fighting for, yet the name is engraved in history. Louis XVI was kindly, pious, modest, by no means stupid. He would have been happy as an honest artisan; in quieter times, he might have been the very pattern and exemplar of a constitutional figurehead. But, by general agreement, he was flabby of

History

flesh and will, and utterly commonplace. Yet we cannot ignore him. Through the irony of fate, ten centuries and the interests of millions were summed up in that cipher. He was the reverse of a "hero," but he was a symbol.

Even in the case of those "Providential men," to use the words of Napoleon III, those heroes who were conscious of their mission, their place in history does not depend solely upon their personalities, but upon circumstances beyond their control. This is hard to demonstrate, since no valid argument can be based on what might have been: if we say that the Revolution gave Napoleon his chance, it might be retorted that he would have created other chances for himself. In a few cases, however, the demonstration is clear. The man tried to make history, and failed; then history made the man.

In 1840, the Napoleonic Legend was at its height. Louis Napoleon attempted to turn that impressive spiritual force into a political movement; the result was his fiasco at Boulogne, even more miserable than his Strasbourg gesture four years before. Had he died then, history would have contemptuously shrugged her shoulders at the ludicrous episode. In 1848, he was triumphantly elected to the Presidency. For twenty years, he was the focal point not only of a great nation, but of all Europe; and his action extended from China to Mexico. He was the same man, with the same principles; but in the meantime, the Revolution of February 1848 had broken out, and the insurrection of June. In 1923, Adolf Hitler and Ludendorff made a bid for power. The wounds inflicted at Versailles were unhealed; the occupation of the Ruhr had made them smart more cruelly; the Cause was there, and the Man fated to serve the cause. And the result was the *Bierhalle Putsch,* a feeble farce. Ten years later, the lance corporal was Chancellor and dictator of Germany, a menace to mankind. There had been no growth in his mental stature. But the American economic crisis had destroyed hope and confidence throughout the world, leaving convalescent Europe no alternative but dull despair or wild adventure. The Hitler boom was born in Wall Street in October 1929.

Education of a Humanist

I have never been interested in "debunking." I am not attempting to prove that all great men were small. I do not deny greatness: on the contrary, I believe with De Gaulle that nations should have their eyes fixed on an ideal of *Grandeur,* provided it be a greatness of the spirit. I find it safer to express my faith in less lofty terms: self-respect, the rejection of meanness. My analysis is meant not to destroy but to understand. And, as a result of that effort, I cannot escape the conclusion, so clearly taught by Shakespeare, that greatness is of different kinds and exists on different planes, which may or may not be brought into a single harmonious picture. In the historical role of a "great man," we should distinguish between his personality, his career, his legend.

Of his personality, his intrinsic individual worth, God is the only judge; and He has warned us to expect a startling revaluation of all our mundane values. Journalism registers the career: a man succeeds to the throne, is elected President, becomes Prime Minister, pays taxes on a hundred million dollars, or is the author of a best seller. What happens to him in such capacity is news, even though he be "a sheep in sheep's clothing," or a caterer to very common needs. The public is duly interested, but not deeply moved: there must be kings, Presidents, Premiers, financiers, successful writers: these will do as well as any. But when imagination and passion are fired, then the "strong individuality" or the "high personage" is transfigured. He becomes the Hero—angel or fiend—for or against whom men are willing to inflict and suffer death.[12] It is this transfiguration that I call the Legend.

This aura of passion, which turns the drab course of events into epic or drama, is popular history, no doubt. But scientific history, as a rule, simply fills with scrupulous care the outlines which have been traced by the popular mind. I cannot think of any hero created

---

[12] It might be said that no one is truly a historical character unless he is under the threat of assassination; although mere personages, like Presidents Carnot and McKinley, or the Empress Elizabeth, have been promoted to martyrdom because of their symbolical value.

History

or destroyed by erudition. The historian, and not merely the confessed disciple of Carlyle, takes heroes for granted: history is a game played by great men, with common men as pawns. The conscientious historian examines the career of his heroes with a microscope; as a rule, he does not challenge the legend itself, that is to say, the importance of the subject. The acid needed here would be philosophy, not research; but philosophy is "unrealistic," while research is "scientific." Renan thought that erudition could solve historical problems; of all his works, it was in his *Corpus inscriptionum Semiticarum* that he took the greatest pride. Yet scholars at least as thorough as he remained scrupulously orthodox, and his own learned conclusions had been anticipated by the man in the street. We shall see that the most exhaustive studies of Napoleon are also the least critical. This is no defense of carelessness: it only means that material care is not enough.

Much scientific history, I repeat, is only the roughest kind of popular history richly garbed with erudition. The investigator rushes for minute facts and accepts uncritically the common hypothesis which directs his quest. If we want to be scientific, we cannot take it for granted that Napoleon was great or even that he was supremely important. That remains to be established. On the other hand, we cannot jump blindly into the contrary hypothesis, even though it be the philosophical core of Tolstoy's *War and Peace:* to wit, that in the vastness of collective action, the nominal ruler disappears altogether; or that, when he remains in view, he is a mere cork carried by the irresistible stream. Beyond doubt, some men have greatness thrust upon them: the element of chance, on the human plane, cannot be eliminated. Still, there are circumstances in which personality plays a part it would be hard to deny.

Success does not provide a decisive proof that personality was present: it can always be claimed that the cause triumphed on its own merits, and that the alleged leader merely "muscled in." A negative argument may be more convincing: it seems that the perversion, the excesses, and above all the absence of personality at a crucial moment can deflect the course of history. Surely it is not indifferent that Louis XVI should have been so weak. In 1886, many Frenchmen were looking for a Napoleon and found only a Boulanger. If the General had had more substantial assets than a blond beard and a black horse, the fate of the country might have been changed. After both world wars, an appalling task of material and moral reconstruction faced the world. Only one country could assume leadership, because both her prestige and her power had enormously increased during the contest. It was fateful that in both cases the man in command should be a "ruler by accident," honorable, well-meaning, not without shrewdness, but blind to the larger issues. On the other hand, although even in George Washington himself personality, career, and mission never fully coincided, they could be simplified and harmonized into a grand historcial figure without too rough a distortion of the facts. Martyrdom achieved for Lincoln what a well-rounded life and serene old age had won for Washington: the nimbus obliterated all the contradictions. It must be admitted that Lenin, Churchill, and De Gaulle were at any rate "men of the hour."

It is probable that in the long run personalities are absorbed into the general trends. Napoleon will inevitably join Ozymandias, Sargon, Sennacherib, and perhaps King Arthur. He accelerated or impeded movements which he did not originate, and which proceeded without him. I believe it would already be possible to write a social history of the nineteenth century without mentioning his name. But "the long run" is too conveniently vague. We have not yet gone "back to Methuselah." On our modest scale, individual influences cannot be dismissed, even if they be delusive. For potent delusions are historical facts, and impotent truths are not. [13]

The Legend, as the term is used in history, is not necessarily a delusion, and even less a lie. Etymologically, it simply means "things

[13] It may seem a blasphemy to speak of "impotent truths"; *Magna est Veritas et praevalebit*. As an example of an impotent truth, I have already adduced the Copernican system: it is a truth on the grandest scale, yet without action upon history. The discovery of the planet Pluto affected us far less than *The Protocol of the Elders in Zion* or the Zinoviev letter, of doubtful authenticity.

History

to be read." Both in English and in French, the text which accompanies a drawing is still called the legend. Then it denotes something "worthy to be read," as in the *Golden Legend* of the saints, compiled by Jacobus de Voragine. The uncritical nature of such hagiographies may well have brought the word into disrepute: a legend, in the commonest sense, is a popular tradition without historical warrant. But the favorable meaning has not wholly evaporated, and the aura of the miraculous clings to the idea of legend. So we still call legends the authentic stories that transcend everyday experience: the most orthodox Napoleon-worshipers use the word Legend without qualms, and indeed with pride; when I called Marshal Foch *un héros de légende* to his face, he and the audience raised no protest.

An error, willful or innocent, is not by itself a legend; neither is a cool appraisal, however favorable. The "legendary" appears with the poetic glow that surrounds the facts; and it appears most clearly when there is a discrepancy, or even a disparity, between the facts and the glow. The legend often is pseudo-history; but it may also be deeply felt history, the only one which truly lives: not young Washington and the cherry tree, but the Father of his Country, first in war, first in peace, first in the hearts of his countrymen. When intense feelings cling to obscure or uncertain facts, the legend appears truer than a sober chronicle would be: this is the case with the founding of all great religions.

The effect produced by the legend upon popular imagination is of an artistic nature: a legend is an epic. So the legend picks out of factual history those elements which conform to the artistic canon and brings them into bold relief. If they do not exist in the record, the missing evidence is supplied. It is what the believers in the anti-Dreyfus legend ingeniously called "drawing a check on the bank of truth." Hence the invincible tendency to touch up history and make it conform to the rules of the drama: to create those historical characters that ought to have been there, those historical scenes that ought to have occurred, those historical words that ought to have been spoken. The liberation of Switzerland from the yoke of Austria demanded a hero; and the hero came, two hundred years later, in the guise of William Tell. Traces of his earthly sojourn are shown, just as visitors can see the actual cell of Dantès, Count of Monte Cristo. Lamartine reports in full the last supper of the Girondists, which possesses the same kind of ideal truth as the last conversation of Socrates with his disciples. Victor Hugo records a stirring discussion between Robespierre, Danton, and Marat. Barrère told the Convention not simply that the battleship *Le Vengeur* had been sunk in combat, but the way in which it must have perished for the greater glory of the Republic; and that inspired *gasconnade* cannot be dislodged from popular history.

Legends grow rank among "historical words." The popular mind demands *le mot juste,* the right, the inevitable expression, and coins it if the protagonist happens to miss his cue. Several days after Waterloo, Cambronne was credited with the noble phrase: "The Guard dies, but never surrenders." Modestly, he declined the honor; but posterity's judgment was against him. A whole generation later, the survivors of the epic struggle swore they all had heard the defiant words; indeed, they all had repeated them, like a well-drilled chorus. In the meantime, the sophisticates grew weary of its classic grandiloquence. About 1830, a wag, Genty, offered a substitute: "Do you know what Cambronne really said? He said: *Merde!*" The new version had the appeal of an outrageous paradox; it was in harmony with the Romantic ideal, already found in Longinus: a daring blend of the sublime and the vulgar. So the new legend started on its rival career. Victor Hugo gave it his pontifical blessing in a grand chapter of *Les Misérables.* Cambronne is now safely ensconced in his malodorous glory. It was reserved for Merezhkovsky, with the mysticism of his Slavic soul, to supply the ultimate refinement: *"Merde!* (said the General), and struck by a bullet in the forehead, drops dead." On our prosaic earthly plane, Cambronne remained alive until 1842. [14]

---

[14] Cf. Georges Lenôtre (Louis Léon Théodore Gosselin), *La Petite Histoire: Napoléon* (Paris: B. Grasset, 1932), pp. 233-239; Dmitri Merezhkovsky, *The Life of*

History

When martial glory has faded, General Pershing may yet be remembered as the man who did *not* say: "Lafayette, we are here!"

The legend, as we have defined it, transfigures not men only but events, institutions, causes. There is a legend of the nameless terror that filled men's hearts in the year 1000; there is a legend of the Inquisition and of the Jesuits; a legend of Chivalry (knighthood was in flower, as conscious pageantry, after its fruit had withered away); a legend of the Bastille; and above all, a legend of the French Revolution. Or rather there are two, fighting for the crown: devils and chimeras dire are as legitimate subjects of legends as angels, saints, and heroes. So legends of darkness tussle with legends of light, the Revolution of Victor Hugo's *Ninety-Three* with the Revolution of *The Gods are Athirst*. Julián Juderías has exposed *la leyenda negra,* which besmirched every achievement of ancient Spain, [15] and in the same spirit, José Vasconcelos tried to reclaim the colonial past of Mexico, traduced by the historians of *la Reforma*.[16] "On the ceiling above the grand staircase of the House of Archives at Budapest is a painting which represents the episode of the Communist revolt in Hungary. A mother draws to her heart the frightened children whom snarling wolves attack. Above the group are angels bringing the protection of Heaven to the threatened family. The angels are capitalistic angels, and the wolves are Communist wolves."[17] This quaint error may have been corrected by the present regime.

The legend of Charlemagne is linked with history by the slenderest thread. Between the achievements of the Frankish king and the mighty deeds of the fabulous Emperor, there was a lapse of two hundred and fifty years. The Carolingian epic cycle is no mere trans-

---

Napoleon tr. by Catherine Zregintzov (New York: E. P. Dutton, 1929), p. 302. Two of Proust's aristocratic characters play delicately with "the" word: the name *Cambremer,* they say, starts twice and stops modestly in the middle.

[15] Julián Juderías y Loyot, *La leyenda negra y la verdad histórica* (Madrid, 1914).

[16] José Vasconcelos, *Breve historia de México* (México, 1944).

[17] Sir John Maynard, Preface to *Russia in Flux* (New York: The Macmillan Co., 1948).

Education of a Humanist

formation of chronicle or folklore, but "a free creation of the intellect," heralding the spirit that was to inspire the Crusades.[18] The Charlemagne of heavy flesh and lusty blood was a Teuton, the Charlemagne of Romance a Frenchman. Legend made Charlemagne a saint; history does not ratify the verdict. (He was canonized, but by an antipope, so his halo is spurious.) The real Emperor, with long drooping moustaches, shaved his chin; his epic shadow is much more impressive with a "flowery" beard. All poets will have it, ungallantly, that his mother Bertha had large feet *(Berthe aux grands pieds)*. I doubt whether sober history gave us the size of her shoes.

The most instructive case of legend, however, is that of Napoleon's: it is *la Légende par excellence.* In magnitude, it dwarfs all the others; even Kircheisen could not number all the publications on the subject. The British, coolest to his fame, yet would rather read about him than about Wellington; he fascinates the Germans far more than Blücher; powerful minds, from Goethe to Thomas Mann, show signs of Napoleon-worship. There are few American homes without some Napoleonic item: a statuette, and engraving of Meissonier's "1814" (usually called "The Retreat from Russia"), a copy of Ludwig's best seller. The Legend, after more than a century, still has its mystic side. Dr. R. McNair Wilson vies with Dmitri Merezhkovsky in considering The Man as more than human, a Messiah; his book ends with the solemn words: "The Man had begun his everlasting Empire over the mind and spirit of humanity." [19] This transfiguration took place, not in remote and ignorant ages, but in the well-informed, critical, scientific nineteenth century. After five generations, and wars on immensely vaster scales than Napoleon's, the Legend has not lost its magic power.

I grew intensely interested in the subject as a baffling problem in culture. I was not concerned with the political aspect: Bonapartism is dead; nor primarily in the artistic: Napoleon has in-

---

[18] Cf. Gaston Paris, *Histoire Poétique de Charlemagne* (Paris, 1865), an early work, but masterly.

[19] R. McNair Wilson, *Napoleon The Man* (New York, 1928), p. 585.

History

spired surprisingly few masterpieces. What I wanted to investigate was the interrelation between the popular mind, conscious literature, and history. The origins of the Legend are complex and remain to a large extent mysterious. The facts alone do not suffice to account for it: the victories of the Revolution had been a greater miracle; ultimately Napoleon lost what the soldiers of Carnot had won. The ineptitude of Napoleon's enemies after his downfall, his own masterly dramatizing of his "martyrdom" at Saint Helena, are very important factors, but not decisive. The spontaneous imagination of the people played a curiously small part in starting the Legend. Two folk-like documents are constantly adduced: a song by Béranger and a popular narrative by Balzac; but both originated with very conscious bourgeois craftsmen. There was no work of commanding power that could serve as the nucleus of the new gospel. King Louis Philippe did foster the Legend, for shrewd purposes of his own; but he did not create it, and he nearly ran it to death with the overwhelming Second Burial, "the Return of the Ashes." My own theory is that the Legend arose in the Romantic era and as a manifestation of the Romantic spirit. The Man of Destiny takes his place among the great Romantic themes: Prometheus, Don Juan, Faust, the Wandering Jew. The Messianism which was to give the great efficiency manager such an incongruous halo was not in him, but in the later Romantic atmosphere. Napoleonism is of the same period as the New Christianity of Saint-Simon.[20]

Napoleon did exist in the flesh: the clever little books of J. B. Pérès *(Comme quoi Napoléon n'a jamais existé)* and Richard Whately *(Historic Doubt Relative to Napoleon Bonaparte)* are not positive contributions to history, but valid satires of excessive skepticism in the study of religion. Not only did he live and move among men, but from the moment he emerged into fame to his death, he

---

[20] Cf. my *Reflections on the Napoleonic Legend* (London and New York, 1924), and my *Napoleon III: An Interpretation* (Cambridge, Mass.: Harvard University Press, 1943), in which the theme and many of the instances mentioned above were discussed.

Education of a Humanist

lived in the limelight. We can account for practically every one of his days. We cannot, evidently, account for every one of his thoughts. We shall never know whether he did commit his worst blunders on the advice of Talleyrand, and to what degree he was sincere in his negotiations with England, Russia, or, in 1813, Metternich. Even the story of his attempted suicide in 1814 is blurred by conflicting testimonies. But, on the whole, the margin of incertitude is less with him than with most great characters in history.

The facts, then, are certain. In their interpretation, plain partisanship can easily be detected and discounted. We are on the firmest historical ground. The mysterious element is the aura which does not obliterate the facts, but transforms them altogether. Why is it that defeat adds even more to Napoleon's stature than victory? It is because we are not appraising events realistically, but in terms of sentiment, picturesqueness, drama. The Egyptian expedition was senseless; Napoleon suffered a humiliating setback at Acre; he left his army doomed to inevitable capitulation; yet the Oriental mirage enhanced his prestige. The Russian campaign was ill-conceived, ill-prepared, ill-managed: it does not take a genius to lose an army in the Russian plains. Yet the suffering and death of a half million men increased Napoleon's glory.

The most orthodox Napoleon-worshipers, many of them well-trained scholars, can tell the facts unflinchingly; but they never allow paltry facts to shake their faith. Three instances will suffice. General Colin R. Ballard[21] tells us that Napoleon was a play-actor and no gentleman; incapable of self-sacrifice and high ideals; "his plans failed because they were based on ignorance"; as a soldier, he lost six campaigns out of twelve. (The General might have added that four times he abandoned his army altogether.) But General Ballard asserts without hesitation: "I think he is the greatest man that ever lived."

Louis Madelin has written many books on the Napoleonic period, from his early *Fouché* to his recent *Talleyrand;* he has been en-

---
[21] Brigadier-General Colin R. Ballard, *Napoleon, an Outline* (New York, 1924).

History

gaged for years on a monumental *History of the Consulate and the Empire,* which is to comprise twelve large volumes. A favorite cliché of his is: "Napoleon created cities by a stroke of the pen," truly an epic touch. The Man from Missouri, searching for these fabulous cities, finds that they shrink into one, Napoléon-Vendée or La Roche-sur-Yon, a dismal county seat. Four years after the "stroke of the pen," Napoleon wished to see the result of his imperial fiat. Millions had been spent, but he found only a mud field. He drove his sword through the crumbling mud walls, raged at the engineer, slapped him in the face, and lost all interest in Napoléon-Vendée. I have seen the cities that Marshal Lyautey created in Morocco "by a stroke of the pen." It is a totally different story.

F. M. Kircheisen devoted his whole career to Napoleonic studies. He compiled an impressive bibliography, an iconography, a large-scale history, and a number of more popular volumes. He is no poet, but a plodding, conscientious worker. In his *Napoleon*,[22] a very convenient epitome, he tells us: "One of the many riddles in Napoleon's life is furnished by the problem why, with few exceptions, all in the Emperor's service, French and foreigners alike, were eager to lay down their lives for him." On the same page, twelve lines below, he quotes a letter from Napoleon to Clarke, the Minister of War: "Out of 747 recruits from the Aube Department, 485 have deserted. Give orders to have them arrested and sent back to the army." And that was in 1808, when the Emperor was at the peak of his glory: the eagerness of these young men to die for the demigod was very artfully disguised. I think we may trust Napoleon's figures rather than Kircheisen's opinions.

My study of the Napoleonic Legend was a by-product of my life-long interest in the Second Empire. Napoleon III was undoubtedly the heir of the Legend, although the Legend by itself could not have carried him to the throne. He revealed qualities of his own, radically

[22] F. M. Kircheisen, *Napoleon* (New York: Harcourt, Brace, and Co., 1932), p. 519.

Education of a Humanist

different from his uncle's; but, without his prestigious name, he would have been a minor Socialist reformer, a lesser Louis Blanc, perhaps a mere Cabet. Romantic imagination, by reshaping into a Prometheus the figure of a martinet, prepared the incredible career of Louis Napoleon.

At one miraculous moment, in December 1848, the confusion that was in Louis Napoleon's character mirrored exactly the confusion of the popular mind: an end to insurrections and to wordy debates; no new upheaval, but no return to the ancient regime; peace, without any sacrifice of dignity and even of prestige; the defense of property against the communists, but with a more generous social program than Orleanist timidity and selfishness could possibly offer.

The result was an equivocal regime (but is it not the very nature of all regimes to be equivocal?), gaudy, materialistic, oppressive, and corrupt in many ways; yet with a surviving glow of the Forty-eighters' dream, with a vigorous grasp of immediate realities, and an unexpected power to peer into the future; the paradoxical alliance of the Army, the Church, and the Stock Exchange, led by a gentle dreamer who was "Saint-Simon on horseback." That regime gave France twenty years of order and prosperity. As late as May 1870, it won a sweeping victory in a free plebiscite. An attaching and disquieting period, mottled, damaged, with great achievements to its credit, and promises which the Third Republic has dimmed.

Now, Napoleon III is the victim of a legend of darkness, as much as Napoleon I is the beneficiary of a legend of light. For the last fifty years, competent historians, particularly F. A. Simpson in England and Paul Guériot in France, have dealt very fairly with the enigmatic Emperor. Octave Aubry, a very capable popularizer, gave an excellent epitome of the period which was widely read in France and in America.[23] Yet the Black Legend remains: automatically, even good scholars (not specialists in the field) cannot refer to the Man of Sedan without a sneer. Victor Hugo's deadly antithesis—Napoleon

---

[23] There is little to recommend Philip Guedalla's *Second Empire,* except its coruscating and truly Jacques Offenbach style.

the Great, Napoleon the Little—still rules our minds. Even H. A. L. Fisher, conventional but well-informed and shrewd, ends on that note his little book on Bonapartism.

Opinions and personal preferences may easily be dismissed, and I shall not attempt to compare the ideals of the two sovereigns: let us be realistic. Most readers will be shocked if I assert that pragmatically, on the basis of plain, palpable facts, the Second Empire was more successful than the First. It lasted longer. It was better supported by public opinion: the plebiscites of Napoleon I were the merest farces— open registers upon which, in certain cases, the names of the whole precinct were written by the same hand; the first and the last plebiscites in favor of Louis Napoleon, his election to the Presidency in December 1848 and the vote of May 8, 1870, were unquestionably free. Profiteering and graft were rife under the nephew, but corruption was even worse under the uncle; Talleyrand among civil servants, Masséna among the military, are only outstanding examples. It cannot be doubted that the Second Empire increased the prosperity of France far more than the First. The great Napoleon left hardly a single completed building in Paris: he was satisfied with "strokes of the pen"; the Little Napoleon transformed his capital. The Second Empire did much for the people, even in the way of elementary education; the First grandly ignored such cares altogether. Under Napoleon I, public opinion was completely stifled; all the great writers were in opposition or in exile; under Napoleon III, although the press could be fined for peccadilloes, although critics had to use the rapier of allusion and irony, thought and expression were remarkably free. The important point to remember is not that Baudelaire and Flaubert were haled before imperial courts of justice,[24] but that, under the "tyranny," they could write as they did, be published, and find a public.

To carry the paradox further—and by paradox I mean an unfamiliar truth—even in "the field of glory" the Second Empire

[24] Flaubert was acquitted, Baudelaire sentenced to a trifling fine (50 francs), which the Empress offered to pay.

Education of a Humanist

came off actually better than the First. The Conquering Hero lost not only everything he had grabbed, but everything also that the Revolution had acquired by 1795; if Napoleon III lost Alsace-Lorraine, he had won Savoy and Nice. Napoleon I lost six campaigns out of twelve, Napoleon III one out of four (the withdrawal from Mexico was not due to military defeat). Both Emperors suffered a crushing disaster in their last battle, which caused the collapse of their throne. But, after Waterloo, Napoleon I fled, leaving his routed soldiers to shift for themselves (it was the fourth time); at Sedan, Napoleon III sought death and shared the fate of his army.

I am not attempting to prove that Napoleon I was a nincompoop and Napoleon III a genius too great for his times. Both regimes and both men were strangely compounded of good and evil. I am simply attempting, as an old student and teacher of history, to define history. And I find that historians, scrupulous and clear-sighted as they may be in the handling of details, are as a rule governed by the common prejudices of their time. They conscientiously bring their hodful of documents, but they do not question the fundamental assumptions, Napoleon the Great, Napoleon the Little. Their preconceptions are proof against the facts; they soar above the facts; they belong to another realm altogether, the realm of imagination and passion, the realm of epic, drama, and romance, the realm of legend.

In such a realm, glamour, not goodness and truth, is the final argument. The prestige of the Hero is of the same order as that of the Fatal Beauty. The elders of Troy whispered, as Helen passed by in the perfection of her loveliness: "For the sake of such a woman, it is meet that a city should perish." I have read many books on the French Revolution, from Burke's *Reflections* to Katherine Anthony's and Stefan Zweig's, in which the single lodestar was the charm of Marie Antoinette. She might be frivolous, vain, swayed by caprice, wholly out of touch with French thought and feeling, arrogant, obstinate: every biographer becomes a Barnave or a Fersen. Even the slightly soiled Josephine has her meretricious halo. Walter Geer summed up her "legend" in his contrasting titles: *Napoleon and*

History

Josephine: The Rise of the Empire; Napoleon and Marie-Louise: The Fall of the Empire. People smiled maliciously at Victor Cousin, long the dictator of French philosophy, who, in his old age, fell in love retrospectively with those amazons in furbelows, the great ladies of the *Fronde*. Who has the right to jeer? Every Dryasdust worships the stars of the historical screen.

There is a Hollywood side to historical prestige; there is a philosophical one as well. It was Vico who first taught clearly that legends were not mere fables and willful lies, but the expression of deep experiences in the collective soul. The hero would remain but a picturesque character, like Lawrence of Arabia, and the great feat but a chance episode, unless they stood for something greater than the man or the deed. They must transcend the level of the factual, they must be transmuted into symbols to assume their full historical stature.

This is the meaning of *myths,* and myths are the warp and woof of history. Louis XVI is not a well-meaning lump of a man: he is Monarchy, ten centuries through which France struggled to achieve consciousness. In another light, he appears to us as the arch-defender of intolerable abuses. Napoleon is the Revolution with sword and crown, the Prometheus of Democracy. Napoleon III is the Super-Policeman protecting the moneybags, in trappings filched from his uncle. They are all figures from noble allegorical paintings or rough political cartoons. If they were but what they are, who would give them a second thought?

In the popular mind (and we are all "common men" in this respect) abstractions have a tendency to turn themselves into human characters: the Incarnation is a perpetual miracle. Every code of laws posits a lawgiver: Moses, Lycurgus, Draco, Numa, Napoleon. Independence needs a leader: the bucolic Swiss evolved William Tell, and sensible Uruguay, nearly a century after the event, voted that Artigas was to be the national hero. The Bolshevist Revolution, against its own principles, has now a shrine: the tomb where lies the imperishable body of Lenin. The gradual process of invention is focused into a single name; people forget that Stephenson simply entered his *Rocket* for a locomotive contest, and believe that the locomotive sprang from his demiurgic brain as Minerva, full-armed, from the aching head of Jupiter.

Language, even at its tritest, is a code of symbols, and so is history. But abstractions are not invariably embodied into gods, demigods, heroes, and fiends. They have a life of their own. The thoughtful historian who seeks to escape from the purely biographical believes in "spirits" (also known as "ghosts") such as "Christianity," "France," or "the Revolution." Every collective movement is a myth: the material reality is made up of so many men who said or did certain things. Yet their individual action is not history: that Jacques Durand, journeyman tailor, went from the Palais-Royal to the Bastille is insignificant—unless it happened on July 14, 1789. The mob, the day, the spirit, become the essential facts. History is the life, the struggle, and the death of such gigantic shadows.

This is emphatically true of the protagonists in modern history, the nations. A nation is an act of faith: it exists only in so far as men are willing to work, suffer, and die for their faith. A nation can be drawn and painted on the map, which is a symbolic picture: but did Nature make Oregon and Florida one, or separate Arizona from Sonora? The United States would vanish like a dream if we no longer believed in the United States. The Congo Free State had all the material paraphernalia of a nation: a territory, a flag, even a sovereign "with flowery beard": but it had no life. Poland, torn asunder, maintained herself in the minds and hearts of men for over a hundred years.

The Romans had a *genius* or spirit for every act in life and every institution: they erected an altar to "the Genius of Indirect Taxation." We do not express our mythology in such formal terms; but our faith reveals itself through our works. Men are willing to give their wealth and even their lives for the defense of the Profit Motive; they accept compulsory military training in order to maintain Free

History

Enterprise. A Russian pauper will be sent to slaughter for the sake of Communism, although he has no decent share of earthly goods; and he will be taught to call his vague millennial dreams Dialectic Materialism.

This is no satire, but a candid inquiry. History is a fascinating science, but the realities which form its subject matter are myths and legends. Dispel man's dreams of terror and bliss: history shall dissolve, leaving not a rack behind.

VAE VICTIS!

> Whatever is, is right.
> Die Weltgeschichte ist das Weltgericht.

To assert, as we have done, that the proper field of history is the impalpable realm of symbols is not to question its validity. Science does not evaporate in the impalpable. Medicine now ascribes certain diseases to filtrable viruses, which are not obvious to the naked eye; and modern physics deals with the innermost mysteries of the atom, which elude common instruments and the common mind.

Before myths and legends achieve the dignity of history, they have to fulfill two conditions. First, they must command or have commanded belief: else their place is in the vast and delightful domain of fiction. There are miracles recorded in *Vathek*, in *The Shaving of Shagpat*, in *Le Voyage d'Urien*, in *Jurgen:* but no historicity is claimed for them. In the second place, the myths must translate themselves into the world of facts, as guides for the efforts of men. However intense it might be, a purely abstract belief, without proof and without influence, would not be history. It would not be religion either; its sole refuge would be metaphysics. On the contrary, fiction, even when it is frankly fictitious, becomes an element in history if it urges and directs action. A novel with a purpose, if it truly serves its purpose, becomes an event. *Uncle Tom's Cabin*, it was said, was worth an army.

Education of a Humanist

My contention, therefore, is that historians cannot be indiscriminate fact-collectors: they must use judgment. Conscious deeds, which constitute history, are directed by opinion; and opinion rationalizes our hopes and fears. Confessors and judges must investigate intentions. The same act—the killing of a man—may be a pure accident; the result of negligence; legitimate defense; "honorable" duel; the unpremeditated outcome of a sudden quarrel; deliberate murder (with a whole gamut of possible motives); the execution of a lawful sentence; military duty. If the historian were to present the case in terms of the murderer's own code, he would be an advocate, not a judge. There are some sects which believe that it is pleasing in God's sight to exterminate His enemies; and the anarchists who killed Carnot, the Empress Elizabeth, and McKinley were heroes in their own eyes. Penetration and sympathy are great virtues, but they will not suffice if they are one-sided. They must also apply to the victims, who may have thought themselves entitled to life, liberty, and the pursuit of happiness. They must also apply to the judges and executioners, who performed their duty in disposing of the assassins. It would be a very rudimentary kind of history that would note, statistically, so many people were killed in automobile accidents; so many at Dachau and Buchenwald; so many at Hiroshima. History is not merely a process, it is a trial: perhaps, as in Kafka's nightmare, a trial in which neither the accusation, the judge, nor the law is ever defined. History has often been called a court; surely no Christian and no scientist will acknowledge it as the tribunal of ultimate jurisdiction.[25]

[25] Schiller's famous phrase, "World History is World Judgment," both in the various translations and in the original, is ambiguous. (*Schiller* in German is "changing of colors, opalescence, iridescence.") *Gericht* can be rendered either by "sentence" or "court" (it also means a "dish"—in Biblical language, a "mess"). It is often understood to mean that History (that is, the chain of events) is self-retributive; if an empire falls, it is because it deserved to fall; history simply exposes the fatal weakness. Or it may mean that History (as an activity of the human mind) passes judgment upon the events. The just man may be martyred, as Socrates was; so may the just nation, as many believe was the case with Finland; the higher court of History quashes the brutal verdict. In his poem "Resignation," Schiller holds that

History

I must insist, for "scientific" historians vehemently deny that they are showing any sense. I must repeat that random facts are not history, and that, if we want to tell how *it* actually happened, we first have to define the *it*. To dismiss certain characters or events as irrelevant is not merely using judgment, but passing judgment. There is no heavier sentence on a man or a cause than declaring they do not count: oblivion, in history, is the death penalty. It is true that many historians write their decisions according to a law which they do not openly confess. They might be said to describe historical facts as "relevant" to a scheme of relevancy which does not exist, just as Kant said of art that it was *Zweckmässigkeit ohne Zweck,* adequacy to purpose without purpose. But, avowed or not, the pattern is there that gives consistency to the historian's thought.

In order further to exasperate my learned colleagues, I shall call that hidden pattern their "implicit Utopia." All of them use artful variations of the formula which runs like a thread of gold through that masterly satire, *1066 and All That:* "It was a good thing, because . . ." Because it conformed with what in their minds was inevitably right. Yet the "bad thing," a challenge to that necessity, is a reality also; it registers in history only because it seemed at one time to have some chance of success. History records attacks against the vested interests of institutions, nations, and men: it cannot report any violation of the law of gravitation. In history there is an alternative, which does not exist in the physical sciences. Even in biology, the element of dramatic suspense intervenes. If a man is stricken with a deadly disease, it is "inevitable" that he should die—unless a competent doctor be called in time, who proves that the disease was not deadly.

"Whatever is, is right," is one of those solemn affirmations which, behind their impressive masks, are vacuity itself. Government, justice, science, religion, are all engaged in a fight against alleged

---

man must choose between Hope (idealism) and Enjoyment (materialism). In this context, his line might be interpreted as: the material record of the world (History) is the condemnation of the world.

necessity. They choose sides according to certain principles: science does not admit that astrology is as good as astronomy, or witchcraft as efficient as medicine. A "good thing," even though premature and doomed to defeat, is one that favors the processes of which we approve: for Protestants, Wyclif and Hus were good things, in spite of their failure. A "bad thing," even though well meaning and apparently successful for a while, is one that has a retarding effect: I have come to believe with Goldwin Smith that the French Revolution was a bad thing. For William L. Langer, our Vichy gamble was a good thing, because, from day to day, it was consonant with American interests as he understands them: his implicit Utopia. For those whose retrospective Utopia is the thirteenth century, every development is a bad thing if it carries us away from that ideal. For those whose ideal is Péguy's—the Universal Socialist Republic—everything is a bad thing that hinders the coming of that millennium. Every historian who has any sense has a sense of right and wrong (not necessarily coinciding with ours); therefore, he is a philosopher in spite of himself, and what he holds to be right is his Utopia.

There are innumerable philosophies of history, but they may be roughly classified under five heads: the theocratic, the liberal, the economic, the racial, and the GOK.[26] The *theocratic* is most clearly typified by Bossuet's *Discourse on Universal History,* but it is found in Carlyle, Hugo,[27] Michelet, Péguy, Merezhkovsky. The *liberal* was quasi official for nearly two centuries: Montesquieu, Voltaire, Hume, Gibbon, Macaulay, Lecky, Woodrow Wilson, Justo Sierra (I mention Justo Sierra because he has been officially proclaimed *el Maestro de las Américas;* for those who believe in continental solidarity, that includes us among his pupils). The *economic* is at present threatening to strangle all its rivals. The first brilliant victory

[26] GOK: a lady kept very accurate and well-balanced accounts. Her husband was intrigued by a constantly recurring entry: GOK. "Oh! that means *God only knows."* Goethe and Robert Browning, by the way, when asked for the meaning of some poem of theirs, joined the GOK school of exegesis.

[27] The victor of Waterloo was not Blücher or Wellington, but God. Napoleon was in God's way: *Il gênait Dieu.*

History

of that school was Rousseau's *Discourse on Inequality;* for Jean Jacques, the turning point in world history, the origin of all our ills, was the creation of private property. An "awful example" of the *racial* is Houston Stewart Chamberlain's *Foundations of the Nineteenth Century*. But racialism is rampant everywhere: Anglo-Saxon pride, the White Man's burden, Slavophilism, Judaism, anti-semitism. As for the GOK historians, their name is Legion. Few philosophies of history are absolutely pure; elementary mathematics will tell us how many combinations of those five elements are possible.

But, rather than in the Five Philosophies, I am interested in two essential attitudes which affect all historical writing: the sentimental and the realistic.

We have already touched upon the sentimental when discussing heroes and fatal beauties. People write and read history by the canons of the epic, the romance, and the drama. This may cut right across a man's philosophy. He may be a Liberal, or an Economist, yet be unable to resist the fascination of Marie Antoinette or Napoleon. By sentimental, I do not mean soft and mawkish: the tough man may be swayed by his sympathy with the tough hero. The fanatical loyalty of many Nazi murderers to their Führer was unquestionably sentiment.

The great law of history seems to be Aristotle's law of tragedy: we most enjoy, as a spectacle, the downfall of a good man, when the fall is justified by some flaw in his being, and especially when that flaw is an exaggeration of his chief virtue: "The pity of it . . ." The most perfect example, because it is the simplest, is the story of Roland: the great paladin perished, gloriously, because he was too proud to sound his horn in time. The grandest is the Napoleonic saga: the daimonic ambition of the Corsican raised him to the pinnacle, then induced him to gamble away the world he had won.

Sentimental history can be soft; it revels in a good cry; it dotes on martyrs, defeated heroes, lost causes: Mary Stuart, the Jacobites, the French aristocrats on the scaffold, Napoleon at Saint Helena, Kosciusko's dying cry: "Finis Poloniae!" (he did not say it, and he

Education of a Humanist

died twenty years later; but it would be callous to spoil a good tale); in Mexico, the abortive revolts of Hidalgo and Morelos, the boy heroes dashing themselves from the heights of Chapultepec; in our own country, the Confederacy and Robert E. Lee. It is as difficult for a successful hero to enter Valhalla as for a camel to go through the eye of a needle. Washington performed that miracle, but Lincoln needed Wilkes Booth. The glorification of the fallen is human enough, without dragging in the masochism which lurks in every man. For the defeated, an orgy of self-pity is their only compensation; the victors take conscious pride and pleasure in their own chivalrousness. When it does not conflict with our interests, we are for the underdog, even though the underdog be the vicious one.

Sentiment is an enormous factor, but so erratic that the final result may be blurred or even negative. It picks out its heroes and its villains almost at random: at one time we were tempted to place Rommel far above Montgomery, although the pursuit was a more arduous task than the retreat. It turns against them with ferocity: at one time Lamartine, Napoleon III, Bazaine, Trotsky, Pétain were popular idols. During the First World War, we transfigured all Frenchmen and Belgians into angels with flaming swords (the British were only second-class angels). Then, ashamed of our orgy of sentiment, we claimed that we had been gulled by lying propaganda, and the reaction was disastrous.

Historical best sellers reek with sentiment. But in serious history, the realistic deformation is far more prevalent, more insidious, and more damaging. Realism is chivalry in reverse: already in the Middle Ages, the high-flown romances had their counterparts in the mocking, bawdy, cynical tales. The realistic spirit consists not merely in noting defeat as a fact, but in jeering at the defeated, in gloating over the *fait accompli,* even though it be manifestly a crime. Thus we escape, in our hearts, the obloquy of defeat; we are one with the victors, like the small boys who, cowering, applaud the bully.

It is a commonplace of history that, after a miraculous start, the career of Lafayette was a constant series of disappointments and

History

failures. This made him the laughing-stock of all tough-minded historians. The fool believed in liberty, decency, generosity: therefore he was despised by Mirabeau and Talleyrand—there was no nonsense about *them!* He was distrusted by the Queen, driven into exile by the Revolutionaries, kept in obscurity by Napoleon, brushed aside by the returned Bourbons. He failed, not because he was wrong or because he was weak, but because the good and the wise, in their halfheartedness, denied him their support. They preferred to follow more "vigorous" leaders, Marie Antoinette, Danton, Robespierre, Napoleon, who led them into disastrous blind alleys. Repeatedly, and as late as 1830, he could have snatched power: he refused to do so, not out of cowardice, but out of honorable and perhaps quixotic scruples. Had the "enlightened" classes been true to their own spirit, which was that of Lafayette, the Revolution of 1789 would have been bloodless and permanent.[28]

In my opinion, the outstanding case of the *Vae Victis!* is our treatment of the European revolutions of 1848. We have left "the Spirit of 1848" triumphant in February. Woe to the defeated! It is a commonplace of history that, to quote Franz Werfel, not the murderer but the murdered is guilty. The social and democratic Second Republic was killed in June: therefore it deserved to die, like Socrates, like Lincoln, like Madero, like Jaurès, like the Spanish Republic. I am of a paradoxical turn of mind: I am not convinced that every assassin is inevitably God's chosen instrument. After all, the Devil too has his share in human affairs.

It is easy enough to sneer: "What would you expect with a poet at the helm?" Remember that the poet, Lamartine, against the shrewd practical people, had pointed out the dangers of the Napoleonic Legend; that against Thiers, he had understood the future of

[28] I know too little about Russian affairs to venture an opinion about Kerensky. We now admit that Kornilov, who first stabbed him, was wrong. Are we certain that Lenin, who gave him the *coup de grâce*, was right? A striking example of the *Vae Victis!* attitude was our indecent haste, in 1940, to consider the fall of France as deserved doom. Only the Channel saved England from the same fate. If trial by the sword proved France wrong, it proved Hitler right—which is absurd.

Education of a Humanist

railways. For a few weeks, Lamartine provided a definite, moderate, and at the same time generous leadership. It is easy enough to say that the new leaders were inexperienced. They were only too willing to secure the collaboration of the old hands. But the trained statesmen of the fallen regime either held themselves aloof or rallied to the new order with the clearly expressed purpose of sabotaging it. It is easy enough to say that the revolutionists wanted a sudden and total upheaval: only it is not true. The masses showed remarkable forbearance. There were no massacres, no looting, no confiscation. The people would have been satisfied with a very short step at a time, provided it had been a step in the right direction. In 1848 as in 1789, the working classes were not opposed to gradualism; but they could not tolerate the total denial of the principles for which they had fought, and which had just been officially proclaimed.

It seemed as though February 1848 had marked the triumph of generosity over meanness. But meanness soon reasserted itself. The survivors of the Louis Philippe era did not turn against the Revolution because, after a fair trial, it had proved a failure: they made it fail, through concerted, deliberate efforts. And the "sound" men of 1848 did not condemn the Revolution a priori because it was bad, the explosion of brutal instincts: they condemned it because it was good, the dream of "idealistic" fools who believed that there was something higher in the world than the pursuit of immediate, material, personal profit. As good "realists," they proclaimed: "Evil, be thou my good!" They committed the Great Refusal.

The focal point of the struggle was the fate of the National Workshops. These, indispensable as an emergency relief measure, received a name borrowed from Louis Blanc: but they were not even a caricature of his scheme. Entrusted to a man whose sole desire was to prove the folly of socialistic planning, they were systematically made futile. When the absurdity became flagrant, the National Workshops were suppressed, as they had been managed, with a willful clumsiness that was intended as a challenge. The workers knew that this was a final showdown. With "the right to a

History

job" made a farce, it was all the promises of the social and democratic Republic that were destroyed.

The Parisian working men rose to save the four-month-old revolution, just as, on July 14, 1789, their grandfathers had risen to check the return of the ancient regime. A soldier, trained on Algerian battlefields, was put in command. General Cavaignac was an honest man and a good republican. But he did not understand that the workers were standing for the essential principles of the new republic. To his military mind, insurrection was anarchy. He repressed the uprising with unexampled ferocity, and deserved to be called "the butcher of June." Order was restored: but it was the old order. The democratic and social republic was dead. The equivocal regime which dragged on its life for three years longer had but one thought: the hatred and fear of democracy. The Second Empire, which at any rate had touches of daring and generosity, came as a relief.

It is not invariably idle to inquire what might have been. History is past politics, which once were present; and we know that present politics can take a wrong turn. When we read the program, when we recapture the spirit, of the men of '48, we feel that on all essential points they were in the right against the victors. What they were striving for, we are struggling for now. "They were ahead of their time?" No: they were their time. It is the alleged elite who were behind. Had the substantial, the competent men placed their technical skill, without mental reservation, at the service of the new ideas, we might have had, in the fifties of the last century, a federal Europe, free and fraternal, democratic, liberal, fearlessly seeking social justice. The wrong choice of a ruling group may retard human development by more than a hundred years.

In June 1848, France, that is to say, the *bourgeoisie* and the peasant proprietors, deliberately chose privilege as its goal. Generosity was condemned as romantic, sentimental, and utopian. Meanness was glorified under the name of "realism." Henceforth, for two generations, realism ruled art and literature; but it also dominated the political and economic world. Adam Smith, the father of the competitive system, was optimistic and benevolent; he believed in the "guiding hand" that harmonized the interests of men. Orthodox economics now assumed a somber Darwinian hue: a pitiless struggle for life and the survival of the fittest, that is to say, of the most ruthless. Bismarck, who had helped sabotage the Congress of Frankfort, substituted for the generous aspirations of the Forty-eighters a "realistic" policy of blood and iron. The profiteers of the Second Empire improved on Guizot's gospel. Get rich, but, since financial success is the supreme good, get rich quickly and make a splurge.

The worst of this transformation was found in Socialism itself. It denied its own inner light and borrowed the harshness of the bourgeois victors. The generous aspirations of Saint-Simon, Louis Blanc, Proudhon, were spurned as "Utopian." Socialism became as realistic, as scientific, as its rival Manchesterianism. It gloated over the iron law of wages and the inexorable processes of dialectic materialism. Humanity, democracy, religion, brotherhood? Nonsense. We must be "realistic," and every wise man, after the terrible lesson of 1848, knows that only meanness is real: material order, material gain, material power.

For a hundred years the most capable men have been asserting: "Generosity is a foolish dream." Not profiteers and politicians merely: this would be justifiable as a plea *pro domo;* but teachers, historians, philosophers, who ought to know better, and to whom cynicism brings no reward. The very best strike a compromise: they profess an *Excelsior!* rule of life on Sunday at eleven o'clock. "Of course, we are devoted to religion, to humanity, to democracy, to the service of our fellow men. But on Monday, we must be realistic. We have a rendezvous with destiny; but that can wait. In the meantime—in the *mean* time—there are a few deals to be closed. Shady or not, who cares? One must not be a perfectionist."

Romantic idealism, defeated, refused to die. It avenged itself by poisoning its conquerors. It survived as a remorse. Baudelaire and Flaubert were shamefaced, tormented Romanticists, masochists

History

flagellating their own undying and despised Romanticism. In politics, the realistic generations indulged in a debased form of Romanticism, the worship of power in its most brutal form, imperialism. The materialistic France of the fifties and sixties wore a gaudy mask of pseudo-Napoleonic glory. Manchesterian England came to be ruled by a spurious Romanticist with an Oriental imagination, Disraeli, who manufactured the bejeweled and unconvincing imperial crown of India. Germany gave up the genuine idealism of Frankfort for the make-believe idealism of the Wagnerian opera; and Bismarck, who posed as the arch-realist, created a monstrosity—an Empire with medieval trappings to govern a scientific and industrial nation.

The spirit of 1848, repressed, reviled, was not extinguished. My earliest definite recollection goes back to 1885, when I saw the funerals of Victor Hugo. The homage of the great city went first of all not to the poet, but to the Forty-eighter, in whose soul the service of God and the service of man were one. The leaders of the Dreyfus crusade, Zola, Jaurès, even Clemenceau, even Anatole France, were the conscious heirs of 1848. So was Charles Péguy, the Catholic poet, who dedicated his first *Joan of Arc* "to those who have labored and suffered for the Universal Socialist Republic."

The reader may have thought that in this discussion I was indulging in sheer destructive criticism, which could only lead to Pyrrhonism, irremediable and barren. "History is a pack of lies agreed upon," said Napoleon; and the American Napoleon, Henry Ford, echoed: "History is bunk."

It will be seen that my conclusion is positive enough: I am the reverse of a skeptic. And that conclusion is very simple: history is the tale of human deeds, and the historian cannot help being human. Because he is human, he is bound to err; but he is not bound to persevere in error. Because he is human, he cannot be excused from the disciplines which guide his fellow men: he must use his mind and not merely his pack of slips. He must have a

Education of a Humanist

sense of values: facts for him must have a significance. Like the engineer, the scientist, the judge, he must not cheat himself or other men. He must test his facts according to the strictest rules of evidence. But the facts must be relevant.

So I am simply pleading for Humanism in history; for history to me is the core of humanistic studies. History is an essential part of culture as defined by Matthew Arnold: "a pursuit of our total perfection, by means of getting to know, in all matters which most concern us, the best which has been thought and said [*and done*] in the world; and through that knowledge, turning a stream of fresh and free thought upon our stock notions and habits."

We shall not recover our integrity until our free critical spirit be made valid on Sunday, and until our spiritual inspiration pervades our working week. Our religion, our science, our political system, our social regime, must be brought into harmony. The defeatist realism that triumphed in June 1848 makes for disruption. We must seek unity again, not in the syntheses of the past, not in any single dogma or doctrine, but in an all-embracing spirit. This is the goal of the Humanities. When we realize that intellectual chaos is weakness, that greed is sin, that privilege is mutilation, that generosity is wisdom, then we shall be again on the high road which we missed in 1848.

What awaits us on that high road? The millennium? If the historian has learned anything, he must shake his head: the quest is unending. We shall encounter more trials, greater trials perhaps, but at any rate on a less sordid, less stupid plane. In human terms, progress has but one meaning: to discover nobler causes of suffering.

VAE VICTORIBUS!

Harold Nicolson closes his reminiscences of the Paris Peace Conference [29] with the signing of the Versailles Treaty. Here are the last words of that disenchanted chronicle: "Celebrations in the hotel afterwards. We are given free champagne at the expense of the

[29] *Peacemaking 1919* (Boston: Houghton Mifflin Co., 1933), p. 371.

History

taxpayer. It is very bad champagne. Go out on to the boulevards afterwards. To bed, sick of life."

We have won an even more sweeping victory, the greatest of all time, in the magnitude of the struggle, the nobility of the professed aims, the completeness of the enemy's surrender; and our souls also are sick unto death. I do not believe in historical laws, because history, forever in the making, cannot repeat itself. Still, there are blurred recurring patterns, which may serve as warnings. One of them is aptly figured by the Nike of Samothrace, the glory of the Louvre: ready to take wing, and decapitated. Victory is frustration. Had the ritual champagne served to Nicolson been of the best, the morrow would none the less have brought its inexorable *Katzenjammer*.

For this feeling of mingled bewilderment and shame, there are many obvious reasons upon which I need not dwell. Overstrain, nervous exhaustion, do not go far to explain it. A great effort might be followed by welcome rest of body and peace of mind instead of a dejection "void, dark, and drear," tinged with torturing anguish. The cause lies deeper than a purely physical reaction. To a large extent, its root is unconfessed remorse. In a death struggle, scruples are silenced. Retaliation, and the will to conquer, absolve and indeed sanctify every deed of violence or treachery. When the need is removed, the means appear in all their horror. "Marching through Georgia," attempting to starve millions of women and children through a rigorous blockade, blasting German, Italian, Japanese, and French cities were necessities so dire that they leave a humane conscience uneasy. Then victory is the reward of sheer power, and power is brutal. We have not won the argument. We have forced Germany and Japan into unconditional surrender, by convincing them not that our aims were loftier, but that our instruments of torture were more effective. Victory only confirms the Bismarck-Hitler conception: Might is Right.

Worst of all, it is not merely the need for unstinted effort that disappears with victory: it is also the ideal that inspired and sustained our endeavor. War, sordid and feral in execution, offers undoubted elements of heroic grandeur. Our armed forces were not impelled by the Profit Motive; the civilians themselves accepted discomforts and sacrifices in a stoic spirit. Looters abroad and profiteers at home were a minority, and universally condemned. We were uplifted by the promises of the Atlantic Charter and the Four Freedoms. Without such an incentive, our enormous potential would have remained useless, as it was in the shameful days of isolation and neutrality. The essential element of power is will power, which implies a purpose, a conviction, and a dream. But as soon as the roar was stilled, the small shrill voice of the Realist was heard. "Arguments of a sentimental or ideological character are dangerous if they are made the basis for foreign policy. They have validity only if they can be made to coincide with real national interests." And by *real* is meant *material* and *immediate:* what can we get out of all this in the form of power, prestige, and wealth? All our professions of fighting for liberty and justice, then, were sheer hypocrisy, tricks that were justified only if they paid. But other tricks, like the Darlan deal or the Yalta surrender, seemed at the time even more clever and more profitable. The dignity of man everywhere, the desire to breathe freely in a free world, are not "real" but "ideological and sentimental"; hope at long range is sheer Utopia. We had expected our men to be heroes, to seek the highest perfection of their nature, with death as the supreme test: "Greater love hath no man. . . ." Then we turned abruptly round and proclaimed that perfectionists were fools.

The worst elements of war were projected into the peace era: power politics, secrecy, jealousy, and fear. But the redeeming features of the grand alliance were scornfully eliminated: the spirit of sacrifice, the merging of minor differences, the subordination of petty interests, global planning. So the new world, for which mankind was so desperately waiting, died at birth in San Francisco of congenital realism. Every hope served by the sword is in peril of the sword. I am not preaching absolute pacifism or Christian

History

anarchy. Man may be justified in destroying wild beasts, especially when they hunt in packs and wear human masks; never forgetting, however, that a metaphor is an illustration, not an argument. As a friend of Nicolson's, Eddie Marsh, put it: "Success is beastly, isn't it?" For triumph means vulgar gloating and breeds hatred. We have yet to learn the wisdom taught by Paul Verlaine and Woodrow Wilson: there can be no peace founded on victory.

All this applies to victories won in battle. But the same disenchantment arises even when no blood is shed. This deeper frustration will be the subject of the present inquiry.

To start with a personal experience: the bitterest day in my life was December 6, 1938, when a treaty of peace and amity was signed between Daladier's France and Hitler's Germany. For three decades, I had been urging a Franco-German understanding. At last my hopes were fulfilled. It was as though a man should meet, after a long absence, the girl of his boyish dreams, turned prostitute.

It is possible for victory to lose all power to save, even though bloodless and unsullied, when it has been too long deferred. It is a strange truth that even the purest causes do not "keep." There was something in the Versailles Treaty more disappointing than the few and minor infractions of Wilsonian self-determination: it was self-determination itself. It had turned rancid in the form of exclusive and petty nationalism, "Ourselves alone." The principle that the peoples have the right to shape their own destinies, to unite or secede as they see fit, was ripe at the end of the Napoleonic wars. It should have prevailed at the Vienna settlement in 1814-1815, for the liberation movement throughout Europe had been a people's crusade. But the pre-Revolutionary doctrine of dynastic legitimacy was imposed upon the continent by men whose cleverness had paralyzed their intelligence, Metternich and Talleyrand. 1848 seemed for a brief season the belated triumph of the peoples. Europe could have become then, according to the luminous dream of Michelet, a group of free and friendly families. But reaction prevailed again; Russia made the world safe for Francis Joseph and Bismarck; and the chance was

Education of a Humanist

lost. By 1918, nationalism had not lost its validity; it was as true as ever that an Italian should not forcibly be turned into a German, or a Yugoslav into an Italian; but the idea had lost its primacy. The fully organized countries, like England or France, took nationalism for granted, as a corollary of democracy; the problem now was to curb its excesses. The nations still struggling for full recognition, from Ireland to Poland, had been arrested in their thought because the solution was overdue. The pressing question was to organize Europe, economically and therefore politically. What was needed, for instance, was not to break up the unity of the Danubian basin, but on the contrary to extend the benefit of free trade in men, goods, and ideas all the way from the Russian border to the Atlantic, and from the Pole to the Sahara. Cultural autonomy, possibly on a personal rather than a territorial basis, should have been recognized as a matter of course. But the main issue was left untouched. So Europe was actually farther from integration in 1919 than in 1914. The victory which should have been achieved in 1814 had lost its virtue a hundred years later. Nationalism had not progressed with men's thoughts, so it had turned into a reactionary factor. Europeans realized that their incredible efforts and sufferings had only retarded the evolution of mankind. So "to bed, sick of life."

On the fourth of August 1789, feudal privileges were formally abolished, and bourgeois liberalism had at last a free field. The Revolution was over then, in less than a hundred days, opening an era of freedom and good will? Nothing of the kind. That memorable victory was not real but ghostlike. In 1789, there was nothing left of feudalism but a few harmless trappings and a few annoying abuses. The vitality of the feudal regime (if ever it had been a regime) had waned by the thirteenth century, with the growth of the cities and of royal power. By the middle of the fourteenth century, the principles of bourgeois constitutionalism were perfectly clear: the Great Ordinance of 1357, in France, was no Utopia. Between Etienne Marcel and Abbé Siéyès, both champions of the Third Estate, there elapsed four hundred and thirty-two years. A confused mixture of decadent

History

feudalism and fitful absolutism prevailed, with bourgeois hard work and hard sense as the steadying element. When the laggard victory appeared at last, it was lame and toothless: the rule of the *bourgeoisie* had become antiquated before it was formally recognized. With Rousseau and the fundamental doctrines of the American Revolution, democracy had already been proclaimed. The problem was no longer to destroy the feudal system, but to steer the world beyond mesocracy or the dictatorship of the middle class. But the bourgeois, assuming full power at last, looked obstinately backward: it is hard for men whose forefathers have fought for a worthy ideal to realize that their cause has become, not wrong indeed, but secondary and even obsolete. As late as 1848, the great philosophical historian Guizot taught that the whole trend of European civilization culminated in the triumph of the moneyed *bourgeoisie (Enrichissez-vous!)* and in the ministry of Monsieur Guizot.

In 1789 again, all the restrictions on economic activities were removed. The old guilds were medieval survivals; their traditions had become petrified; instead of protecting all parties—the producers, the middlemen, and the purchasers—they had been turned into citadels of privilege. And the regulations imposed by the monarchy were likewise hindrances rather than incentives. Against that ubiquitous and cumbrous tyranny, emancipation was the obvious remedy. Political thought and economic trends were in harmony: *Laissez faire, laissez passer,* free the individual from the trammels imposed by feudal lord, absolute king, or antiquated craft. So economic individualism was born, a sturdy and even rugged infant, still dear to some of our best citizens. Unfortunately, it was born too late. It was meant to work, and would have worked admirably, in an economy of independent workers—peasant proprietors, merchants with little stores all their own, craftsmen at their own bench or their own smithy. This would have been an unqualified blessing as late as 1700. But in the second half of the seventeenth century and throughout the eighteenth, two economic

Education of a Humanist

revolutions had their start: modern finance first, and then the immense expansion of the machine. Under Louis XVI, the Industrial Revolution, although not so advanced as in England, was already well under way. Now the very essence of modern finance and industry is collectivism, the company, not the isolated individual. The village blacksmith, who "owes not any man," has still a legitimate place in our world, but it is a minor one. To apply rigidly the rules of competitive individualism in a country which already had such vast enterprises as Anzin and Le Creusot was arrant anachronism. The urgent task was to save liberty and dignity in a collectivistic age, a difficult adjustment which neither Russia nor America has yet been able to make. Because the problem was not frankly and fearlessly faced at the right time, we had the "dark Satanic mills" and all the horrors of what Lewis Mumford calls the paleotechnic era. Adam Smith was not the prophet of our world, but a hundred years behind the times.

I trust that by this time the pattern of the "laggard victory" is beginning to appear. I must repeat that it is offered as a suggestion, not as a doctrine. The concept I am attempting to define—a form of the "cultural lag"—does not open every door in history. But even in cases when it plays a minor part, it is not wholly negligible. And it offers at least an indication in the case of problems so highly controversial that no scientific solution can be hoped for.

The first of such instances is offered by the Reformation of the sixteenth century; not the only reformation in Christian history by any means, nor probably the greatest. The Church, from the days of the Apostles, has been in constant need of self-purification, for a divine purpose can never be served with absolute perfection by a body of erring men. In particular, the late Middle Ages were keenly aware that abuses and superstitions had crept into the practices and governance of the Church Militant. The spirit is deathless, but garments have to be renewed. Another return to essentials was needed. That Reformation was clear in many minds in the thirteenth and fourteenth centuries; it inspired groups as diverse as the Walden-

History

sians, the Franciscans, and the Lollards. It was exactly that spirit, rather than theological quibbles, that later animated Martin Luther. But by that time, the purification of medieval faith and discipline no longer was the paramount issue. The Renaissance was in full swing, and it carried the human mind beyond, and not back to, the literalism of Bible-worship. The problem was to integrate the spiritual data of the faith with revived pagan wisdom and with the enormously expanded scientific horizon. Erasmus and Rabelais were looking forward: Luther and Calvin were engulfed in the past. However justified their criticism of current abuses may have been, however cogent their thought within its self-defined circle, however powerful their personalities, their influence hampered human thought then and hampers it to this day. Their victory came five or six generations too late.

After 1848, there was in Europe a wave of philosophical, political, and artistic "realism." It was due in part to the collapse of the great romantic humanitarian dream of that "mad and holy year," in part to the manifest triumphs of science and industry. Marx saved socialism from the wreck of 1848 by giving it a modern, scientific, realistic garb. No more utopian dreams of "harmony," no more apocalypse in reverse after the fashion of Charles Fourier: instead of all such wistful thinking, hard facts and inexorable laws. As a strategic move, this fusion of science and socialism was successful to a large degree. The defenders of orthodox economics were outflanked. Unfortunately, when Marxism became at last not a mere sect of the Catacombs but a major ideology, one of the poles of modern thought, it was still wearing the outmoded garb of the 1860's, complete with impressive whiskers. It is too valuable to be called mere junk; it has not attained the serene remoteness of a classic; its proper place is Ye Antique Shoppe, along with horsehair sofas. Eric Bentley rightly says that behind Wagner's Valhalla one can descry the Crystal Palace. In the same way, the materialistic determinism of the Marxians is one with the harsh intellectual machinery of Taine and Littré, of Fechner and Haeckel. Socialism, which is

Education of a Humanist

a living spirit, cannot tear itself apart from Marxism, which is a corpse. But the corpse, in ghostly fashion, speaks louder than the spirit, and is far more impressive to the unwary: for it is easier to memorize dead formulas than to pursue elusive truths. A man like Léon Blum, a free mind but a timid soul, hints at times that Marxism should be put away so that socialism may live; but invariably the Fundamentalists manage to outvote and overawe the heretics. No one can tell how long Marx, a contemporary of Napoleon III, will prevent men from using their own reason.

The San Francisco Charter is the latest of these laggard victories. The Dumbarton Oaks plan, forced upon the assembled nations, was conceived in a 1920 atmosphere. The man who had to be placated, and therefore who actually dictated its terms, was Senator Henry Cabot Lodge, many years in his grave. So a new League of Nations was proposed, rather feebler than the old. It was so plainly out of date that it was ignored, as a matter of course, from the very first: the Potsdam agreement, and our support of the Monarchists in Greece, by-passed without a qualm the new Parliament of Man. The United Nations is not an infant that will gather strength: it was born decrepit. It might have met the problems of 1919, just as the Maginot Line would have stopped the Germans in 1914. The world, weary of war, had consciously moved beyond that stage. It might be said in extenuation that the delegates knew nothing about the atomic bomb: but they should have realized that aviation and the radio had already made the old conception of nationalism obsolete. Countries can no longer be sealed in absolute isolation: the plain, fresh, and vigorous mind of Wendell Willkie needed no atomic bomb to discover that this was, in the most literal sense, "one world." Instead of a true Federal Republic, we were given a globe parceled out among fifty states, five at least of which have jealously preserved their full sovereign rights. The United Nations of today would have been a step in the right direction if it had come soon after the first Hague Conference, half a century ago. Now it cumbers

History

the path toward peace. Another "victory" with leaden feet, wearily looking backward.

The very concept of victory is an attempt to arrest the clock. While men fight, they cannot think, and events pass them by. The "leader" of sect, party, or nation, too busy "leading," does not realize that he is trailing behind: evolution came to an end when he assumed command. So every "victory" is eternal in its own eyes of stone. The true historical spirit does not bid us walk in our fathers' footsteps: it cannot be done, for the course of time is irreversible. If you shoot at a moving target, aim ahead of its visible position. Build bridges before you expect multitudes to cross them; and do not worry overmuch about the rivers you have left behind.

V. World Citizenship

TRUST THE EXPERT AND KEEP YOUR OWN COUNSEL

I started my career in this country as a French teacher of French; I ended it, forty years later, as an American teacher of world citizenship. There was no revolution in my thought and in my work: only a sharper consciousness and a larger opportunity. But this shift in emphasis raises the question of my credentials. In my narrower field, I had official warrant: I could show beautifully engraved parchments and formal letters of appointment. I was something and somebody: that most respectable character the *Fachmann,* in recognized control of a neatly labeled compartment. In my later capacity, I was roaming the world at will. This might imply that I had forfeited my academic standing. *Lehr- und Lernfreiheit:* teaching and learning must be free, but within prescribed limits, and the narrower the better.

For the benefit of those who are still thinking in departmental terms, let me first dismiss, as a mere biographical detail, the question of my University status. I never held a position in the School of Social Sciences. But my colleagues in that immense field—or shall I call it that jungle?—very courteously acknowledged me as a licensed privateer or auxiliary. I was frequently asked to lecture in the Stanford course on Citizenship (later Western Civilization). I was invited to join symposia of Social Scientists, where I found that, although every discipline used a jargon of its own, it was not impossible to attain a modest degree of mutual understanding. I

Education of a Humanist

reached the dignity of Bishop *in partibus:* there was no actual diocese under my charge, but I was entitled to wear the amethyst ring if I chose. Saint Theresa was granted her Doctor's degree three centuries after her death; Gallieni and Maunoury received their Marshal's baton posthumously; perhaps Stanford, about 1980, will appoint me retroactively to a chair of World Citizenship, with all the rights and privileges thereunto appertaining. If the news reaches the myrtle groves, it will greatly rejoice my shade.

Now in this book I am discussing my experiences as a qualified teacher, not my opinions as a man. I am not offering a personal Utopia, but the testimony of a trained investigator: this is not my *Bottle in the Sea.* So, to justify the presence of this chapter, the keystone of my enterprise, the very core of humane learning, I had to establish my professional claims. But this involves two previous questions. Is it possible to keep man and teacher separate? And: what is the "authority" of the expert, even when he is recognized?

I am, I repeat, offering this report as a teacher, not as a man. The dichotomy, if made too sharply, would be absurd. I do not claim to know how far such a cleavage would be valid in the case of preacher, lawyer, diplomat, or soldier. These professions have definite codes of their own, which may sharply diverge from the common law. Good men are praised for actions which, in the laity, would be reprehensible, including deceit and wholesale murder. Father Gaucher, in Alphonse Daudet's pretty little tale, was authorized to get drunk for the good of the community; ambassadors lie for their country; sailors are allowed one wife in every port. There are few such dispensations attached to teaching. The one instance I can remember is that I was permitted to read *Ulysses* with a good conscience, at a time when the majesty of American justice had pronounced such reading a transgression. There is, in every American, a Miltonic, Byronic, or Baudelairian strain, which finds pleasure in defying the laws: Prohibition and the O.P.A. were great boons. But there is a still loftier pleasure: the calm certainty of being not against but above the law. However, that thrill

World Citizenship

came only once in a lifetime. When *Lady Chatterley's Lover* appeared, I was so sure I had the moral right to read the forbidden text that I never felt tempted to do so. I was satisfied (more or less) with the edition expurgated *ad usum Delphini*.

Candidly, I never was conscious of changing my personality when I was entering the classroom. I never believed either that what I had learned and taught in my professional capacity had no bearing whatever upon my private life. In my experience, man and teacher almost coincided. The center of my teaching was the critical spirit, so I could not be accused of forcing my opinions upon my students. The critical spirit was their protection against me; it was also my protection against outside interference. It gave me the privilege to challenge, without any reservation, any doctrine I might happen to encounter. In forty years, my right to question has never been questioned. Let my Presidents, Trustees, Deans, and Departmental Heads be collectively and severally blessed for this perfect record of academic freedom.

Naturally, although there was no split in my personality, there were inevitable differences in attitude. There are subjects upon which I can claim a limited degree of expert knowledge. I have investigated some of their aspects at first hand, and thought about them, methodically, with my own head. World Citizenship is one of these subjects. This gives my opinion a certain density, a certain weight, as well as an even more certain ponderosity. For the latter I refuse to apologize. Pedantry is the mark of our trade, our inevitable and honorable professional deformation. Every specialist, when he appears as such, is a caricature, for one feature in him is developed out of proportion with the rest. The teacher who, for fear of being pedantic, simply chats with his students, is not true to type and not true to his calling. Socrates was not guilty of such an error; only the grand old fraud cloaked his cogent reasoning in the guise of artless conversation.

There are matters, therefore, which concern John Doe closely, and about which I know more than John Doe. If John is not im-

Education of a Humanist

pressed, it is his fault and his loss. I believe that no important decision involving technical problems should be taken without expert advice. If you want a bridge built, it is wise to have a trained engineer examine the site, test the soil, and calculate the stresses. If democracy were, as Emile Faguet defined it, "the cult of incompetence," it would infallibly go down before a better equipped system. Fortunately, in our democracy, the cult of incompetence prevails only in a parasitical domain, that is, politics. In all things that really matter, in business, industry, law, medicine, we believe in efficiency, not in the party system.

Am I advocating "Technocracy" in the more general sense of the term—government by experts? No. Only an engineer is qualified to design and construct a bridge; but the previous and essential question is: do you want a bridge built and are you willing to pay for it? The answer does not rest with the technician. Here John Doe must assert his rights and assume his responsibilities. The expert is a consultant, not a dictator. His business is to tell the common man: "The thing you desire can—or cannot—be done by the means at present at our disposal. If it can be done, here is an estimate of the cost." For the Paris Exposition of 1937, it was proposed to erect a tower seven thousand feet high. I suppose it was feasible. The people preferred to put their money into other ventures, possibly no less foolish. Cram wanted to have all our colored citizens moved back to Africa: a proposition about as reasonable as Zionism. The material difficulties are not insuperable: our war effort was on an even larger scale. The cost should be figured, and not exclusively in terms of dollars. Sociologists should be consulted, as well as specialists in transportation, finance, agriculture, and public health: but it is not they who should have the first word, or the last. A third instance, in my opinion far less remote than the other two: the World State is a possibility, if only John Doe desires it. It will enormously reduce the insurance premium against war, thus releasing energies and resources for constructive purposes. John Doe, I believe, is aware of this. But the fact should not be overlooked

World Citizenship

that it will involve the sacrifice of cherished prejudices and of treasured privileges as well. The cost will be high. Here are fairly detailed blueprints, with an estimate. The decision is up to you.

In Hohenzollern Germany, the worship of the *Fachmann,* the specialist in a definite field, was ubiquitous and deep. None but professional army men had any say about army affairs. This is the dream of the military mind all over the world; I sympathize with Clemenceau's counterstatement: "War is too serious a business to be left to the generals." Diplomacy is a deep mystery which the initiated alone should discuss. Mr. Cordell Hull was greatly irked by those busybodies who were prating about American principles and thus interfering with his masterly game. To the present day, few are the men who thoroughly endorse the Wilsonian ideal of open diplomacy. Now this blind reliance upon the expert is extremely perilous. Faguet, after writing *The Cult of Incompetence,* had a companion volume, *The Dread of Responsibilities.* But it is the excessive trust in competence that fosters irresponsibility: leave everything to the man who knows. The admirable discipline of Hohenzollern Germany resulted in the slavishness of Nazi Germany. Every expert was absolute in his compartment and respected the absolute authority of others in their compartment. The layman had no voice; and everyone was a layman except in his limited sphere. So if a man was told to destroy lives by the hundred thousand, he did so without a qualm and with undoubted efficiency. "His not to reason why."

The first principle, in world citizenship as well as in national citizenship, is: the common man has to decide. The trouble is that the common man, as a rule, is inert. He does not think until he is roused; and, as soon as he is roused, he stops thinking. (Politicians and journalists call this cataleptic state "grim determination.") That is why he needs pricks and prods—not in order to take the decision out of his hands, but in order to keep him alert and remind him of his responsibility. Of his own accord he could not even voice a definite desire; he could even less formulate the terms of a choice.

Education of a Humanist

He needs propagandists (or apostles: the words are synonymous) to point the way, and experts to throw light on the proposed way. But apostles and experts should act only as scouts, pathfinders, blazers of trails, not as slave-drivers.

Consult the expert, and beware of the expert. First of all, we must remember that no expert is infallible, even in his own field; and that the unanimous agreement of experts at any one time may itself be mistaken. The history of science is cluttered with manifest errors which once were solemnly taught. There were experts in astronomy for interminable ages before Copernicus, and experts in physiology before Harvey. Fortunately for the progress of the human mind, experts do not present a united front. Their rivalries restore our freedom. It was Marx's outstanding service to science to have established one essential point: to wit, that the classical school of economics was not in undisputed possession of absolute truth. It was said that whenever British economists met, at least three conflicting opinions were expressed, two of them Maynard Keynes's.

Even when technicians agree within their own field, they have a tendency to exaggerate the importance of their subject. No problem can be settled on the technical plane unless all secondary considerations are eliminated; but these "secondary considerations" are part of life, and to other minds may seem of primary importance. Specialists were probably right in isolating Profit as the sole motive of *Homo œconomicus*. But this did not explain why, between 1919 and 1939, the people of Danzig would gladly have committed economic suicide in order to be reunited with the Reich.

Finally, when technicians most arrogantly assert their authority, it is in virtue of their experience, their accumulated knowledge, their established superiority, that is to say, their past. Their position is a vested interest, a citadel to be defended against all comers. Naturally, all theologians, even the most liberal, will rally to the defense of theology, all military men to the support of armaments, all diplomats to the justification of diplomacy. Whenever you seek a new path to truth, you must expect to find it obstructed by the bulk of expert opinion. That is why we need "experts in humanism" to break down the unconscious and invincible parochialism of the specialists. (I taught in the School of Humanities: the reader will appreciate how consistently I follow my great model, Monsieur Josse.)

I said that John Doe, suffering obscurely, hoping vaguely, had to be roused out of his apathy by apostles and advised in his quest by experts. Two very different types of minds; in this chapter and in this whole book, I am claiming my modest place among the experts. But no sooner do we draw a distinction than we realize it needs to be qualified. There are pure apostles, no doubt, and pure experts also. The pure apostle preaches the substance of things hoped for. The expert deals with the evidence of things actually seen. He knows all about his subject and is indifferent to its applications. The authority on ballistics is interested in guns, not in men—except as servants or targets for guns. As a rule, however, the apostle has facts to justify his hope; he is an observer, an experimentalist, a teacher, as well as a preacher. The technician who is not a mere cog in his own machine loves his craft, believes in it, seeks to promote its influence, and, to give it dignity, hitches it to a star: everyone knows that gun makers are the most ardent of idealists, eager to uphold either Karl Marx or free enterprise. Except in Kant's conception of art, "adequacy to purpose" is not found "without purpose." I am not an artist, and I have not labored for Art's sake only. I admit that, if I have investigated certain aspects of world chaos and examined certain proposed remedies, I was not seeking pleasure in the pure algebra of thought. I was conscious of preventable human suffering; which may be a flaw in the armor of scientist or scholar.

Yes, if we want to be conscientious workers, it is indispensable that we distinguish what in our minds is preconception or prejudice, what is the fruit of scrupulous research, what is aspiration or ideal. It is indispensable, but, I repeat, it is also highly artificial. A man is at the same time his own past and his own future. As a scholar, I

Education of a Humanist

should like to believe that all my ideas are by now so objective, so carefully tested, that they possess universal validity. As a riper scholar, I know that this is a dream, and not even a beautiful dream. I have worked sedulously all my life on the problem of world organization: when I realize how little I have changed in a half century, I shudder.

Once I heard a man who had occupied the highest position in his country quietly affirm: "My thoughts were formed by the time I was eighteen. I have seen no reason to question or revise them." To me, it seemed a dreadful admission, although I had surmised as much. Yet my own case is not radically different. The illustrious personage spoke with complacency, and I speak with misgivings: I have constantly challenged my own principles. But the result is identical: my preconceptions have resisted every questioning, and I too am the same as I was at eighteen. My explorations in varied fields—philosophies, religions, political and social systems—have, I hope, enriched and not merely cluttered up my mind; but they have not transformed it. By 1898, I was set. In other words, I am a period piece, a fossil.

A fossil? My one comfort is that I am a fossil in a world of fossils. There are with us today Thomistic fossils, Reformation fossils, Adam Smith fossils, Jeffersonian fossils, Karl Marx fossils: they can be neatly labeled and dated. Only the unthinking live wholly in the elusive present. Every worthy fossil looks forward with his fossil eyes, and is a Utopian. An economic individualist, for instance, is not merely a survivor of the Manchester era: he wants to give *laissez faire* the full trial it never had, even in mid-Victorian England. Christians and Communists are not looking backward: they are striving hard to fulfill prophecies and to impose patterns. The *laissez-faire* millennium will never dawn if we simply trust to *laissez faire*. We have to make people do something about it: *laissez faire* is not *laisser aller*. The ineluctable processes of dialectic materialism will bog down unless there are Marxes, Lenins, Trotskys, Stalins, to prod them on. Even for the most orthodox, God's plans

World Citizenship

need us as conscious instruments. I do not mind being a fossil, so long as I am working for the future.

I have related elsewhere how internationalism was forced upon me in self-defense. I had been brought up, at home and at school, as a very orthodox patriot. Perhaps I did not clearly visualize what it meant to "die for one's country"; but I knew it was a very fine thing to do, and I was—vaguely—prepared to do it. Then the Dreyfus storm broke.

Soon the lines were sharply drawn. No doubt intermediate positions could have been defended: "Of course, we must place justice above all other considerations; but justice has decided, and Dreyfus has been legally and properly condemned." "Of course, we do not challenge the supreme claim of the country, the necessity of army discipline, the secrecy which must envelop matters of national defense: but none of these things would be endangered if a plain miscarriage of justice were righted." Between such reasonable opponents and defenders of Dreyfus, an agreement could have been reached. The military, however, chose to make it a test case: let no mere civilian challenge what the Army had decided.

Individual guilt and individual stupidity no doubt played no small part in raising this momentous issue. But the high officers responsible for that fateful course were in truth the representatives of great principles. They stood for the divine character of established authority against the anarchism of free and critical thought. That divine authority—to their great regret—was no longer vested in the Church and in her secular sword, the anointed king. But the same sacred power survived in the *nation,* which had been fashioned through patient centuries by the united efforts of Church and King. The nation is an absolute: it is not above the law, is it the supreme law. Of the nation's existence, the army is the symbol and the shield. Weaken the army and you threaten the very life of the nation. Stephen Decatur put it pithily: "My country, right or wrong!" In terms of practical conduct, in any controversy, do not balance—

rally to the flag. There can be no truth or justice above or against the country. If a man's religion made him falter in the service of his country, that religion would be false and he would be a traitor.

The conflict imposed immediate duties upon us. It did not raise at once the problem of international organization. The Universal Republic of Victor Hugo, Tennyson's Federation of the World, remained in our minds *myths* in Georges Sorel's meaning of the term: spiritual truths guiding action, but not themselves the object of immediate action. The direction was set, the impetus given, but the goal would forever recede. Not that the goal was a delusion: but the process itself was the achievement. This tallied very well with the dawning influence of Bergson and with the gradualism of the Fabians. We knew that a supranational world was growing in the vast fields of science, industry, commerce. We thought that, spiritually also, that world was gathering consciousness. The Dreyfus case seemed a perfect demonstration of that increasing moral unity: in every part of the earth men had felt that the injustice against one unknown man was their concern.

The fanatics of the national idol were defeated. It was a season of unlimited hopes. Alas! How closely akin are *unlimited* and *indefinite!* The first Hague Conference held out promises that armies, like kings, might fall into innocuous desuetude. The Paris Exposition in 1900 was the occasion of innumerable gatherings: practical, scientific, cultural, all commissions of a mighty Assembly yet to be convened, the true Parliament of Man.

That this inchoate Parliament had no formal power did not strike us as a fatal weakness. Anarchism in many forms had lured us in the nineties; bomb throwing had merely the name in common with the radical individualism of Spencer or Ibsen, with the evangelic contempt of Tolstoy for all forms of materialistic power. We thought of gradually dissolving the local state, rather than creating the super-state. We were naïve enough to believe in government by consent. If I have abjured that form of idealism, it is for the present

World Citizenship

emergency only. Rule by force, in however mild a form, is rule by terror. Any master who can make me do what I hate to do is a dictator, whether his title be corporal, Duce, Führer, or Majority. We talk with virtuous horror of the Police State; but every state is by its very nature a police; and what we mean by the World State is a World Police. I have reluctantly come to believe that we need such an instrument in our stage of civilization; it certainly does not represent my ideal.

It is now obvious that we had misread the signs of the times. We thought that war was a disease in full regression, surviving with virulence only in backward countries. It could be held in check, and even stamped out, through sanitary measures, in the same way as yellow fever. Japan was not yet a menace. Turkey, the model of the state founded on conquest, was manifestly decadent. Germany had the antiquated panoply of a military empire; but she was developing tremendously on scientific, industrial, nonmilitary lines; her Social-Democratic Party, officially committed to internationalism, was the strongest in Europe. From the dim and remote confusion of Russia, only two voices reached us: Tolstoy's, with his gospel of nonresistance, and the Autocrat's, cooing like a dove to summon a great peace conference. England and America were of course our towers of strength. England believed in free trade and the United States in free immigration (at any rate for "Caucasians"): these were the two great instruments for the automatic adjustment of economic inequalities, for the gradual waning of nationalistic prejudices. The Spanish-American War had not shaken our faith. It appeared as another crusade for liberation; democracy was destroying by the sword the last trace of rule by the sword. The Boer War was a worse trial. We found comfort in the fact that almost for the first time prominent statesmen, and not merely irresponsible agitators, had openly rejected the "My Country, right or wrong!" blasphemy: Sir Henry Campbell-Bannermann and David Lloyd George had dared to denounce the brutal policy and the ruthless methods of their national government. The world was still stumbling; but it was facing in the right direction, and gradualism would suffice.

So my interest was centered in immediate and definite problems: a Franco-German reconciliation, a Franco-British Entente. By 1900, the latter seemed the harder task. Yet, in spite of the Fashoda crisis and the Boer War, it was realized in 1904. It pointed to that complete union of the two ancient enemies, prophesied by Henri Saint-Simon, very seriously discussed on the eve of the Second World War, and proposed at last by Winston Churchill in June 1940, just a few weeks too late. The Franco-German problem was not insoluble. Our generation had rejected the thought of a military *Revanche:* even the Franco-Russian alliance implied that renunciation. Had Germany granted Alsace-Lorraine a generous measure of administrative autonomy and cultural freedom, we should have been satisfied. There had never been in France any blind hatred of the Germans; there had been, on the part of great Frenchmen, Michelet, Quinet, Hugo, Renan, a profound love for the German spirit. I have never ceased to work for such a *rapprochement,* even in the most tragic hours of the two world wars; and this moderate objective seemed at least realized at Locarno.

America, when I arrived in 1906, confirmed my pragmatic optimism. The country which was fast becoming the richest and most powerful in the world was attached to peace. The martial spirit of 1898 had been but a flutter; military glory had no appeal. President Taft's treaties of unlimited arbitration, not excepting matters concerning national honor, seemed to me necessary and sufficient: my very first public address in this country was in their support.

In those days, I called myself a pacifist: the word meant then a worker for peace, not a nonresister. I have not met a consistent nonresister yet. If evil should not be curbed in international affairs, it should have a free field at home as well. Pacifists welcome police protection for their life and property; they do not object to the arrest of criminals; they would not hesitate to shoot a wild beast

World Citizenship

crouching to pounce upon a child, even though the wild beast wore a human countenance. Half-confessed nonresistance, purely negative measures such as the outlawry of war or disarmament, struck me from the first as dangerously insincere. No step is effective unless it involves definite responsibilities. Arms are the fruit, not the seed, of the war spirit. The policy to oppose international aggressors "by all means short of war and that will not lead to war" was to my mind a perfect example of muddle-headedness. If resistance was not to be futile, it would lead to war; if the rejection of war was absolute, it assured the aggressors that their path was clear.

Had the peace-minded nations, before 1914 and before 1939, been clear in their thought and firm in their action, the two world wars would not have happened. I share to the full the guilt of that confusion, with far less excuse than John Doe on his Middle-Western farm. We were "unrealistic," not because we pleaded and worked for peace, but because we did not plead and work hard enough. We failed to see that gradualism would not do, and in our moderate, leisurely, scholarly way, we lost the race with catastrophe. It took a first World War, or rather the failure of a first World Peace, to destroy my complacency. Others needed a second and sharper lesson. Many are waiting for a third.

THE LANGUAGE APPROACH

In 1901 or 1902, in London, a friend of mine handed me a red-covered penny pamphlet about Esperanto. I had, I am proud to say, all the natural responses of a scholar and a gentleman. I smiled with just the right degree of supercilious indulgence. Scholars and gentlemen have a good command of language: I used mine, full blast, in the defense of good taste and sanity. I do not remember what were the synonyms of "crackpots" then in fashion, but I am sure they were vigorous and colorful enough. My friend, with a smile of his own, asked me: "Have you really given the subject a thought?"

Education of a Humanist

No. I had not. I had vaguely heard of Volapük: the word is in Renan. Esperanto was not even a name. I took the pamphlet home. No stroke of lightning converted Saul into Paul. But I started thinking quietly about the problem, and I have not stopped. I am still meeting men of the keenest, freest intelligence whose natural reaction is the same as mine was nearly half a century ago. It is as inconceivable for a properly educated person to take the question seriously as it would be for him to wear a red tie with a full dress suit. A fearless spirit might be praised for challenging Aristotle, St. Paul, St. Thomas Aquinas, Napoleon, or Karl Marx. But there are two points he must not question, if he is not to lose caste: the holiness of the party system, and the utter foolishness of artificial language schemes.

As a minor but persistent activity, I did not a little research on the subject, before and especially after I wrote my *Short History of the International Language Movement.* I corresponded for years with the authors of the systems I took most seriously, particularly with Giuseppe Peano and Edgar de Wahl. I hunted up, in a workers' quarter of Paris, a Polish family which for three generations had kept alive the tradition of Solresol—Solresol, the most fascinating language that ever could be played on a saxophone. Thanks to David Starr Jordan's magnificent freedom from prejudice, I was allowed to teach at Stanford an experimental course in Esperanto. It duly figured on the catalogue and carried regular university credit: my dear old colleague Ewald Flügel wept tears of shame at the thought. When my interest showed signs of flagging, I was inspired to renewed efforts by the clear-sighted, unselfish devotion of Dr. Frederick G. Cottrell, then Director of the National Research Council. I kept in close touch with the International Auxiliary Language Association, and in 1940 spent a sweltering summer in New York probing interlinguistic difficulties, driven by the gentle but relentless lash of Mrs. Dave H. Morris. I attended Esperanto meetings and could speak the language with creditable fluency, especially before those who were not acquainted with it. Once, in

World Citizenship

Paris, when a streetcar refused to heed my signal, I hurled at the driver the expletive *Sentaugulo!* which unfortunately was lost in the wind and the rain. I had specimens of marvelous Esperanto submitted to me by two prodigies, William James Sidis and Winifred Sackville Stoner. If I had been challenged to do so, I could have produced a workable *lingua franca* of my own. I smuggled an interlinguistic paper into the highly respectable *Publications of the Modern Language Association,* browbeat H. L. Mencken into taking one for *The American Mercury,* and even planted the green star flag over the grave of Ralph Waldo Emerson in *The American Scholar.* It was good serious work, and earnestly meant. At the same time, it was also a pleasurable exercise in irony. My friends suspected a trick, and could not expose it. They wondered how I could be so absurdly right, when by all the canons of learning and taste my thesis was so manifestly wrong.

I first considered Esperanto purely as a labor-saving device, a convenience of the same order as shorthand or a telegraphic code. I had no personal need of it, but I saw no reason why it should not be encouraged. Exasperation and enthusiasm seemed to me equally out of place. Gradually, I realized the ramifications and the implications of the problem. There are several questions involved, on different planes; and although ultimately they are fused, it will be well to present them separately.

The most obvious is the problem of language in international relations. There is nothing cranky or visionary about this difficulty. In the good old phrase, it is not a theory but a condition. It arises whenever two people happen to meet who do not speak the same vernacular. It may be settled in a variety of ways: most obviously through the services of an interpreter, if one can be found; and of a whole battery of interpreters, if more than two languages are involved.

This strictly practical problem has become at the same time infinitely more pressing and infinitely more arduous in our own days. International relations are no longer ignored by the multitude; they have become so intense as to overshadow purely home affairs. What did Italy, for instance, have to vote on in 1948 if not U.S.S.R. or U.S.A.? Bombs are evidently the tersest of international languages, but they are inadequate for the finer shades of meaning. There are no hermit kingdoms left: Korea, Tibet, Afghanistan, Iowa, can no longer take pride in their splendid isolation. Not only has the airplane abolished oceans and mountains, but the movies carry Hollywood to Punta Arenas and Timbuktu, and the radio has annihilated distance altogether. We are all thrown together in a gigantic agora; but we carry with us everywhere the last, the most impassable of all frontiers, the barrier of speech.

While the need for world communication increased immeasurably, the solution was actually receding from us. The situation is now worse than it ever was in the last two thousand years. For nearly twenty centuries, any man of standing—Roman administrator, priest, scholar, diplomat—could travel through the vast and complex domain of our civilization with the aid of that incomparable Esperanto, Latin. For two centuries, French held the same position in society, polite learning, and diplomacy. English plays a similar role today in business transactions, which dominate to a large extent political activities. We have a stranglehold on all markets. But it is neither probable nor desirable that the present economic dictatorship will be permanent. In a truly competitive world, we shall have to learn Spanish and Portuguese as fast as Latin America is learning English: it pays to meet your customer halfway. At present UNESCO remains faithful to the bilingualism of the defunct League: French and English. But the United Nations had to admit five languages from the start, and it is obvious that the list is not closed.

For—and this is the most discouraging feature of the situation—there is no sign that the number of languages will be reduced through a Darwinian process of natural selection. Every tongue once considered minor claims full equality of rights; and how long will

World Citizenship

German, Italian, Portuguese, Japanese, Arabic, and Hindustani be kept artificially among the "minors"? Every dialect aspires to full national status: I expect H. L. Mencken to petition the United Nations for the recognition of the mighty tongue he has done so much to study, defend, and illustrate. Languages which yesterday were slowly dying, like Irish, have been revived by drastic remedies. Others which, like Hebrew, had long attained classic dignity and repose, have been rudely dragged from the library and the temple to fight their way in an era of violence. This is "One World" indeed, but that world is Babel.

Everyone knows that we cannot use for international affairs the hundreds of languages, the thousands of dialects, now current on earth. There must be a selection of as few as possible, and ideally of one. I repeat that this is a practical problem before us today, not a wild leap into Utopia. Per se, it involves no ideology, and it promises no millennium: we know, through the example of our respective governments, that affairs can be mismanaged even when all parties speak—roughly—the same idiom. It implies no sentiment either: our mother tongue, with its cherished associations, will remain in sole possession of its traditional domain. Young Americans will not be expected to read Shakespeare or Milton in Esperanto translations.

When it comes to the selection of an auxiliary language, the basic principle has been expressed with matchless clarity by I. A. Richards, and I cannot improve upon his words: "It [a common language] must be clear from any threat to the economic, moral, cultural, social or political status or independence of any person or any people. It must carry no implications of intellectual, technological or other domination. No one, in learning the world language, must have any excuse for feeling that he is submitting to an alien influence, or being brought under the power of some other groups."[1] This is realism of the highest order. The reader knows that I have

---

[1] I. A. Richards, *Basic English and Its Uses* (New York: W. W. Norton and Co., 1943), p. 11.

no sympathy whatever with jealous, hate-filled nationalism. But nationalism is justified in resisting imperialism, the imposition of an alien pattern upon a reluctant and helpless people. Linguistic imperialism is the one which carries most clearly the boast of superiority —financial, military, or cultural. It will be resisted tooth and nail. The first condition of an international medium, according to I. A. Richards, is scrupulous neutrality.

The second problem is: Can a language be made to order, by a conscious act of the human will? What has been called the Topsy school, the believers in obscure growth, rebel at the thought; that is to say, they refuse to think. Of course, they say, you cannot make a language any more than you can, by a stroke of the pen, make a city or a constitution.

I was taught never to reject a hypothesis a priori. If it was absurd, its inner contradictions would soon be brought to light. The test might be swift and unmerciful; still, there ought to be a fair test. Men have found it profitable to investigate non-Euclidean geometries, although for centuries Euclid's postulate seemed identical with common sense. Other men are working out the possibilities of imaginary numbers. I saw no reason why the "Enlightenment," that is, clear thinking, should capitulate to the "Obscurantists." The comparison of city, nation, constitution, language, with organisms is a romantic metaphor, not a scientific truth. Even though these things have a life of their own, they are also instruments. Man, who uses them, is manifestly free to alter and discard them; new words are deliberately coined, just as new laws are passed and new streets constructed. No worshiper of "unthinking" (there are very shrewd thinkers among them) is free from the taint of planning.

No laboratory has ever produced a Homunculus or a Frankenstein monster. But we build robots in the shape of machines and machine tools. We can devise mathematical and chemical formulas and agree on signal codes. As a matter of fact, a scientific paper dealing with the most abstruse and intricate subjects is written, in its essential parts, in an artificial international language, clear to the adept, a dead letter to the uninitiated. Only the connecting links are in a "natural" tongue, and for that reason they cannot be deciphered by a foreign scientist. In Giuseppe Peano's *Formulario Mathematico,* the share of the "natural" was practically eliminated.

On further investigation, I found that the radical opposition between "natural" and "artificial" was grossly exaggerated. In a seminar which I conducted for years on the subject of Literature and Language,[2] my students and I were driven to the conclusion that the so-called "natural" languages were to a large extent artificial. They have a logical structure which appears in their grammar: not even English is a haphazard accumulation of idioms. "Exceptions" confirm the existence of "rules." Parts of speech are categories of thought; conjugations are not wholly anarchical; words have legitimate families of derivatives. All these standards are recognized and imposed by groups possessing prestige and authority; they are codified and transmitted by grammarians; they are most unnaturally forced upon the young. When the social order is not stabilized, when it breaks down into barbarism, language is set free and evolves with startling rapidity: this is true of certain tribes, of the Roman Empire in decay, of the nursery, and of ephemeral slang. But in civilized ages, that anarchical freedom is checked, and standards prevail. Dante is still intelligible after six hundred years. Natural evolution has been retarded, almost arrested, and replaced by the deliberate enforcement of a norm.

On the other hand, the languages of the Esperanto type are not artificial in the same sense as the formulas of mathematics and chemistry. They are not arbitrary (but consistent) sets of symbols. Every science aspires to such perfect symbolism: a full-grown science is a well-made language. But common speech, necessarily looser, will never reach that degree of logical precision. Esperantos are not invented algebras, but natural languages simplified and regularized. There is nothing hateful about simplification. It is not a return to

[2] See above, Chapter III, Literature, second section, *Literature and Language.*

the crude; it may mean a move into the higher levels of consciousness. Otto Jespersen showed convincingly that progress in language could be achieved through the removal of useless complications. English, his chosen field, and the perfect example of a *lingua franca,* provided him with a luminous example. The German definite article, in the singular, has four cases and three genders; in the plural, the genders disappear, but the cases remain. There ought to be sixteen forms in all; there are only six, *der, die, das, des, dem, den,* because, in a most confusing manner, one form may be used for several different meanings. English has the single word *the*. This does not argue that the language of Shakespeare is in this respect inferior to that of Schiller. A regular verb is just as precise as an irregular one: *to love* is a satisfactory instrument, although, grammatically speaking, it is steady and not erratic. And a derivative like *goodness* is all the more intelligible for being logical. Our English adjective, sensibly enough, is invariable: in most other languages, it decks itself with various unprofitable endings. On the other hand, our eccentric accentuation is a torment, even to the native-born; French accentuation is perfectly regular, and the music of Ronsard, Racine, Hugo, Baudelaire, Verlaine, is not impaired thereby.

An "artificial language" is made up of traditional elements, both in vocabulary and syntax. But it is functional and discards all the excrescences which serve no visible purpose. In a report on the cattle trade, there is no advantage in preserving the plural *oxen* or reintroducing the plural *kine*. I am not advocating the ruthless simplification of our native language: I know that the disruption of our habits would outweigh the advantages.[3] But if we have to acquire

---

[3] The same argument has been urged against the adoption of the metric system, and so far it has proved invincible. The comparison is correct in theory; in practice, there is a vast difference in the scale of the problem. I for one spend whole days without making computations in inches or ounces; but language is needed at every turn. To convert the necessary records into the metric system would be child's play compared with the rewriting of our whole literature. The adoption of civilized weights and measures is an attainable goal; so would be a modicum of simplified spelling; but the complete removal of grammatical exceptions and irregular con-

a second language, it does make a difference that learning its grammar be a matter of minutes instead of years.

Those who firmly believe that an artificial language is guilty even if it should be proved to be innocent assert that, a crude thing at best, it could never express the complexities of modern civilization. The worst complexities—far beyond my reach—are those of the higher mathematics and organic chemistry; and they are translated into formulas which are frankly artificial and practically international. The complexities of thought do not depend, for their precise presentation, upon any absurdity of form: no irregular plural or preterit adds to the force or to the subtlety of an argument. This is no longer a matter of opinion. A difficult passage from Theodor Gomperz's *Griechische Denker* was translated into several languages, including Esperanto, then retranslated by other competent scholars into German. The version which had passed through the Esperanto filter was closest to the original.

There is one last ditch for the die-hards to defend: granted that such a code could be made accurate, still it would remain hideous; and aesthetic considerations have their legitimate share in guiding human action. I doubt whether any artificial language could be quite so harrowing as a "natural" language spoken unnaturally. A lady insisted on forcing her broken French upon Ambassador Jusserand until tears came to his eyes. He begged of her: "Madam, I beseech you, desist: you are making me too homesick." I am sure Esperanto would have been a great relief.

But is there any reason why an artificial language should be ugly? Professor G. D. Birkhoff, who attempted to apply the statistical method to aesthetic problems, submitted to his students lines which were scrupulously meaningless, so as to isolate the element of pure phonetic beauty. The one voted most pleasing vaguely resembled Hawaiian; the one utterly damned had a distant and delusive

---

jugations is hardly feasible. As for the most objectionable feature of our home language, its weird pronunciation, even the authors of Basic do not dare to suggest its reform.

Education of a Humanist

kinship with Magyar. But that is sheer prejudice: to those who know Magyar, it must have power and charm. Anatole France asked an advocate of Esperanto to translate the beautiful lines in *Phèdre:*

> Ariane, ma sœur, de quel amour blessée
> Vous mourûtes aux bords où vous fûtes laissée!

The young man did his best. The aged word-artist raised his eyebrows, and, with his justly famous Irony-and-Pity, passed the verdict: "You see, my friend, it cannot be done." If the disciple had dared to play a trick upon the Master, and translated the lines into Rumanian or Portuguese, Anatole France's judgment would have been exactly the same. There are not a few adversaries of artificial languages who do not know Greek: if you were to read a few lines of Homer to them, and if you told them it was Volapük, they would exclaim, as expected of scholars and gentlemen: "How horrible!"

The truth is that much beauty in literature lies in the thought, in the images that are evoked, in the depths that are reached, not in the pure sound. Puns wither when transplanted. "The Yonghy-Bonghy-Bò" and "Ulalume," two of the most hauntingly musical poems in our language, are strictly confined within the boundaries of English. But deeper notes—"Let there be light"; "To be or not to be"; "The rest is silence"—would call for the same response in any tongue, even Solresol. It is not necessary to reduce ourselves to such austere simplicity. Take such beautiful lines as

> "Silent, upon a peak in Darien..."
> "Voyaging through strange seas of thought alone..."
> "Tel qu'en lui-même enfin l'éternité le change..."
> "Ueber allen Gipfeln
>   Ist Ruh..."

the intellectual content, the emotional depths, are of far greater importance than the melody.

World Citizenship

No one expects an Esperanto to be beautiful: let it be functional and we shall be satisfied. However, even the most elusive kind of beauty is not barred out forever. Granted that the notes of such a language are without overtones: even with such a simple instrument, a true artist could express some of the music in his soul. The overtones would come later, when poet and audience had grown attuned to each other, when a tradition had been formed, when a statement could be delicately shadowed by an allusion.

Just as the accuracy of Esperanto was demonstrated by experiment, so was its capacity for beauty proved by experience. A literature has grown, rich in translation, but also in original fiction and poetry. This, however, cannot be asserted as a scientific fact, for it is purely a matter of taste. I can testify that there is a difference between correct Esperanto, elegant Esperanto, beautiful Esperanto. No one can appreciate these shades unless he knows the language and has abjured prejudices. A Samoyed, a Bantu are excusable if they cannot tell apart O. Henry, Henry James, James Joyce, and Joyce Kilmer. Theoretically, the possibility of beauty exists in all languages as soon as they become familiar. I claim no privilege for Esperanto. Dr. Zamenhof, its creator, was a solitary genius, an oculist by profession, with an extensive but superficial knowledge of linguistics: his solution is an individual work of art, which happens to please me, as Volapük does not. Even its oddities and absurdities give it a flavor all its own; and the very features that experts rightly condemn have endeared it to many of its followers. Its flaws, which are obvious, are venial compared with those of the best "natural" languages. But I should be the last to maintain that blemishes are a condition of beauty, clarity, or strength. There is no reason why a better language should not be adopted if one can be devised.

In this, I am a very orthodox disciple of the *Majstro,* as the faithful call him. He never believed in his own infallibility. He did proclaim that the essentials of his language, the *Fundamento,* should remain unchanged, until the matter be taken up by an appropriate authority. Then the idea would be safe, and the battle won: he would not care whether his own scheme were touched up, radically modified, or discarded altogether. This plea for provisional stability was not conceit or mulishness, but masterly strategy. It enabled Esperanto, after Volapük, but on an immensely larger scale, to provide a practical demonstration. No one who cares to look into the subject can now claim that people learning the language could not understand one another if they came together: there have been innumerable gatherings, including large international congresses, and although the participants had in many cases acquired Esperanto by themselves, in faraway places, no difficulty was encountered. No one can affirm either that a manufactured language would necessarily split into local dialects, or that it would change from one decade to another: Esperanto discipline, which is purely voluntary, has proved an effective substitute for the force of tradition; the Esperanto of fifty years ago is still the norm throughout the Esperanto world. This demonstration is invaluable. The unique place of Esperanto in the interlinguistic movement is secure, because the demonstration will not have to be repeated.

For the willfully blind, Esperanto has become a term of derision; and the worst among them were certain seceders or propounders of rival schemes. Esperanto, they asserted, was laughed out of court; it failed because of its manifest and ludicrous faults. This again is a misstatement. It is a fact that Esperanto has not conquered the world, but its weaknesses were not the decisive cause of its defeat. So long as mankind seemed to be proceeding steadily and peacefully toward a better understanding, Esperanto grew with our hopes, not as a fad, but as a force. By 1914, it had over a hundred magazines, some of them mere propaganda sheets, but not a few of very high quality. Official recognition had already been won from business and political circles. If the membership was fast increasing in numbers, its quality was improving even faster: scientists were growing interested in the idea, and scholars were following at their own gait, *pede claudo*. It was expected that the tenth International Congress, to be held in Paris, would be a decisive manifestation and open a new era. Alas! The date was August 1914. Dr. Zamenhof was turned back at the frontier; the members, already gathering in their thousands, had to disperse and attend to the more realistic business of killing their fellow men. Esperanto was engulfed in the disaster that overcame a peaceful and orderly world. The language has not fully recovered from the staggering blow. Neither has mankind.

Even before 1914, and while recognizing to the full the necessity of Esperanto discipline, I believed that scholars should continue to investigate the technical aspects of the problem, against the day when it would be finally considered by a competent and official body. The impregnable rock of the Holy *Fundamento* never blocked my freedom of inquiry. Esperanto is not the only project worthy of consideration; nor is it, at present, intrinsically the best. It is entitled to our gratitude, not to our superstitious reverence. Edgar de Wahl, an Estonian, was a perfect epitome of the whole interlinguistic movement. He worked with the various groups, modestly, patiently, over many decades; and he finally evolved a scheme of his own, *Occidental,* which commands the respect of all serious inquirers. Giuseppe Peano, the mathematical logician, following the hints given by Descartes and Leibniz, arrived at a simplified *Interlingua* or *Latino sine Flexione.* Since the core of his system are the Latin words that survive in English, it can be read, practically at first sight, by anyone who knows Latin, or English, or any one of the Romanic languages. Conversely, it can be used as an introduction to classical Latin. Every priest throughout the world could at once understand it and teach it. From the aesthetic point of view, it is by far the scheme which most appeals to me. The International Language Association, which owes so much to the reasoned and persistent enthusiasm of Mrs. Dave H. Morris, has placed the whole problem on a scientific basis. A competent staff has been at work for years. Elaborate lists of word-frequency and concept-frequency have been compiled. All existing schemes have been studied and compared. The advice of prominent philologists and semanticists has

Education of a Humanist

been sought, and they form an impressive rostrum. The Association has achieved much. Its position is that of the true expert, who is not a propagandist and not an executive. When a world authority recognizes at last that the language obstacle can be overcome, it will find all the materials ready for a final solution. Hardly a week goes by without my receiving a message from some lonely and courageous fellow worker, in Switzerland, in Mexico, in Sweden, in Yugoslavia. They have no reward but their unconquerable hope.

I found Interlinguistics—the conflicts, the contamination, the coöperation of languages—a complex and fascinating study. With a background of history, geography, and sociology, it raises many curious points in etymology, semantics, and general grammar, which is another word for logic. I may yet be able to organize my voluminous papers and more voluminous notes on the subject. But, although I recognized Interlinguistics as a fruitful branch of philology, the technical side of the international language problem never was uppermost in my mind. I was chiefly concerned with its third aspect: its contribution to the consciousness of world unity.

In this my guide was Dr. Zamenhof himself. He had definitely proclaimed that Esperanto was a language, not a faith; but it was his faith that led him to create the language. An Esperantist is simply a man who uses Esperanto for any purpose and in any spirit he chooses, futile, selfish, scientific, or religious. Dr. Zamenhof himself was a Jew; but, from the very first, there were Esperanto groups of Protestants and Catholics, and the idea found great favor with the Bahaists. The French Touring Club and the Paris Chamber of Commerce endorsed it, while young Stalin, an internationalist in those days, looked into it with sympathetic curiosity. During the First World War, I received a vast quantity of pro-German propaganda in Esperanto; the Allies had to retaliate in kind. But behind that perfect neutrality there was what Dr. Zamenhof called "the inner idea" of Esperanto. The visible need for international communication indicated the existence of a world community. The man who has oil interests in Saudi Arabia, the one who seeks to spread Buchmanism or Communism, the scientist and the artist, all, whether they confess it or not, are world citizens.

For Dr. Zamenhof, artificial obstacles between man and man had a vivid, a tragic significance. He was born at Białystok, where Poles, Germans, Russians, and Jews lived close together, in mutual diffidence and enmity. He could see, in the form of pogroms, the result of blind hatred. That hatred was born of ignorance and prejudice: he knew that his Christian neighbors were not all evil men, and that his coreligionists desired to live quiet, orderly, and useful lives. When he moved to Warsaw, he could see the language problem in a larger perspective. Whole nations were tormented by it. If Austria had adopted a liberal policy toward the Polish upper class, Russia and Germany were attempting to kill the Polish nationality by stifling its language. In Prussia, children were flogged for praying in their mother tongue. Poland was not the only sufferer: the Poles in their turn tried to polonize the Ruthenians.

The linguistic map of Central and Eastern Europe was a crazy quilt; and no map, however intricate, could convey the full bewildering reality. Cities were of different speech from the countryside; within the cities, quarters were at odds with quarters, and streets at latent war with streets. In Transylvania, there were Saxon islands within the Magyar islands surrounded by Rumanian masses. The Banat of Temesvár baffled the linguist and the ethnographer. Around Salonika, once officially Turkish and then Greek, there were Yugoslavs (in bitterest feud among themselves over dialectal differences), Kutzo-Vlachs or Rumanians, Albanians; the chief commercial element in the city was Jewish and spoke not Yiddish but a Spanish jargon; the language of culture was French. Everywhere, the policy of the governments was to impose an official "national" language, in the hope that it would create national consciousness and loyalty. It was considered a great victory for civilization if a Pole were made to speak bad German; and it was a triumph for freedom if a man refused to learn the language of Kant and Schiller.

Education of a Humanist

From this witches' caldron of politics, race, language, with class and religion added at times for good measure, arose fierce and ubiquitous hatred. Dr. Zamenhof thought of a first method of relief: let freedom of speech be restored. Let everyone speak without hindrance whatever language he, for practical or sentimental reasons, happens to prefer. Let members of different groups meet as equals, on neutral ground, through a common auxiliary medium. From the local conditions that he had observed, Zamenhof rose to a view of Europe as a whole, and of the mighty globe itself. For him, language conflicts were but the symbols of all artificial conflicts between men of good will: the problem was essentially the same with class, caste, color, sect. He did not believe that all men could learn wisdom overnight and dwell together in peace and amity; but they could at least be liberated from the self-imposed obligation of fighting for arbitrary divisions, the results of superstitious traditions. He was a realist: men are men, while nations are shadows, languages mere instruments, faiths but converging paths. Let men struggle, if struggle they must: but let it be for ideas, and by means of ideas. The notion of dictating sentiments and imposing inequalities by force—legal, military, financial—is damnable and must go.

Zamenhof expressed his ideal with simple eloquence in a great speech before the Races Congress (London, 1911), and with touching directness in the "anthem" of the movement, *La Espero*. Men rallied to his Green Star because of the hope it symbolized. Its chief appeal was that it offered at the same time a practical means as well as a distant goal. By learning Esperanto, you were actually breaking down a barrier; you could from the first correspond with likeminded people, *samideanoj,* fellow thinkers and fellow citizens, throughout the world. Symbol and instrument were one. The greater reward would be for future generations, but you could enjoy at once the fruit of your effort.

So the Esperantists started at once "building Jerusalem" within every nation. They gave immediate if sporadic reality to that "great Republic of Humanity at large" proclaimed by George Washington.

World Citizenship

Esperanto was by 1914 "the living language of a living people," and if circumstances had been favorable to gradualism, that people would have conquered the earth. The Universal Esperanto Association already had its practical side. Esperanto "Consuls" were beginning to lend their services to the members. The flag with the green star evoked deep loyalty. Interlinguistic romances were the by-products of Esperanto congresses; children were born who, first lisping in Esperanto, afterwards spoke English with a marked Esperanto accent. If much of this enthusiasm now seems naïve, we must note that the same spirit of boundless hope prevails in every new movement—Christianity, democracy, socialism—that truly reaches the people. Esperanto never was a fad among the sophisticates. It was endorsed by men like Max Müller, Leo Tolstoy, Boirac, a philosopher and university president, Sébert, a general and member of the French Academy of Sciences; a resolution was proposed to the League of Nations, expressing its sympathy with the idea, and among the signers were Lord Robert Cecil, Wellington Koo, and Beneš; so the movement did not lack intellectual standing. But the rank and file were common men, for whom the hatred of war and the oneness of mankind were articles of faith.

Thus the Esperantists of the heroic period had quite simply refuted in advance the fallacy of the great, subtle, tormented, and tortuous theologian, Reinhold Niebuhr. Niebuhr, paradox incarnate, is among the World Citizens who deny the existence of the world, among those Children of Light for whom Darkness alone possesses reality. He said: "National and imperial communities all have ethnic, linguistic, geographic and other forces of social unity. The universal community, however, has no common language and no common culture—nothing to create the consciousness of *We*."[4] This is the pure doctrine of Joseph de Maistre against the Enlightenment, the Revolution, and the Rights of Man. For De Maistre and Niebuhr, to be a Russian, a German, a Frenchman is a reality; to be a man is a meaningless abstraction. Yet a man of flesh and blood

[4] "The Myth of World Government," in *The Nation*, March 16, 1946.

must remain a man until he dies; but he may change his creed, his language, his allegiance; and many do. De Maistre, a Frenchman by culture, who was in the service of the King of Sardinia, lived for many years in St. Petersburg. Among the servants of the Tsars, he must have met Germans galore; Swiss; Frenchmen; a Livonian of Scottish descent, Barclay de Tolly; a Corsican, Pozzo di Borgo. Bernadotte turned from a typical Gascon into a model Swede and remained a man for all that. Both De Maistre and Niebuhr are Christians; they hold that Jesus died for us: what could create a deeper "consciousness of *We*"? Obviously, Niebuhr is spurning religion and philosophy, which are his spiritual homes, and which posit the unity of man. He chooses to move anachronically in the murky mystic atmosphere of German romanticism, according to which national cultures alone have life.

Yet the world unity to which the Esperantists were committed and which Niebuhr denies is plain for all eyes to see. Terence's *Homo sum* has never lost its validity. Men constantly and spontaneously say *We* when they mean the human race. According to Ségur, people wept for joy in the streets of St. Petersburg when the Bastille fell. Father Gratry said: "So long as Poland is martyred, we shall live in a state of mortal sin," and today the power of Franco weighs us down with shame and remorse. The planet felt the wound when Dreyfus was unjustly condemned, and great meetings were held in Paris to plead for Sacco and Vanzetti. Niebuhr himself, as the head of a relief committee, urged us to accept food restrictions because we could not face the thought of being replete in a starving world.

This feeling, I must insist, is not the privilege of an elite; it is more ardent, more spontaneous, among the masses than among the men of gentle breeding. The world community does exist; there is a humanity common to all men; to defend it against disaster and self-destruction is our common cause. This community is unorganized, because our political institutions lag a century or more behind our political consciousness, because we are still governed by ghosts, and above all because these ghosts alone have control of deadly weapons. "That community has no common culture"? If science and technique be part of culture, this is nonsense: Danes, Russians, Germans, Italians, Frenchmen, Japanese, as well as Englishmen and Americans, labored at the atomic problem. If Niebuhr means the arts: our museums are filled with foreign masterpieces, and the air is alive with German or Italian music. If he means literature: I have had Chinese and Iranian students who had been deeply moved by *Les Misérables*. "That community has no common language"? This is true also of India and the U.S.S.R.; it is a great handicap; and it is exactly the obstacle that interlinguists, facing a real problem realistically, are attempting to remove. Of course we need a common language, both as a symbol and as an instrument. And a common language shall be provided.

A FREE EUROPE, AND REGIONAL UNIONS

No child in Europe can be indifferent to international affairs. They loom like an eternal nightmare which, even for the richest and safest of nations, bodes catastrophes. Every neighbor is a rival and a potential enemy; he compels us (and we compel him) to arm and to place "cannon above butter," that is, to sacrifice such luxuries as social welfare and education to the jealous god of defense.

I have previously stated that two problems were haunting us when I was a student in Paris: France's feud with Germany and her enmity with England. Virulent nationalism at home made us realize that France would never enjoy genuine liberty unless she had peace; and that peace was not a matter of guns but of reconciliation. Hatred and fear are the hardest of taskmasters. After fifty years, that poisoned atmosphere has not been dispelled in Europe; indeed, it has grown denser. Now it has reached America as well. We too, at the summit of our power and glory, are devoured with anxiety and paying heavy tribute to our distrust and dread. *Morbus Europaeus* has become *Morbus Mundialis*.

I soon discovered that the Franco-German and the Anglo-French problems were inseparable. To treat one evil by itself only made the other worse. About 1900, France and Germany were manifestly drawing closer; but Anglophobia, thanks to the Boer War, was rife in both countries. With the accession of Edward VII, the Entente Cordiale became possible. But it did not clear the ominous clouds. There had been, throughout the nineteenth century, a strong pro-German feeling in England, with Carlyle as its most vehement spokesman. It turned to bitterness, because Germany, flush with military, scientific, and industrial success, would not brook England's invincible assumption of superiority. France was not allowed to be neutral; Germany, unable to strike at England across the inviolate sea, threatened to treat France as a hostage. It was a maddening puzzle: you could shake two balls into their proper holes, but never all three.

Many Frenchmen, many Europeans of my generation believed that if this equation with three unknown and capricious quantities could be solved, the peace of the world would be assured. This was not so provincial as it may now seem. It did not imply that only those three great powers counted and alone had to be satisfied. We fully knew that some of the smaller countries were actually more civilized than the giants in heavy armor. They did not have to be preached the gospel of peace; but, in spite of their moral superiority, they could not establish and maintain peace among their huge and surly neighbors. Some of the "little fellows," on the contrary, were more quarrelsome even than their "big brothers": the Balkans had an unenviable reputation in those days. But if the larger nations had been in agreement, these local feuds could easily have been adjusted. An Anglo-Franco-German reconciliation would immediately have integrated the whole of Europe; neither France nor England felt any hatred for the allies of Germany, the Hapsburg dual monarchy and Italy. Russia was barely discernible in Cimmerian twilight. But France had a defensive alliance with her; Germany had repeatedly sought her friendship; and robust, sensible England might some day cease to hear in her sleep the footfall of the Bear crossing Afghanistan. Moreover, the vast tenebrous empire, ill-compacted, ill-governed, was no match for a United West. We did not ignore or belittle America: we believed she was free from our curse. Preserving the peace in her own continent, she had no thought of disturbing the peace in other parts of the world. So, with England, France, and Germany firmly united, war on a large scale became almost inconceivable.

Two obstacles stood in the way: the Alsace-Lorraine question and the colonial problem. For Germany, Alsace-Lorraine had a symbolical value: it was the prize of victory, the keystone of the new Reich. For the French also, the two provinces meant far more than territory, wealth, or prestige. Their history had been checkered; but in 1871, they had expressed their choice, freely, emphatically, both in the French National Assembly and in the German Reichstag. *Revanche* never meant *revenge:* it meant vindication, justice. France could not accept the *status quo,* and Germany could not permit it to be questioned. Had the German ruling caste been civilized, had a generous autonomy been granted to the provinces, time would have assuaged the bitterness of the feud, and neutralization might have followed. As it was, the French felt that members of their spiritual family were held in bondage; and, a short time before the outbreak of the First World War, a German official blurted out that Alsace-Lorraine was still *Feindesland,* enemy country. The baleful figure of Bismarck grew more despotic after his downfall and death. His romantic medievalism, turned into a "vital lie" by a modern scientific people, paralyzed thought and inflamed primitive passion. The epigones of the Bismarckian age, stiff in the Iron Chancellor's crushing armor, could not afford to give up a particle of his heritage. Bismarck-worship and Napoleon-worship must be obliterated. Napoleon's work has been undone; so must Bismarck's. The huge barbaric memorials, the Bismarck-towers which dotted Hohenzollern Germany, were idols demanding the blood of millions.

On the colonial issue, Germany and Italy had a legitimate grievance. They had achieved their unity too late to grab their proper share of the spoils. The grievance, be it noted, was a matter of feelings, not of interests: how idyllic this world would be if it were governed sensibly by economic considerations! Germany was prospering brilliantly, although her colonies were all but useless. Italians found at that time unlimited opportunities in North and South America. The flag is not needed to create trade: England found in Argentina a more profitable field for trade and investment than in most of her possessions. There were no more empty, fertile, temperate continents waiting for the pioneers; no new Eldorado to lure the conquistadors. It was purely as a matter of pride that Germany and Italy wanted to assume their rightful place among the robber barons.

It is not easy to satisfy the pride of others without some sacrifice of your own: prestige consists mostly in keeping others humble and mindful of death; and what is called national honor is usually little more than saving national prestige. There might have been two ways out of the colonial difficulty, one "realistic," the other sensible (I swear there is a sharp difference). It would have been "realistic" to give the two insistent claimants their share; and England had thought—a masterstroke of *realism!*—of dividing with Germany the possessions of her ancient ally, Portugal. But "realistic" concessions breed further "realistic" demands; and England was determined never to give away anything of her own. The Bulldog Breed had adopted the motto: "What we have, we hold." It would have been sensible to liquidate empires by promoting home rule and assuring to all equal economic opportunities. But pride cannot be realistic, and greed cannot be sensible. The Entente Cordiale was sealed by swapping Morocco for Egypt—countries to which neither party had a right. Germany and Italy were left out in the cold.

World Citizenship

All this, to the American reader of the present generation, is the story of a world before the flood. New contenders have appeared: we ought, even in 1900, to have been more sharply conscious of their increasing presence. Out of the far and fabled East and out of the Middle Ages, a formidable Japan was rising. Russia, the loosely knit and dim-sighted giant, lurched into disastrous wars and miraculously emerged out of a thirty-year ordeal disciplined and dynamic. And we had not fully realized, half a century ago, that three antagonistic forces were tugging at America's soul: pacific isolation, imperialism (continental or global), and world citizenship. The star performers of yesterday, England, France, and Germany, have all but disappeared from the center of the stage; at best, they are the supporting cast, not the protagonists.

And yet, in this radically altered world, the terms of fifty years ago still define our problems. Now as in 1900, an intimate combination of England, France, and Germany could integrate liberal Europe. Such a Union, independent of American support, would have nothing to fear from Russian aggression. An equilibrium would become conceivable, thanks to which world activities could peacefully grow. Granted that Europe, in this century, has through her insane divisions forfeited power and leadership, she has at any rate preserved a certain preëminence in evil. A non-European war can be localized; but any major European conflict, whatever may be its starting point, is bound to set the world aflame. Europe is still the open wound; if she could be healed, mankind, with or without formal institutions, could learn the ways of peace.

Many political thinkers, from Pierre Dubois in 1306 to Coudenhove-Kalergi and Winston Churchill today,[5] have proposed a European Union as a decisive step toward durable peace. The remedy may seem paradoxical: the very hatreds which are the cause of war appear to preclude union. It must be remembered, however, that these hatreds are not in the blood: Germans and Poles, when transplanted

---

[5] Pierre Dubois thought of union as a prerequisite to a crusade against the infidels; so does Mr. Churchill.

to France or to America, soon forget their hostility. Hatred arises out of distrust and fear, which themselves are the results of ignorance. When people are thrown together and compelled to know one another, they discover what they secretly knew before: that folks are folks on either side of an arbitrary line. It is just because the ancient prejudices are so strong that they must be shattered by a deliberate effort. The reality, infinitely deeper than all prejudices, is that Europe, in all essentials, is one, far less heterogeneous than either the U.S.S.R. or Hindustan. It is impossible, as Arnold Toynbee has shown, to write an intelligible history of a single European people, or of a single literature, in complete isolation. All the great cultural movements in Europe have been Pan-European. This, for many years, has been the burden of my song, and I need not intone it again.[6] But the "idealistic nonsense" of yesterday has now become a commonplace voiced by the shrewdest politicians and businessmen. We are no longer preaching to the deaf, but to the blind. They understand that union is strength and peace, but they cannot find their way.

For two conditions have to be fulfilled if union is to be attained, and the practical men refuse to face them. The first is absolute equality: equality of status, equality before the law, of course, for we hold this truth to be self-evident that all men were not created equal. There must be no assumption of superiority, no claim to privilege, on the part of any national group. It was the dream of hegemony that proved the destruction both of Napoleon's *Imperium* and of Hitler's New Order. Without such equality, there can be no true liberty and no self-respect. The second condition is that the abolition of privilege cannot be expected, without sustained pressure, from the agencies whose *raison d'être* is the defense of special interests and privileges, that is, the national governments. Need we rehearse again the mottoes which everywhere sum up the tradition of

---

[6] Cf. *The France of Tomorrow* (Cambridge, Mass.: Harvard University Press, 1942), Part III; and *Europe Free and United* (Stanford University Press, 1945).

nationalism? "Ourselves first, last, and all the time!" "Ourselves alone!" "Ourselves above all others in the world!" "Ourselves, right or wrong!" This is exactly what must be broken down. And it can be broken down only through an appeal to the European people.

A nuclear economic union of Great Britain, France, and Benelux, to be joined later by Italy and the rest of Europe, including Germany, would be an excellent approach to the European problem, if we were still in a period of comparative sanity and peace, of liberty and comfort, such as the last decade of the nineteenth century and the first decade of the twentieth, "Europe without passports." In those happy days, gradualism would have been wisdom. But we are in a state of war: before the shadows of No. 2 have dissolved, those of No. 3 are gathering. In a catastrophic situation, leisurely methods are inadequate. The integration of Europe is a pressing need if we want to avert Armageddon; and statesmen—guardians of ancient skills, defenders of vested interests—are still balking at European integration.

The world is still thinking in terms of pacts between sovereign nations. Paper helmets! Pacts, if they were truly binding, would destroy the sovereignty of the separate states. So long as we respect the Hay-Pauncefote Treaty, we cannot do as we please with our own Panama Canal; but we would not respect it very long if it clashed with our national purpose. The sovereignty of nations makes every pact a scrap of paper as soon as an essential interest is involved; and every nation remains the sole judge of what constitutes an essential interest. *Sacro egoismo* is the supreme law, indeed the very definition of the national state. That is why the world is so skeptical about the most solemn covenants: not one of them, in a crisis, is worth the paper it is written on. Under Napoleon, when the guns of the Invalides were booming the news of some fresh triumph, the French wearily shrugged their shoulders and sighed: "Another victory!" Today, when nations assemble to outlaw war, establish justice, and proclaim eternal amity, the people sneer: "Another treaty!"

Education of a Humanist

The road to our hell was paved with dishonored agreements. The Briand-Kellogg Pact was the outstanding example. A sickly infant, it died in its cradle. It was exhumed for the Nürnberg trials, fitted with a preposterous set of posthumous teeth, and hastily buried again. Did Secretary Marshall ever remember its existence? There was a magnificent treaty of eternal peace and friendship, in December 1938, between Daladier's France and Hitler's Germany: "permanent," in the language of diplomacy, has the same ironical meaning as in the jargon of the beauty parlor. There was a bond so close that it amounted almost to a union between England and France on the eve of World War II: it did not stand the shock of defeat. England hastily withdrew all her planes to protect her own cities, and France signed a separate armistice. There was a Nazi-Soviet entente. There are still, for all I know, two unshakable alliances between England and Russia, between France (on the initiative of General de Gaulle) and Russia. There was another indestructible treaty at Dunkirk between France and England: who gives it a thought? There was a solemn peace, bearing our honored signature, settling for all time the fate of Trieste; the ink was barely dry when we changed our minds, because Trieste was a convenient bait for Italian votes. There was a formal promise, with the whole moral and material power of America behind it, for the creation of a small but independent Jewish State. We took it back, we restored it, in a series of masterly fake-double-reverse plays. Every nation reserves *in petto* the right of being "realistic" at the proper time. A new pact invincibly reminds us of the inebriate husband: "Yes, darling; I know I broke my promise; but I'll make you another *just as good*."

No European order can be founded on a precarious, and inevitably treacherous, agreement between nations. It must exist above the nations. In other terms, it must deny the fundamental dogma of nationalism: absolute sovereignty, a memory of monarchical days. It must seek the bedrock of democracy. There will be a Europe as soon as the Europeans, not the governments, are free to declare: "We, the people . . ." This declaration (which is not in sight) is

World Citizenship

both necessary and sufficient. When the people of Europe asserts its will to be recognized, it matters little what political forms are adopted at first. The war, which compelled us for a few years to unite or perish, was waged with improvised institutions: if only they had been preserved at the end of hostilities! England manages to muddle through somehow without a written instrument. The source of power is not paper, but the will of men.

The will of the European masses to live and work together has existed for two generations at least. It has been betrayed, it is again being betrayed, by the diplomats, guardians of the dynastic tradition, and by the politicians, defenders of selfish parochial interests. When a people discovers that it is not truly represented by its government, the result is a revolution. Such a revolution is needed at present in Europe. The Sons and Daughters of the American Revolution shudder at the thought. But revolutions do not necessarily mean bloodshed. In 1789, Louis XVI was resigned to the curtailment of his absolute power before there was any uprising in the country; the privileged orders freely abandoned their feudal rights on the fourth of August 1789. In Russia and Brazil, the abolition of serfdom and slavery—a major revolution—did not cause a civil war. England is particularly noted for sweeping yet peaceful adjustment. The "revolution" of 1832 was not won on the barricades. The Lords were shorn of their power without being sent to the scaffold. Socialism is being introduced without disturbing Church bazaars, Court ceremonies, and the Lord Mayor's Show. It is still possible, in Western Europe, for public opinion to assert itself apart from, and even against, the official governments. Fortunately, "subversive elements" have not been fully purged away, as they are under the various forms of totalitarianism.

There is a famous bit of French humor: *Le guillotiné par persuasion*. By gentle means, the upholders of ancient wrong may be induced to commit suicide. At any rate, it is well worth trying. The European Federalists were well inspired in calling together the States General of an integrated continent. There are new departures in history; but even precedents do not fully condemn such an attempt. It was a self-constituted committee that, in March 1848, summoned a *Vorparlament,* prelude to the Frankfort National Assembly; and Frankfort came very near success. One liberal country, France or England, might very well play the part of Virginia and Maryland in our constitutional history. The goal is within reach, if only people would realize that, in desperate straits, timidity is not invariably wisdom.

It is late. It is not too late. To unite Europe now is an immensely more difficult task than it would have been six or seven years ago; but it is also more imperiously needed. Imagine a Marshall Plan, with no Truman Doctrine attached, proposed by this country as soon as we went into war! Europe could have been created on these shores, as was, some twenty years previously, the Czechoslovakia of Masaryk. We had a chance to outbid Hitler's New Order. We could have offered the Germans a more intelligent alternative than "Unconditional surrender!"—that mask of grim and proud determination concealing a craven refusal to think ahead. There would have been no peace treaty, but a European settlement gradually elaborated by the European assembly. When the task was easy, we shrugged it away as Utopian. Now that it has become the one way of salvation, the difficulties are almost insuperable. Yet the tremendous efforts and sacrifices that the creation of United Europe would entail are trifling compared with the cost of World War III. We may learn some day that it is "realistic" to build bridges ahead when we expect multitudes to cross a river. Opportunism, crying "It is too soon!" until it changes its tune to "It is too late!" is the infallible art of missing opportunities.

There have been three developments in the last few years affecting the problem of European union: two favorable, but not decisive; one adverse, but not wholly disastrous.

The first is that the United States has withdrawn its unspoken but determined opposition to the scheme (when we consider how unaccountable the policy of great nations is, the word "determined" assumes an ironical overtone). It would have been natural for the American Union to favor a similar organization overseas. The reverse was the case. As Dr. Lin Yutang put it, it seemed as though preventing a European Union were one of America's unconfessed war aims. Perhaps there was some unconscious Machiavellism in such an attitude: we wanted to keep a good thing for ourselves. Thus France, before 1870, was proud of being "one and indivisible," and sternly resolved that Germany should not be. It was rather an instance of our inveterate conservatism; a new departure is "radical," and this nation, born in radicalism eight score and some years ago, still indomitably radical in science, education, and technique, is a very Metternich in the political domain and fervently clings to the past. We have learned wisdom at the eleventh hour: America declared herself proud of Secretary Marshall's bold and generous statesmanship. The Marshall Plan was hampered, and almost frustrated, by the Truman Doctrine: Washington spoke with two discordant voices, thus adding to Europe's incredible confusion. But the Plan was first offered irrespective of ideological differences; and it is not inconceivable that, much mischief done, wiser counsels may prevail.

The second development is that England has discovered at last (still in a slightly muzzy fashion) that historically, culturally, economically, and above all strategically, she is part and parcel of the European continent. Pride and prejudice, as well as misunderstood self-interest, had long favored "splendid isolation." Even the Channel Tunnel was dreaded by philosophers like Herbert Spencer as well as by soldiers like Lord Wolseley. Insularity in the twentieth century is a delusion, and the rocket bombs destroyed the last trace of it. But before World War II, even Coudenhove-Kalergi, who had inspired the Briand Plan of European Federation, believed that England should stay out; and Winston Churchill, in sponsoring Coudenhove-Kalergi's crusade, confirmed that view: "You have our blessing; but we, of course, live in a world of our own." Such a position was hard to defend, but Winston Churchill never made any claim to consistency. We cannot imagine that any British statesman, least of all Winston Churchill, could have favored or even tolerated the formation of an independent block, three hundred million strong, within twenty miles of England's shore. To dispel such a nightmare, the rights of the small nations would have been virtuously invoked. England would have shattered European unity as the disinterested champion of San Marino, Andorra, Liechtenstein, and Monaco.

As sheer isolation lost its splendor and became untenable, some Britons veered toward an English-speaking Union. The idea is attractive, and so long as it remains on the cultural plane, it meets with universal favor. Not so when it is translated into definite political and economic terms. Mr. Winston Churchill's Fulton speech roused no enthusiasm on either side of the Atlantic. Good old-fashioned Americans balked at "rescinding the Declaration of Independence." Others hesitated about foreign entanglements with what seemed to them a bankrupt concern. The British fully realized that in such an association the senior partner would be expected to play a minor part. And England went socialist, with the rest of Europe, at the very moment when America was trying to wash away the least trace of pink in her make-up.

The supreme argument against England's joining a European Union was the existence of the British Commonwealth. That admirable body, it must be noted, has not become better integrated, politically, in the present generation. On the contrary, the Dominions, under the Statute of Westminster, have been recognized as fully independent nations. The bonds between the members of the Commonwealth are historical, cultural, sentimental; and these bonds would remain unimpaired even though England were closely linked with the European continent. Canada is associated with the United States by the need of a common defense policy and by many practical ties; yet there is no thought of disloyalty to the symbolic British Crown.

From the economic standpoint, preferential tariffs within the Commonwealth are a comparatively recent policy (Ottawa 1931),

World Citizenship

which, because it was so halfhearted, has produced no sensational results. England, of course, would continue to trade with the Dominions, as she did before preferential tariffs were established. But a free market of three hundred million at her very door would appeal to her realistic mind. The pooling of the British, French, Dutch, Belgian, and Portuguese colonies would immensely expand the opportunities of British manufacturers.

The other major states in Europe would welcome the new New Order, provided it be free from the curse of preponderance. It would dispel the French nightmare—only too justified—that Germany might revive as a military power. The only safe solution of the baffling German problem is to abolish Germany altogether as an entity organized for war, and to absorb the Germans into a larger whole. In a United Europe, there would no longer be a separate German Army, great or small, overt, hidden, or potential. There would be no separate German industry, the backbone of modern warfare. But German-speaking citizens of Europe would have that *Gleichberechtigung,* that absolute equality of status, which they have a right to demand. The haphazard boundaries cutting across river valleys would lose their tragic significance. The absurd barriers between iron ore and coal would disappear. The problem of the Ruhr and of the Saar could at last be approached intelligently.

The chief gainers would of course be the small states. They would no longer be used as pawns in the game of power politics. Their theoretical equality with the larger nations, now a mockery, would become a reality. For within a Union, such as ours, force is not the final argument. As a consequence, smallness entails no loss of prestige and no sacrifice of economic advantages. Delaware does not feel itself "inferior" to Pennsylvania; Connecticut is not sacrificed to New York; Rhode Island is not under the thumb of Massachusetts.

But, in one respect, the situation has greatly deteriorated within the last ten years. Before the Second World War, Russia was opposed to the formation of any hostile group along her borders; she did not

Education of a Humanist

explicitly object to a friendly European Union. As late as 1943, in the palmy days of war, when people were not ashamed of being farsighted, bold, and generous, such a Union could have been planned with Russia's guarded consent. In a decade, much ground has been lost which cannot be recovered without conscious effort.

Russia had good reason to be guarded. For years, she had been the victim of aggression. The Western Powers supported every White adventurer they could discover. They encouraged Rumania, Poland, Turkey, to snatch whole provinces from the prostrate and bleeding giant. Our own attitude, although ambiguous at times, was on the whole much more sensible. Woodrow Wilson urged to the willfully deaf ears of Clemenceau and Lloyd George that the Russians be treated as men, struggling to emerge out of Tsarist chaos, not as a pack of wild beasts. And America refused for many years to acknowledge the secession of the Baltic countries, which had originally been engineered by German armies. But England and France bear a crushing moral responsibility. It is easy enough to forget the wrongs inflicted upon a great people; that people cannot be blamed if it remembers.

At last, Hitler's incredible folly made Russia and the West companions at arms, and reconciliation became possible. We almost grasped that miraculous possibility; perhaps Franklin Roosevelt, with his unique blend of generosity and cleverness, would not have let it slip altogether. We and Russia became acrimonious friends, then angry strangers, and at last open nonbelligerent enemies. It is difficult to tell when the rift began, for the new causes of suspicion merged all too easily with the old. The conflict was inevitable, not, I repeat, because of a clash in ideologies, but as the natural outcome of "realistic" power politics. When there are only two Big Fellows left, they are bound to snarl at each other. Once more, if Russia had emerged from the ordeal completely ruined, and England strengthened, Britain today would be the enemy.

Perhaps the turning point was the Polish problem. The West backed unreservedly the heirs of Pilsudski. They were not acceptable

World Citizenship

to Russia because they stood for imperialism abroad, reaction at home, and irremediable hostility to the Soviets. Had we frankly accepted the Curzon Line and a government of the Polish people by the people and for the people, Poland might be today the cultural and political link between East and West. In Hungary, Yugoslavia, Rumania, Greece, Italy, we made it plain that our sympathies went to the conservative elements. We did not realize that they were not "conservative" in the American sense, but feudal and anti-democratic. In Eastern Europe, Senator Taft would be a firebrand of radicalism.

As a result, Russia has turned against the West the bad old policy of the *Cordon Sanitaire*. She has favored pro-Soviet elements in the neighboring lands, just as we have been favoring anti-Communist classes and parties throughout the world. We must not forget that through the greater part of Europe, socialism is today the most urgent task of democracy; our State Department has at last recognized that Europe, thanks to the blind selfishness of its privileged classes, has gone socialistic. And for the European masses, Communism does not mean subjection to Russia, which no one in his senses desires; the Communists are simply the shock troops of social democracy.

Europe should by all means have extended as far east as the Curzon Line. Poland, Hungary, Rumania, Czechoslovakia, the northern part of Yugoslavia, felt themselves culturally one with the West. Warsaw, Budapest, Prague, even Bucharest, were European cities in tune with Vienna, London, and Paris, and not with Moscow. Now they are gone from us, for a while at any rate; and they cannot, they should not, be reconquered by force. Thanks to our mismanagement, Europe has shrunk by at least one third.

If what remains were to be organized as a fighting force against the Soviets, it would be an irretrievable disaster; for it would bring about the war we all dread and deprecate. In such a war, Russia would have one great advantage, proximity; and a still greater advantage, the fact that in the West she would find at least one third of the population in her favor, and another third divided.

Education of a Humanist

Western Europe—Germany and France at any rate—would be overrun in a few weeks. With our monopoly of atomic power, we could of course blast our way to ultimate victory by turning Paris into a Hiroshima. Strangely enough, the prospect fails to appeal to the Western mind.

If we truly want European peace, without which our own peace would be exceedingly precarious, let us heartily support some kind of a Marshall Plan on an even more generous scale. "A quart of milk for every European" would be a much safer investment than atom bombs and universal military training. But such a plan must be purged from any trace of the nefarious Lloyd George–Clemenceau–Hitler–Mussolini–Franco ideology. It must be made manifest that the Union of Western Europe is not directed against Russia, and desires friendly relations with Russia.

We must recognize also that Socialism, and its marching wing Communism, so long as they do not resort to violence or advocate violence, cannot be outlawed in a liberal state. A democracy ostracizing one third of its citizens, as would be the case in France or in Italy, would look dangerously like totalitarianism. As John Foster Dulles emphatically said, we have not declared war on Communism as such; we have expressed our undying hatred of tyranny wherever it may be found. Tyranny in its double form, imperialism and the police state. We stand against it wherever it raises its head, in Russia (no "appeasement" with what we believe to be wrong!), in Spain, in China, and above all in our own country. For a free world is one founded on consent, not force. We have the right—a right which Russia possesses also—to have our friends everywhere. But there should be no attempt to bribe or coerce European voters to support our friends. Bribery and coercion do not deserve, and never command, gratitude or loyalty.

The present division of Europe, created through our blunders, may help repair our blunders. Instead of having on the Curzon Line a sharp ideological frontier, which might easily have turned into a battlefield, we may have a gradual shading between the embattled orthodoxies of Russian and American doctrinaires. Already in the western belt of the Soviet Union, the Baltic Republics, the Communist system is mitigated. In the countries now within the Russian orbit, non-Communist parties are tolerated, although Communist leadership asserts itself with a heavy hand. In the West, the Communists, who have fought hard for liberation and worked hard for reconstruction, are entitled to a proper share in the government. Driving them out of power in France and Italy was a shortsighted policy, for which Czechoslovakia was made to pay the price. Driving them underground would be "worse than a crime: a blunder." France is a socialistic and democratic country with a strong tinge of Communism; England is a socialistic and democratic country in which Communism has little power. Through France and England, both lands of liberty, Socialist Europe can remain in close and friendly relations with capitalistic and democratic America. As General Eisenhower said: "A house divided cannot stand; but there may be houses of different colors on the same street."

The greatest threat to European unity, world reconciliation, and world peace is the fact that we have been trapped, without a calm, full, and free deliberation, into making anti-Communism a national doctrine. And for those whose sole idol is national prestige, it is extremely undignified for a great country to climb down. Let us remember that America is not without practice in that very difficult exercise. There was once a Washington-Jefferson Doctrine, not opposed to the World Republic, but deprecating special "foreign entanglements": our commitments in Greece and Turkey were a plain reversal of that ancient and wise tradition. There was a Richard Olney Doctrine, according to which our Fiat was law throughout the Americas: it did incalculable harm and was ultimately replaced by the Good Neighbor Policy. There was a Woodrow Wilson Doctrine, which we applauded during the First World War, and which won us devoted friends abroad; our Senate failed to endorse it, and it fell into disrepute. Only yesterday, isolation and neutrality were cardinal American doctrines that would never change. We are not afraid of the hobgoblin consistency. Let one more forgotten doctrine join one more forgotten man in the merciful limbo of history.

I have been concerned for years with the unity of Europe. For the regional system applied to other parts of the world, I felt sympathy, but with a touch of academic aloofness. I never looked upon it as a substitute for world federation. I never believed either that it was a necessary step toward world federation. The two ideas are excellent and can be applied separately. In my opinion, they will work infinitely better if they are combined.

Many planners on the cosmic scale divide the earth into a number of regions, nine, twelve, fifteen, twenty, with due regard for balance and symmetry. This may be a convenient scheme for purely electoral purposes: we want to get away from the nations with their petty interests and tremendous inequalities, and the globe as a whole is too large a constituency to have any meaning. A healthy federalism would welcome a drastic simplification of the political map.

In March 1942, when it was proposed to create a Supreme War Council, I suggested that it be turned into a Council of the Free Nations, with seven representatives, one for each of the following groups or regions:

1. The British Commonwealth
2. China
3. Free Europe, or Europe in exile, West of the U.S.S.R., including Republican Spain and those Germans who were Hitler's first victims
4. Iberic America
5. India
6. The United States
7. The U.S.S.R.

If the chairmanship of such a council had been offered to Franklin Roosevelt, it would have been advisable that he resign from the Presidency of the United States so as to devote himself entirely

World Citizenship

to the gigantic task of the combined war effort. Thus we should have had the nucleus of a world government, sorely needed for reconstruction as well as for victory. It would have existed, informal and effective, before the enactment of definitive institutions. At that time, it must be remembered, the tasks facing the Allies were far more intricate and difficult than would be those of a peacetime government. If a shipping pool could be managed when the seas were infested with mines and submarines, it would have been child's play to continue its services when hostilities had ceased. It is strange that capable men find it so difficult to think sanely, except to the accompaniment of gunfire.

This rudimentary government was based on the regional principle, so as to have as compact a body as possible representing the whole of civilized mankind. I have come to believe that the inclusion of the British Commonwealth was "unrealistic," that is, not in accord with the palpable facts. The Commonwealth, that supreme achievement of wise statesmanship, is not a constituted or even a potential "region." It is *sui generis,* a miracle, not a pattern. There is a Commonwealth feeling; there is no Commonwealth policy.

Of these six regions—omitting the British Commonwealth—four were already in existence: China, India, the United States, the U.S.S.R. Although India has since been split, it is still to be hoped that the two sections, which have so many traditions and so many interests in common, will find some acceptable *modus vivendi* and act as one in world affairs. These four are the "super-nations" of today; the would-be autarchies on a lesser scale are manifestly obsolete. Europe, in my opinion, should form at once a fifth region of the same class.

Of the same class: but there is no thought of imposing upon the five the same constitutional pattern, just as we cannot expect the provinces of India to attain, on the map, the marvelous simplicity of Colorado and Wyoming. Iberic America, the sixth partner, has a definite geographic and cultural unity, even though it uses two dialects of the same language, Castilian and Portuguese. There is no reason to force upon that group any closer political or economic bond. If the Latin republics choose to federate, they are free to do so. When you meet Latin Americans in the United States or in Europe, you are struck with their close kinship, and they feel it themselves. I had in my department at Rice a Peruvian and a Chilean at a time when their countries still believed themselves eternal enemies: in an "Anglo-Saxon" atmosphere, they realized they were at least first cousins.

The above arrangement recognized the plain facts: I did not invent a Lemuria, a Gondwana, an Atlantis. It did not disturb the political habits of the enormous majority of mankind. It left vast zones without formal organization: the Middle East, Africa, Indonesia. For many practical purposes, these could have been recognized as regions: but not in the same definite sense as China, India, the United States, and the U.S.S.R. Both Russia and ourselves provide intermediate steps between dependencies and full-fledged members of the Federation: autonomous republics, territories. The world state could very well adopt a similar arrangement.

These regions exist, therefore, not in the imagination of an ingenious prophet, but in the political world of today. For immediate purposes, my pragmatic definition of regions will serve: *the largest areas in which free circulation of men, goods, and ideas is at present attainable.* According to that definition also, the British Commonwealth is not a region, for there are tariffs and immigration barriers between its members. In the more distant future, the regions would be liquidated, for complete freedom of circulation will ultimately extend to the whole globe.

But again, I consider the arrangement as practical, voluntary, not compulsive: let the sons of Bolívar accomplish his noble dream if they choose. In Europe, the situation is different; it is pressing; it is tragic. Unless Europe unite, she will have to fight again; and imagination recoils at the thought of such a morrow.

Union will save Europe from catastrophe. But it has more to offer than safety in dinginess. It will bring a new hope, not to Europe alone, but to the world. The present book is the candid report of a student, not a piece of propaganda. So I shall close this section with a statement which would be my undoing if I were a candidate for office. I profess to be, as a disciple of Washington, Goethe, Hugo, a world citizen; and I believe that this One World, lost in a dark forest of hatreds and fears, needs leadership. Such leadership cannot be provided by distracted India or by war-torn China. But Russia and the United States, the two contenders, have both forfeited their claims. Not because, with their antagonistic systems, they block each other's way; but because those two Workers' Republics are too much alike. Both are frankly materialistic; both are blatantly doctrinaire; both believe in conformity, "hundred-percentism," imposed by force, be the pressure insidious or brutal. Above all, both are "Great Powers," the only Great Powers, and power corrupts. Europe, with her extraordinary variety and historical depth of culture, Europe, chastened by unexampled suffering, has at least a chance to seek and find a new path. But Europe must first be made free from want and free from fear. A liberal, a pluralistic Europe, if she could integrate herself, might bring harmony to the world. Arnold Toynbee expressed such a hope—in cautious terms, for the hope is faint. But it might well be our last, our only hope.

THE ATOMIC REVOLUTION

On August 5, 1945, Hiroshima was blasted by an atomic bomb. On the following Sunday, Robert Hutchins, Chancellor of the University of Chicago, participated in a Round Table discussion on *Atomic Force: Its Meaning for Mankind*. The great educator confessed that, until the preceding Monday, he did not have much hope for a world state: the bomb was the great light on his road to Damascus. To him, the formidable new weapon was what he called, after Léon Bloy, "the good news of damnation." "It may frighten us into that Christian character and those righteous actions and those positive political steps necessary to the creation of a world society, not a thousand or five hundred years hence, but now." On August 18, Freda Kirchwey wrote in *The Nation:* "In the space of a day, the World Security Organization grew from childhood to senility. Now it must be replaced ... A new conference of the nations must be assembled to set up a World Government, to which every state must surrender an important part of its sovereignty. In this World Government must be vested the final control over atomic energy. And within each nation, the people must establish public ownership and social development of the revolutionary force war has thrust into their hands. This program will sound drastic only to people who have not yet grasped the meaning of the new discovery. It is not drastic. We face a choice between one world or none."

The reaction voiced by these two intellectual leaders was quasi-unanimous. We have previously discussed the concept of self-determined periods: there are moments when mankind is conscious of crossing a threshold—or a Rubicon. Just as Rabelais had exclaimed, "We are out of Gothic night," so did we all feel, when we heard the momentous news, "We are entering the Atomic Age." The goal, Mankind United, had been clear for centuries; it had been defined by George Washington, Tennyson, Wendell Willkie, and a host of others; but the bomb completely altered the conditions of the problem. Instead of a distant ideal—Mortimer Adler, who had taught America "how to read a book," had said that it might perhaps be realized in five hundred years—the World State became an immediate issue. It was no longer sufficient to dream about it, or even to think about it: something had to be done. The tables were turned: it was the traditionalists, the opportunists, the gradualists, the safe-and-sane, the middle-road men, the muddlers, who appeared "unrealistic." When Louis XVI heard that the Parisians were storming the Bastille, he remarked: "So it is a riot?" "No, Sire," came the reply, "it is a revolution."

The reader would have tossed this book away long before this if he had no sympathy with my fundamental assumptions: that human thought and human will are factors in human history; that national-

World Citizenship

ism must be curbed and transcended; that definite evils such as ignorance, poverty, disease, war, must be fought by definite means, and, through eternal vigilance, can be held in check. I need say no more about what must be obvious to all thinking men. I have done, I am still doing, my bit of propaganda work: in an emergency, everyone must serve, even if he is not particularly qualified for the task. But this book is no place for propaganda: I take it fully for granted that my readers see the necessity of organizing mankind against the recurrence of war. My purpose is to examine the difficulties in our path. I shall do so without a trace of defeatism: the battle must be won. But it will not be won merely by the irresistible power of an idea. If it were sufficient to be right, the Christian spirit would be ruling the world today. Practical forces have to be harnessed, practical means have to be devised, practical obstacles have to be overcome.

One decision has to be taken: There must be a World State. The governments, and their advisers rich in retrospective wisdom, have shirked it. Farsighted in the wrong direction, they have rediscovered Metternich and Talleyrand. The San Francisco Charter created an old-fashioned League of sovereign states, which played from the first the old-fashioned game: deceit and bluster, secret diplomacy and power politics. I have chosen my course. But, much as I admire those great mystics Léon Bloy and Robert Hutchins, I was not moved to do so by the fear of hell. All fear is craven, and this is a time for greatness. If I were told that our path leads to damnation, the right answer would be still, "So help me God, I cannot otherwise."

Our experience since 1945 proves that mankind cannot be deterred from its evil ways simply through the fear of the atomic bomb. Strangely enough, that momentous invention has affected least those who should know it best, that is to say, the military men. We are making pre-atomic weapons at a faster rate than ever before; we are planning, not to coördinate and mobilize our industry, but to train our whole manhood, as though these were the days of Lazare Carnot and Napoleon.

Education of a Humanist

The atomic scientists assure us that there can be no defense against the atomic bomb. They are world citizens, and they are placing—pardonably, yet illegitimately—their scientific prestige at the service of their ideals. Once more, consult the expert and keep your own counsel. No ultimate weapon will ever abolish war. Artillery made cavalry obsolete (it took five hundred years for aristocratic army leaders to realize it), but it did not bring peace. When in ancient days a man faced a good swordsman, he knew that an effective sword-stroke would be fatal, as deadly, so far as his own individual life was concerned, as any atomic bomb; but he took his chance of killing his man first. Our Wild West heroes knew that the stoutest heart could be stopped by a bullet; they trusted that they could beat their adversary to the draw. If we cannot make our cities proof against bomb attacks, we can at any rate have the vital organs of national life buried deep in mysterious places. For aught I know, we may already have a secret President hidden in the caves of Kentucky, in case Washington should be wiped out. It will cost billions, but the realistic mind never balks at such details when it comes to thwarting the "idealists."

Defense, it is true, is apt to lag behind offense: the aggressive mind is naturally the quicker. All Maginot Lines would have been impregnable against a previous generation. But defense never is quite out of the race. I have greater faith in the scientists of the Atomic Age than they seem to have in themselves. Perhaps not the very same men who devised the bombs, but others of the same class, will evolve methods of protection. Some super-radar may detect the bomb the very moment it is launched; some wave inconceivable to the lay mind may deflect its murderous course. We are not fighting against uncontrollable elements: formidable as they may be, the new weapons are our own tools. Whether the arms be the stone axe or the death-ray, still the contest is between human wits.

The military know that the atomic bomb threatens to kill war; and since the healthy survival of war is their vital lie, they will rather kill the bomb, eager as they may be to use it. Of course, I know

World Citizenship

that every agreement for the limitation of armaments involves a fallacy: if men could be trusted to humanize warfare, they should be sensible enough to abolish war altogether. The temptation to deal a safe and decisive blow is all but irresistible: we committed the coolest atrocity in history, although Japan was already staggering. But if the temptation is great, the fear of retaliation is more effective still. It was not the deep humanity of Adolf Hitler that prevented him from using chemical and bacteriological warfare, in which scientific Germany was probably second to none. But Hitler knew that the same method could be used against his own people, and he recoiled. (I trembled to the very last, lest he should at the end unleash mad forces of annihilation, in a supreme *Götterdämmerung* gesture.) It is a fact that the world fought desperately for six years and yet managed to stop on the brink of the abyss. On a purely realistic basis, the outlawry of atomic weapons is not an impossibility.

We are now in the realm of hypotheses. I am not asserting as a fact that a mode of defense can be found against atomic weapons, or that a convention against their use would be respected. But these hypotheses are reasonable enough to blur our dread. We have sole possession of the atomic bomb, yet Russia is not abjectly submitting to us. We are aware that Russia knows the secret, or rather that there is no secret; and that the "know-how" may be attained at any time—perhaps a "know-how" simpler and more efficient than our own. Yet we are not hastening to make ourselves masters of the world by means of the "ultimate weapon." I am not belittling the importance of the invention: I believe it is so epoch-making that its destructive aspects will soon sink into insignificance. My point is that we cannot commit our souls, for salvation or damnation, to a robot of our own making. Man is still greater than the work of his hands, and his responsibility remains entire. It is not a gadget, however devastating it may be, that can frighten us into wisdom.

It is a commonplace, and perhaps a truism, that the Atomic Bomb heralds a new age which makes "modern man obsolete."

Education of a Humanist

The revolution does not consist so much in this particular discovery as in the method by which it was achieved. After three centuries of indecisive struggle, the scientific method at last comes fully into its own. It supersedes both the mellowed tradition so dear to scholarly minds and the aimless fumbling of the practical men. When I was a student in England, my British monitors told me with sagacious mien: "James Watt and George Stephenson knew nothing about thermodynamics." Toryism was still the ruling spirit in industry; it had not been fully exorcized from science itself. Atomic research was the triumph of radicalism in the fullest and deepest sense of the term. Against precedent, against the evidence of his own senses, starting from the most abstract hypotheses, man, by taking thought, showed himself capable of revolutionizing the material world. The laboratory proved immensely more effective than the drill ground, the stock exchange, or the council chamber. As methods of directing man's activities, these suddenly appeared antiquated. The formidable power, not of atomic energy merely, but of systematic, lavishly endowed, collective research was fully revealed. The techniques and resources of war—socialism of the most sweeping kind—and those of pure science were for once harnessed together, and the result filled us with awe. After the first shock, we are trying hard to forget the lesson so destructive of all our cherished prejudices. But we cannot. The Shape we ourselves have evoked from the deep will not recede. Henceforth, struggle as they may, the martinet, the huckster, and the prattler are but recalcitrant ghosts.

We, clinging to that ghostly yesterday, are actually striving to ignore the possibilities for good of such a revolution. I must repeat that I am not thinking of atomic energy alone. I do not know when it will be brought into practical beneficent use; tomorrow perhaps, but the rocket and the kite existed centuries before men evolved jet planes. What is uppermost in my mind is the effectiveness of the method for mastering nature. In an odd and vital little book, *A Time is Born,* Garet Garrett, writing before Hiroshima, had hailed a new age, basing his prophecy on organic chemistry rather than on nuclear physics. The same conquering method can be applied in food research and in the biological-medical field. The atomic bomb was but the sensational achievement of a new spirit.

This universal surge of energy was characteristic of the great sixteenth-century Renaissance: inventions, discoveries, scholarship, Reformation, artistic triumphs, all bore witness to the liberation of the human mind. In such times it should be a joy to be alive. When the dawn is so fraught with promise, it is depressing to think exclusively, or even first of all, in negative terms: how to prevent research, how to hamper experiments, how to preserve secrets. A healthy dynamic world cannot be founded upon distrust alone.

This jealous, repressive attitude is self-defeating. No Holy Inquisition can completely stifle discovery. If we do not transcend old-world conceptions of selfish power, we may easily imagine a Nazi or a Communist scientist evading the most rigorous inspection. He could work out theoretical solutions in his closet, and then perform experiments which to him would be crucial, while to the rest of the world they appear harmless or futile. There is no Maginot Line against research: the inspectors we are thinking of setting up would merely be qualified to prevent the invention of the atomic bomb—if it were not already there. We must remember that atomic energy is not the only weapon that science could place at the disposal of evil instincts. The Japanese were working on "death-rays"; chemical and bacteriological warfare, we are told, is an immediate and disastrous possibility. Repression is a blind alley. We must reverse our present attitude of bewilderment and dismay. We should seek salvation forward, by promoting instead of checking research. *Research should be completely released from the secrecy, the jealousy, the potential strife, imposed by national or private greed.*

So I found little promise in the proposed Atomic Commission of the United Nations. It was conceived in a surly and grudging spirit: how far should atomic research be tolerated, so that it would not endanger the crumbling frontiers and the obsolete economic systems of the old world? We should have realized that we were dealing with a new reality, transcending the national state, transcending Big Power politics, transcending both capitalism and communism. These old forms cannot dictate to research: it is they, if they want to survive at all, that will have to adapt themselves to the new conditions. The adjustment should be peaceful, if the waning institutions and doctrines meekly accept their subordinate position. The new world will have more pressing tasks than destroying Wall Street, Buckingham Palace, and the Kremlin.

The first step would be to create a World Research Council, autonomous in its own field, never to be held in subjection by the political states or by economic regimes. The Board of Directors could include, to start with, the Nobel Prize winners in all fields, including Peace and Literature. This Council should be endowed, not with a few paltry millions, but on the new scale inaugurated with the Manhattan Project; something that would be at least an appreciable fraction of what we are spending in preparation for the next world war. In the opening stage, this budget could be apportioned among the members according to the scale adopted for the World Bank, under the Bretton Woods agreement. But this would be purely a transitional measure: as trustee of new inventions, the Council would soon collect royalties on an ample scale and become financially independent.

The Council would create such new research centers as it deems necessary; there should be one at least in each of the main regions of the globe. It would also subsidize existing centers, without depriving them of their autonomy. It would, above all, coördinate all scientific efforts. It would have priority for the materials necessary to its researches, everywhere in the world.

Without having to proclaim such a lofty purpose (I do not forget how mortally afraid we are of being branded as do-gooders), the Council would inevitably be dedicated to the common good. All discoveries made by its members—whether institutes or individual associates—would become the common property of mankind, as it should be and by right is with all scientific truths. No exclusive patent rights. No monopolies.

This, I believe, would be acceptable to the scientists themselves. Great scientists do not primarily think of personal pecuniary rewards: we find no trace of the "profit motive" in Pasteur, the Curie family, Einstein. Even Proteus Steinmetz, who served industry and made millions for others, cared nothing for wealth. It has been my privilege to know three men who showed the same lofty disinterestedness in fields where private gain would have seemed most legitimate: Harris J. Ryan, William F. Durand, Frederick Cottrell. Scientists returned from Los Alamos with scanty thanks and scantier savings, while war contractors became millionaires. Legitimate self-interest, however, need not be ruled out. All scientists should be paid adequately. Participations in great discoveries should bring great rewards, both in honors and emoluments, if the scientists cared to accept them.

The World Research Council then would pool practically all vital inventions. This need not destroy the competitive system in industry for those who are attached to it. The present automobile industry, for example, is highly competitive; yet monopolistic inventions play a comparatively small part in the struggle. All manufacturers have a backlog of new ideas. All cars soon adopt all major improvements, of such a class as four-wheel brakes and balloon tires. The makers compete not by offering radically different features, but through refinements in construction or marketing: reliability, finish, a happy balance of qualities, good service, price. If the Research Council were to give the world a metal lighter than magnesium and tougher than steel, a gas-turbine no larger than a shoebox, indestructible tires, competition would go on as merrily as ever. Such is the case with those pharmaceutical products which are not patentable: each firm strives to acquire and to maintain a reputation. This is also true of books out of copyright: anyone can reprint Shakespeare, but there are indifferent and excellent editions.

Education of a Humanist

Secrecy and monopoly are not in the least essential to free enterprise: indeed, enterprise is all the freer without them. If on the contrary a nation or region should prefer to develop the inventions on a socialistic basis, it would be at liberty to do so. Scientific research goes beyond Adam Smith and Karl Marx.

Applied science would then be the common property of mankind, as pure science already is. Common property would be no mere figure of speech: the World Research Council would be the trustee for that "common wealth" which would be the growing substance of the real world state. So far as technical knowledge is concerned, there would be no hard-and-fast line between the Haves and the Have-nots. Every discovery would at once be accessible to all.

As a corollary of the scientific principle, the rule of the Council would be publicity—not advertising!—instead of secrecy. Even work in progress would be announced; all results, at every stage, would be published at once in technical papers, discussed in scientific conferences. All laboratories would be open to inspection, not by journalists, politicians, and detectives, but by competent scientists approved by the Council. Leading men from various countries could be drafted to work together on a given project. Young men in training would be encouraged to move from center to center, as did the handicraftsmen of old. In the service of mankind through science, technicians from the enemy countries would be welcome at once. It was reported—erroneously, I hope—that cyclotrons had been smashed by our troops in Japan: under the new dispensation, such an outrage would be inconceivable.

Diplomacy, politics, and business are all founded on rivalry and distrust. Even ideologies and religious faiths (in their historical formulation) are causes of division. Science alone completely transcends such antagonisms. To try to hold science in check by political and diplomatic means is absurd. The proper way is to release science from any form of political thralldom. Science alone can make a verity of the formula used over and over again in the charter of the United Nations: "without distinction as to race, sex, language, or

World Citizenship

religion"; and we might add: "without any distinction as to national allegiance, caste, class, or party." Atoms, elements, and genes will behave exactly in the same way before a qualified observer, whether he be white or colored, a Semite or an Aryan, a Christian or an atheist, a Communist or a Manchesterian.

I am not advocating a political dictatorship by the Scientists, such as was envisaged at one time by Ernest Renan. Scientists are but men, and very fallible men. I want them to be free in their own immense domain: I do not want them to abridge our common freedom. Their success will be our gain, and we shall not begrudge them their reward. I do not believe in rank; but I am quite willing that, in a sane and "realistic" society, scientists should outrank administrators, politicians, businessmen. They form a clergy and inherit many of the attributes and powers that the clergy possessed in past ages. Outrank, not supersede: the art of dealing with men is not learned in the laboratories. I am not ready to admit that scientists should outrank philosophers and poets; it is obvious that they cannot supersede them.

THE GREAT REPUBLIC—AND THE PRICE TO PAY

I am well aware that a World Research Council is not the full equivalent for a World Constitution. It is only a Declaration of Independence: the atomic revolution means the preëminence of science in the control of the material world, and we want science to be in the hands of scientists, not of soldiers, diplomats, politicians, and businessmen. If we achieve this—a charter for scientific research —then we may allow the purely political state slowly to wither away. It may not wither for ages; but it has already lost its absolute supremacy. This is not 1215, 1688, or 1787: the scientific revolution was not foreseen in *The Federalist*. If we think first of all of those great precedents, we are out of place in the world of modern thought.

So I never considered a world constitution as a panacea. Not that I was skeptical, or even indifferent. I knew there could be a better and a worse in such matters, and that it could mean success or catastrophe. One brief constitutional article might have saved the Third French Republic. We may be certain that no scheme will ever be adopted, and none will ever function smoothly, simply because it is "perfect" on paper. An excessive belief in elaborate mechanism is the delusion back of Mr. Ely Culbertson's well-meant and very able efforts. The Weimar Constitution was theoretically foolproof, and tumbled down like a house of cards. Our own Constitution failed to avert the Civil War; it has not worked well when borrowed by other lands. It is so loose that the most learned in the land, the judges of the Supreme Court, often disagree five to four as to the constitutional validity of an act. Several of its original provisions have become obsolete without being repealed. It soars vaguely above realities: it does not refer to the most essential feature (alas!) in American political life, the party system.

On the other hand, a loose pragmatic mass of precedents will work if the people show the proper spirit: the classic example is the British Constitution. Even emergency measures may prove effective, although they are not codified. The French Revolution wrote an admirable constitution, consigned it to an Ark of the Covenant of fragrant cedarwood, and deferred its application until the country was saved—the evident assumption being that a constitution is a luxury for easy times. Until November 6, 1945, liberated France did not have even a rudimentary constitution: yet De Gaulle's government was not dictatorial and not chaotic. I have already pointed out that, in the last year of the war, there existed a very powerful government of the United Nations, without any formal instrument except a general proclamation of a common purpose. It would have been much more important first to recognize that inchoate but vital rule as *de facto* sovereign over the whole free world than to draw up, in San Francisco, an impressive and deceptive charter. No more than six words would have sufficed: The Universal Republic is hereby proclaimed.

World Citizenship

My feelings about a world constitution and about a world language are scrupulously the same. Both are valuable, and first of all as symbols. The fact of formally adopting them would be a declaration: mankind, realizing its unity, wants to express it in practical ways. Conversely, by rejecting them, we openly profess that the world community is a dream. No doubt both are "Utopian." But there is a Utopia in every law, for no law can create the good it seeks or abolish the evil it condemns; it can only define a goal and a method. Without our constant striving, the most perfect law would be a dead letter. So it is with a constitution and a language. They have to be used, used skillfully, and used to worthy ends. But, radically different in this respect from the Briand-Kellogg Pact, they are instruments as well as ideals. They translate themselves into terms of definite action. The spirit informs the deed, the deed defines and enhances the spirit.

To me—still at heart an anarchist—the significance of a World Constitution is above all defensive: the constructive work demands other tools. We need such an institution not so much to attain positive good as to check immediate evil. There are conflicting tendencies in man: but the forces which make for war—jealousy, pride, greed—are strongly organized and formidably armed; the forces which make for peaceful development—enlightened self-interest, science, good will, brotherhood—no less real, no less heroic, are not regimented for a fight and possess no weapon. In a crisis, they have as much chance of making their will prevail as a peaceable crowd confronted by machine guns. The remedy is not to arm the faiths, the ideologies, the parties—that would be ubiquitous civil war—but to take the gun away from any one who places some passion or interest above justice. When Stephen Decatur said, "My country, right or wrong!" he gave the one irrefutable reason why the nations should be disarmed. We should simply shrug our shoulders in amusement if Jean-Paul Sartre were to say, "Existentialism, right or wrong!" because he cannot destroy rivals or dissenters. If we want peace and orderly progress, force must be not in the hands of fanaticism, but in the hands of the law: cool reason with a sword. And to establish world law implies a world state. To me, the world state is the police defending "the humanities," the universal commonwealth.

So I was filled with pride and hope when, in December 1945, I was invited to join the Committee to Frame a World Constitution. It was work in which I believed, and which I felt qualified to undertake; it would be my crowning effort in the service of the Humanities.

Two members of the University of Chicago, G. A. Borgese and Richard McKeon, challenged Robert Hutchins to implement his stirring declaration of August 12. Hutchins could not evade the logic of the situation. The Committee was created; Hutchins became its president, McKeon its chairman, Borgese its ardent and indefatigable secretary. The Committee has told its own story in its monthly bulletin, *Common Cause*,[7] and the fruit of its efforts has been made public. It is not for me to distribute palms among my colleagues. It must suffice to say that working with them was a great opportunity, a great reward, and—unexpectedly perhaps—a great delight. Our discussions were earnest and strenuous; in my case, they came between flights or train rides from the Pacific Coast to New York or Chicago and back again. I learned law, logic, anthropology, economics, history, from some of the leading experts in their fields. But my most abiding recollection is one of cheerfulness. We did not wisecrack unduly; but we practiced that virtue named *Eutrapelia* or holy mirth, "mark of the inward joy demanded by God of his servitors." I believe that *Eutrapelia* is recommended by St. Thomas Aquinas himself; and we had among us the staunchest disciples of the *Doctor Angelicus*.

The desire of the common man for a world of liberty under law is clear. It can be gauged by the responses to the popular books of

[7] The title was borrowed from G. A. Borgese's great book.

World Citizenship

Wendell Willkie and Emery Reves. To turn that desire into a working world order is not an easy task. The will must find its way, and first must explore the possible ways. The universal republic will not happen unconsciously, automatically, "organically," according to the lazy fatalistic philosophy of the nineteenth century. A world order is not merely an aspiration: it is an act of faith, an act of will, and a complex technical problem. Many, including mad Emperor Norton, wished for a bridge over the Golden Gate; but the bridge could not be built until it was planned for, blueprinted, voted upon, financed. All this preparation, this listing of obstacles, this definition of terms, this mooting of solutions, is indispensable; and such was the work we were engaged upon. Modestly, without megalomania: we expected no Lawgiver to descend from Mount Sinai with the new Tables of the Law. But while prophetic voices are urging that the work should be done, scientific minds are examining how it can be done. Then will come the statesmen, and it will be done.

A few principles guided me during these two years of intense research and discussion. I could not have signed our project if it had radically departed from them.

The first is that the Great Republic (to borrow Washington's famous phrase) must have sovereignty in its own domain. It must not be a mere League of Nations, with delegated powers which at any moment may be whittled down, nullified, or withdrawn. Because the nations are invincibly attached to the tradition of "sacred egoism," the Great Republic must derive its power directly from the people. When its representatives gather, they must form a genuine Parliament of Man, not a diplomatic conference. This is the one essential step, which was not taken at San Francisco. The rest might be left to "organic evolution."

The division of power between a central government and local or special [8] authorities is the very essence of federalism. The balance between the two is extremely delicate: every Federation, including

---

[8] *Local* and *special*: by this distinction, I mean to reserve the possibility of non-territorial agencies, economic or cultural, as components of the world state.

our own, hovers between the *Staatenbund,* or League of States, and the *Bundesstaat,* which, although decentralized, is in fact unitary. In attempting to trace that elusive line, three tendencies appear among world federalists.

The *Minimalists* demand a limited world government, with only those powers which are necessary for the preservation of peace. It seems to me practically impossible to establish such a distinction. Any conflict—religious, racial, economic, cultural—may become a threat of war. Armaments no longer are purely a matter of actual military forces: they consist first of all of an industry geared in advance to war production. The great danger, for generations to come, will be the survival of the jealous national spirit; a central government too narrowly circumscribed would be unable to cope with it. It is the police that we must strengthen, not the potential lawbreakers. The crucial question is: will the world state have a force at its disposal sufficient to impose the law, even upon the mightiest offenders? If not, we have nothing but a feeble league, and we remain in the chaos of power politics. But if the world state is to have such a force, it can be limited only from within, in the same way as any liberal government is today.

The *Maximalists* (and many Minimalists unconsciously blend the two principles) start from the grand conception of essential human rights. These rights, common to all mankind, are to be guaranteed by world law. If they are infringed by local authorities, any individual may seek redress before the courts of the Great Republic. There is no doubt in my mind that this conception is ideally right. It means, of course, a unitary state: the nations are reduced to mere autonomous provinces, and their activities limited to strictly local interests. No doubt it would be extremely difficult to formulate these rights in a way that would be precise enough to have any legal significance, and yet acceptable to all mankind. Everyone for instance will agree on Liberty. But some will interpret liberty as independence, which is anarchy: the world community, like all communities,

World Citizenship

is founded upon interdependence. As Sir John Maynard points out, for the socialists, the first condition of liberty is economic security; for others, it might be the sacred right of getting rich. Equality means, among other things, racial equality. Will South Africa, in this generation, allow a Kaffir to appeal to the World Courts?

I do not object to the explicit statement of great ideals. It has an educative value: gradually, it will shape the law. The place of such a statement is in a majestic Preamble. But the Constitution is not a homily, it is a law; and its actual articles should contain nothing which is not enforceable. Else, we shall foster that soul-destroying hypocrisy which has been the curse of much "idealism." I wish I could honestly believe in Maximalism. The plain fact is that I cannot.

The third tendency, which might be called the *Constructive,* is to give the World State unlimited scope in every activity that is international or supranational. Let the nations remain supreme in their own sphere: but there is much that lies beyond. The most obvious and most essential of these activities is a world police: the independent nations provide no ultimate basis for their relations except war. But ultimately the police, as it does within a civilized state, would lose in relative importance. An international reality is world trade. The Great Republic should be, among other things, an International Commerce Commission. Trade includes transportation and communications beyond national boundaries: the Shipping Pool of war times should be revived, and a World Air Service created. The keys to international circulation should be under world control: Suez, Singapore, Panama, Gibraltar, Kiel, the Dardanelles, and the Bosporus. This conception was properly extended by President Truman to international rivers, such as the Rhine, the Danube, the St. Lawrence, the Amazons, the Río de la Plata. The world state would have charge of international sanitary measures; it would be entrusted with the repression of the white slave traffic and of the illicit commerce in narcotics.

Education of a Humanist

All this is familiar enough: such agencies existed before the First World War. The difference is that these functions would be coördinated; and above all that they would be exercised by the World State directly, not by grudging delegation from the various political governments. The World State would exist because it would have something essential and definite to do, something which the nations cannot do so well. With its world shipping, world aviation, world bank, world currency, it would be a greater economic power than any of the territorial units; and that power, founded upon intercourse, could not, without defeating itself, be used for selfish ends. Nothing in all this would interfere in the slightest with the way of life of an American, so long as he lived in America and dealt with fellow Americans. But as soon as he engaged in any international or supranational activity, he would *ipso facto* fall under the jurisdiction of the World Republic.[9]

Note that the Rights of Man, which at present cannot be enforced upon the nations, turn into a reality in the vast and ever-increasing domain of the World State. We cannot by law compel a Boer to behave in a Christian manner to a Kaffir; but we can give a Kaffir, in the multifarious activities of the World State, an absolutely equal chance with the Boer. If the Boer does not relish the prospect, he has only to stay within his own boundaries.

The World State would not be concerned exclusively with material interests. It would be the natural trustee for the Scientific Council which we have previously discussed. Other cultural foundations—universities, academies, fellowships, philanthropic and religious bodies—might seek an international charter.[10]

The Constitution framed by our Committee does not emphasize this aspect of internationalism; but it removes obstacles from its path. If it came to a choice, I should unhesitatingly prefer activities

---

[9] As a corollary: all passports for international travel would be issued by the World State, not by the national governments; and for protection abroad, a man would resort to World State agencies, not to consuls appointed by his own country.

[10] In particular, an Interlinguistic Institute.

World Citizenship

without legislation to legislation without activities: reality, even though chaotic, rather than Utopia, however ideal. But the opposition is absurd: the two conceptions must inevitably work together.

In the 1948 elections, both parties, through their presidential candidates, proclaimed their faith in an international order founded upon righteousness and justice. We ought by this time to be familiar with the irrefutable argument: no peace without justice, no justice without law, no law without enforcement. To make justice instead of "My country, right or wrong!" our guiding principle is the implicit recognition of the world state. If we believe in power politics (gangsterism *in excelsis*) instead of liberty under law, then our support of the United Nations, our reproof of the obstructionists, are only sanctimonious masks. Unless the United Nations turn into a genuine world government, it will remain an interminable, confusedly squabbling diplomatic conference, an irritant to the world's ills. If realism were given its true meaning—the power to discern between hard facts and shams, between crumbling façades and living forces—it would be seen that the world state exists *de facto,* although chaotic and torn by civil war. A state may exist before it has a formal constitution: so it was with our own country. The crime of the Nazis was rebellion against "the Great Republic" hailed by George Washington one hundred and sixty-three years ago.

The cost of national sovereignty and power politics is war: a cold war at first, irritating, crushing material interests, numbing thought; and, at the mercy of the merest incident, a shooting war. But do not imagine that law, the sole foundation of peace, does not also exact a price. Law is a curb: we cannot hope at the same time for the profits of anarchy, such as they are, and for the benefits of order. Law is forethought, law is planning; and this is no less true of power politics. If we were taking no thought for the morrow, we should clear out of Europe and scrap our armaments. The choice, therefore, is not between the practical and the utopian, but between two rival constructive programs. It does not suffice to say, "Let us be good!" or "Let us be strong!" Either resolution must be implemented. If

Education of a Humanist

we want to be both strong and good, let us be wise. Therefore let us think ahead: this is the first item in the price for security. Many will find it a heavy one.

The second item is heavier still, for it is of a sentimental nature, and passion "rates" higher than thought. The chief obstacle to peace is that national selfishness ("Myself first, last, and all the time!") has been extolled for over a century as the highest duty of man. If we want the spirit of fierce tribal egotism to wane, we must first work for a world in which no *national* privileges are recognized; for the inevitable effect of these is to harden differences and intensify rivalries. In this respect, the Germans were right after the First World War in their claim for *Gleichberechtigung,* full equality of status. Without such equality, there can be no liberty and no genuine peace: for privileges can only be maintained by force. Treat an American as a citizen of the first class and a Chinese as a citizen of the second class, and you will turn America and China into eternal enemies.

That is the danger of introducing into the proposed World Parliament, or revised United Nations Charter, the idea, mooted by the Dublin Conference and adopted by many World Federalists, of a "properly weighted" representation. If we give a larger vote to a country because of its "greater economic development," we are recognizing power and wealth instead of plain justice. Any legislation which takes that element into account is plutocratic. Be sure the Have-nots will soon detect the fact.

A literacy test is more justifiable, yet it also might be a cause of injustice. Illiteracy is a misfortune rather than a crime: the masses, long kept in ignorance by their masters, would be penalized for their sufferings. I am a bookman, and I can find no proof that book learning is a full guarantee of wisdom. The Chinese evolved such a leader as Sun Yat-sen, and the Hindus have Nehru; prominent members of the French Academy supported Pétain, and the most highly educated country in the world, Germany, submitted to Hitler.

If economic and literacy tests were to be adopted, in all fairness they should apply to individuals, not to nations. Liechtenstein is not the equal of the U.S.S.R. in the game of power politics; but every Liechtenstein subject should, before the law, enjoy equality with every Soviet citizen. Let us then rule—if we dare—that no man has a soul unless he has a substantial income and is able to read *Forever Amber*. But if we assigned differential quotas to *countries,* the result would be absurd. The vote of a Hindu captain of industry would count for less than that of an American pauper, the vote of a Chinese scholar for less than that of an American illiterate. It would be dangerously cynical to enact for the World State civic inequalities which we reject with horror at home. I have no blind faith in universal suffrage, and I do not believe that it is identical with democracy. It is merely a defense against privilege: all self-style elites use their influence to protect their vested interests. If we have any voting at all, let us make no effort to enrich the rich and strengthen the strong: they are quite able to take care of themselves. Let their profits be the reward of their services; and of such services, let the people be judge.

The reactionary proposal of "weighted representation" (as in Prussia before 1919) springs from the fear that we might be outvoted by "Asiatic hordes." There is no reason to suppose that, except on that very issue of equality, the Asiatics would vote solidly against us. Asiatic unity is a delusion. India and China are radically different, and each is even more sharply divided than we are. There are many Chinese who agree with certain Americans better than they agree with other Chinese: Chiang Kai-shek and Colonel McCormick are on the same side of the barricade. One of the meanings of democracy is the readiness of the minority to submit gracefully, without forswearing its beliefs, and without committing suicide. We are teaching that difficult piece of wisdom to our citizens; we must learn it ourselves in the international field.

Juggle representation as we may, there is no method that will ensure that we, one hundred and fifty million strong, shall invariably command a majority in a world of two billion. There is only one protection against being outvoted: the veto. But the veto is the reward of sheer power: no one believes that Russia is intrinsically wiser or more virtuous than Sweden; and, to remain effective, the veto must be backed by effective power. That means that we cannot escape from the welter of rival forces, brutal and deceitful, which is plainly the origin of all wars. Our only hope, as our national leaders have put it, is to establish a world rule that will guarantee justice. Once again, if our advantages are just, they will be safe; if they are not just, they should be sacrificed.

We cannot preserve peace, liberty, and injustice. Resignation to the loss of privileges, or better, a proud acceptance of fair play, is the price demanded for the abolition of war. Are we ready to pay such a price?

First of all, we must give up altogether any thought of dictating a world constitution, of fashioning it exclusively in our own image. There is an ideal of liberty and justice which is universal: else no government would be conceivable. But "God fulfills Himself in many ways, lest one good custom should corrupt the world." It is the damning weakness of Clarence Streit that he cannot conceive of international organization except on the orthodox lines of Anglo-Saxon liberalism, just as the Holy Alliance was unable to look beyond monarchical legitimacy. Against this sectarian view, I have repeatedly quoted the words of that canny Scot, John Buchan, Lord Tweedsmuir—no visionary, but a popular writer, an able business-man, a great servant of the Commonwealth. "It seemed to me," he wrote in his autobiography,[11] "that democracy had been in the past too narrowly defined and had been identified illogically with some particular economic or political system, such as *laissez faire* or British Parliamentarism. I could imagine a democracy which economically was largely socialist and which had not our constitutional pattern." We should go to the world's constitutional convention ready to defend our principles, but ready also to learn from others.

[11] *Pilgrim's Way* (Boston: Houghton Mifflin Co., 1940), p. 222.

World Citizenship

It is my conviction that forms are accidental, and that ideologies are mere rationalizations or working hypotheses. Four things must be present and work together; all four are indispensable, and only those four matter: *will power* in the service of *good will,* while the *critical spirit* and the *experimental method* never relax their vigilance. The authorities of Aristotle, Saint Thomas Aquinas, Adam Smith, Jefferson, Hamilton, Karl Marx, and Lenin are not exempt from the searching test.

I hate compromise, if it means deliberately submitting to some evil, even for the sake of a greater good; but I believe in careful and fair-minded adjustment. Truth is not crude: that is exactly what the sciences, the humanities, and the law courts are attempting to teach us. The World State is our common cause: it must be conceived so as to include all men. A Universal Republic established by one section only according to its own particular principles would be a mockery, even though seats were reserved for the "erring sisters." The erring sisters have convictions of their own, and they too aspire to form a commonwealth embracing all mankind. A Union of the Streit type is nothing but an alliance for the suppression of heretics. Even supposing that our military victory were certain, and that we should be ready to pay the price in gold and blood, the moral cost would be disastrous. For no one has ever been converted by force, neither our own South, nor the Germans in 1918 and 1945. The only justification of victory should be to "bring people to their senses" and "make them listen to reason": why not appeal to reason first of all? Getting tough is no argument; all too often, a tough hide covers a soft brain.

It will not do, therefore, to evade the issue and go ahead "with or without Russia." The very first step is to discuss peaceably, amicably, with Russia. It has not failed, for it has not been given a fair trial. This cannot be done unless we drop the crude and fanatical belief that Russia, at all times, on every point, must be infallibly wrong. (Even when she agrees with Lord Curzon.) There are many things that are right about Russia, as can be learned, for instance,

Education of a Humanist

from Sir John Maynard's thorough and judicial study, *Russia in Flux*. I am not suggesting that we should accept wrong and call it right: this would be appeasement at its most cowardly, not peace. But our one hope is to find out what is right with Russia, that is, the points of possible agreement. For these will be the sole firm foundation for the Great Republic. So it is imperative that we should first of all follow the advice once offered by Mr. John Foster Dulles and make it plain that we are not fighting *Communism,* the belief and practice of the early Christians; we are fighting *tyranny,* as we have from the beginning of our national existence. And the best way to fight tyranny is to establish the reign of freely discussed, freely accepted law.

We are in no such mood at the time when I pen these lines: may they be obsolete before they appear in print! The difficulty is that our conflict with Russia is not at bottom ideological: it is a clash of elementary passions. Both the Russians and ourselves are good pragmatists and care little for abstract conceptions: Lenin and Stalin have repeatedly boxed the compass. Our economy is far from being solidly "individualistic." We are not fully convinced that our political machinery is divinely inspired; and it is obvious that Russia is not the Communist Utopia which is found only in the Catholic religious orders. The contest is purely one of power. Flushed with military and economic victory, we bulge our muscles and frown on all comers, ready to "show 'em who's boss," whoever *they* may be. For those who acknowledge our supremacy, we are all smiles and generosity: *parcere subjectis et debellare superbos.* The nations behave like the kings whose heirs they are, that is, like gentlemen infinitely punctilious about their "honor," and ready to draw if any rival should bite his thumb at them. It is this swashbuckler's conception of prestige that must first of all be purged away.

The first step toward peace, therefore, is to withdraw our declaration of war and to stop the insensate crusade against "Communism." For many red-blooded Americans, this would be an intolerable humiliation: we have scowled so long that a smile would seem a con-

World Citizenship

fession of weakness. For those whose national ideal is not the bully but the true Christian, the scholar, the gentle man, this would be no humiliation, but the end of a nightmare. Let the misbegotten doctrine be sent into the wilderness, a goat for Azazel. Until this be done, the Great Republic will be a dream. The problem today is not "Which is the bigger and the tougher giant?" but "Will the giants have wit enough (a rare commodity among giants) to swallow their pride, forget their awkward bulk, and show as much sense as though they were dwarfs?"

We are now reaching the heaviest item in the bill for peace. Let us suppose the Russo-American problem solved. Let us imagine that a formula has been found that will make the world safe for both the scared giants, safe for democracy in both its forms, capitalistic and communistic. (This, by the way, is exactly what the Hutchins Committee to Frame a World Constitution has been attempting to do.) Safe for democracy: it must be democracy indeed, something far more vital than any election machinery. It implies the rejection of privilege, equality of status, and a fair opportunity offered to all as essential conditions of freedom; liberty under the law; and the law as the relentless quest of justice. The law, which is the common will, tends to sweep aside everything that is not for the common good; our pride, our wealth, have to stand the test. Are we ready to accept the consequences?

The United Nations must soon turn into a world state or die of congenital insincerity. Now, in a world state, we must expect that free circulation of goods, men, and ideas which already exists in some of the regional unions, and particularly in our own country. We may—indeed, we inevitably shall—write into the original constitution that tariff and immigration policies are matters which are reserved exclusively to the national states. But any intelligent constitution provides for its own revision at the will of the majority. Economic and population barriers are far less sacred than political and military boundaries: England prospered for generations under free trade, and we under free immigration. We have to face the possibility that in defending our autonomy on these points we may be outvoted ten to one.

Even the feeble United Nations Organization has given us an inkling of what could be done in that line. There was a country, Palestine, which had ceased to be Jewish nearly two thousand years ago, and which had been Arabic for fully a thousand years. An outside authority decided to force an unwelcome immigration upon it, with the avowed purpose of shifting the majority and changing the allegiance of the land. Liberals in America, in strange alliance with fierce nationalists, racialists, and theocrats, urged that the material power of the United Nations be used to impose that solution. What the world—unwisely, in my opinion—claimed the right to do in Palestine, it could attempt on a larger scale in America. The precedent is deadly.

"Ah! But the comparison is foolish. The Palestinian Arabs, even with the help of all their sympathizers in neighboring lands, are powerless against the might of the giants, the United States and Soviet Russia, united for once (and terribly embarrassed by the fact). Who is going to treat us like another Palestine, compel us to admit Chinese, Japanese, Hindus, in such numbers that a vital part of our territory be made thoroughly Asiatic?" What is the difference? Simply that, according to the good old jingo tune, "We've got the men, we've got the ships, and we've got the money too." A frontier, political, economic, or ethnic, is a fortification of the Haves against the Have-nots and can be maintained only by force. Unless we are ready to share the land and share the wealth, we need the veto in all its rigor, supported by a stockpile of atomic bombs. And this is the negation of everything we are striving for.

If we were thinking in the crude terms of a dilemma, we should have only two alternatives: relentless preparation for war (and we ought by this time to have learned the lesson: *Si vis bellum, para bellum*), or the unreserved abandonment of privilege. Let us sacrifice all our material advantages in order to save our souls. Let the hungry from the whole world flock to these shores, until a common level of misery be established throughout the earth. One generation, atoning for the sins of many, would deeply suffer. The next, starting from the bottom of the abyss, would strive to improve the condition of "Humanity at large" by every available means, the most obvious being birth control.

In the perspective of centuries, this solution might be wise as well as heroic. I love to dream ahead; when it comes to planning, our units of time should be generations rather than millennia. That is why the radical proposal to accept at once the full logical consequences of our principles does not appeal to me. As a realist, I know there is not the slightest chance of our adopting it; as an idealist, I sincerely believe that it would not, within the next fifty years, be of the greatest benefit to the greatest number.

What I have to offer is not a compromise but a dialectic application of the historical spirit. Let us not refuse to move, huddling behind the Maginot Line of our material supremacy. Let us not attempt either to jump into a perfected Utopia. Let us define the goal by proclaiming at once and without mental restrictions the Great Republic envisioned by George Washington. But let us recognize that the existence of that Republic will remain exceedingly precarious until inequalities have been so reduced that the last frontiers may be allowed to crumble, and complete freedom of migration may prevail.

These glaring inequalities, and not the U.S.S.R., are the enemies against which we must wage unremitting warfare. Unless we raise the level of the whole world, the rest of the world will drag us down, by warlike or by legal means. If our advantages are blindly defended as sacrosanct, they will be challenged, attacked, and ultimately destroyed. If on the contrary we consider them as opportunities for service, they will be respected.

Here again, realistic and idealistic considerations are in harmony. Mankind will accept our leadership, on a purely practical basis, if that leadership shows itself efficient for the common good. Then it will obviously be better business to work with us than to plunder us. Morally, our services will justify whatever luxuries we may retain. Working men, in America as well as in Russia, do not grudge the comparative affluence their leaders enjoy.

We in America profess two conflicting ideals: the ideal of service, which is Christian, democratic, and socialistic; and the ideal of competition and unlimited individual profit, which, however smooth its exterior, is that of the jungle. If we want peace, we must unreservedly shift from the anarchistic conception to the coöperative. We have shown ourselves magnificently capable of such a collective effort for the good of mankind in the highest moments of the two world wars. This spirit must be revived and kept steadily burning. Unless we engage in a fifty-year crusade against starvation, disease, ignorance, intolerance, oppression, everywhere in the world, the San Francisco Charter, even though it were amended into a genuine World Constitution, would remain as futile as the Kellogg Pact.[12]

It is the task of the Humanities to educate men for such a campaign. Science will provide marvelous means; but only the humane spirit can direct them to worthy ends. The Humanities must help us transcend the parochialism of sectarian religion, of the national state, of the profit motive, of party politics, of doctrinaire ideologies. Culture is not a luxury: it is a way of life.

[12] This was written before President Truman's great offer of assistance to underdeveloped regions.

NOV 25 1996

NOV 26 1996